PSYCHIC LITERACY

& the Coming Psychic Renaissance

A BioMind Superpowers Book
Published by

Swann-Ryder Productions, LLC
www.ingoswann.com

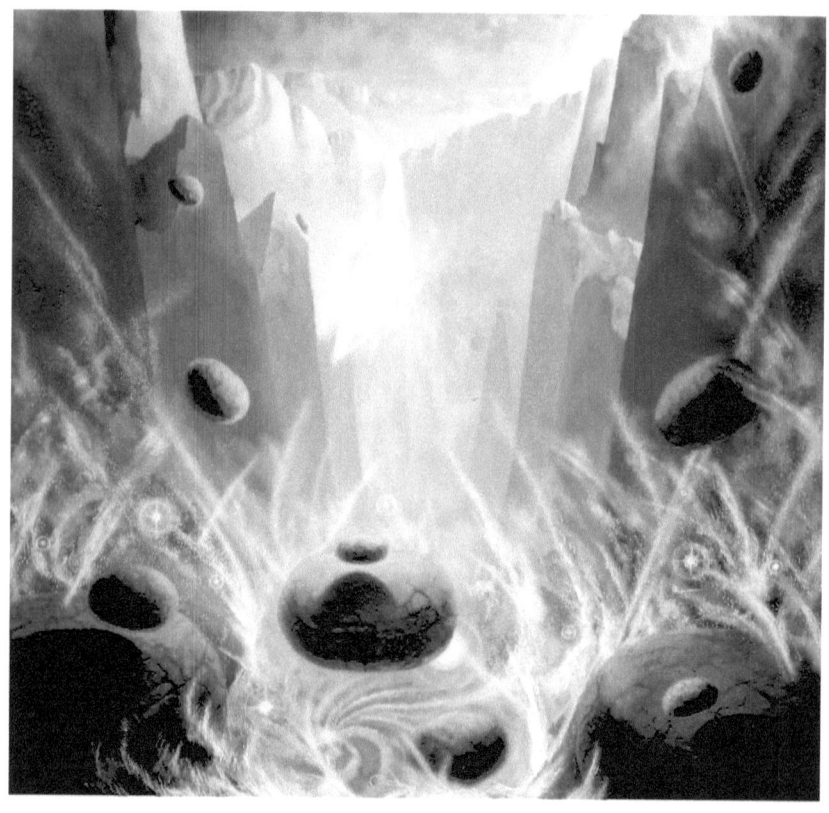

Copyright © 2018 by Swann-Ryder Productions, LLC

All rights reserved. No part of this book may be used or reproduced in any manner whatsoever without written permission. For more information address: www.ingoswann.com.

ISBN-13: 978-1-949214-47-5

First edition BioMind Superpowers Books

Editor: Brian Lord

Cover art: *Floating Canyons* by Ingo Swann © The American Visionary Art Museum courtesy of The American Visionary Art Museum (www.avam.org)

Cover design and book layout by Ender H. Isin

PSYCHIC LITERACY

& THE COMING PSYCHIC RENAISSANCE

INGO SWANN

WITH AN INTRODUCTION BY COLIN WILSON &
AN AFTERWORD BY DEAN RADIN

To Special Collections
in the Irvine Sullivan Ingram Library
at the University of West Georgia

Audaces Fortuna Iuvat
-- Virgil

TABLE OF CONTENTS

EDITOR'S PREFACE   2

INTRODUCTION   4

PREFACE   8

PART ONE

I THE PSYCHIC RENAISSANCE BEGINS   17
- THE TIFLIS EVENT
- THE PSYCHIC RENAISSANCE GETS UP STEAM IN THE U.S.S.R.
- THE INITIAL AMERICAN RESPONSE
- THE WORLD LEARNS OF SOVIET PSYCHIC RESEARCH
- WASHINGTON'S PSYCHIC DILEMMA
- THE PSYCHIC RENAISSANCE EMERGES IN THE UNITED STATES
- PREDICTING A NEW SOVIET VITALISM
- THE SECOND AMERICAN RESPONSE

II AMERICAN PSYCHIC LITERACY   39
- MAINSTREAM ATTITUDES REGARDING PSYCHIC MATTERS
- AN ASTONISHING GAP IN AMERICAN PSYCHIC LITERACY
- PSYCHIC PHENOMENA AS ABNORMAL PHENOMENA
- THE AMERICAN BREAKTHROUGH
- THE HISTORICAL CONTINUITY OF PSYCHIC EXPERIENCE
- REWORKING OUR CONCEPTS OF DISCOVERY
- PSYCHIC MATTERS AND THEIR SURVIVAL VALUE
- TOWARD A "WORKING" PSYCHIC LITERACY

III PROFITING FROM PSYCHIC INFORMATION   63
- SUCCESSFUL PEOPLE USE PSYCHIC INFORMATION
- THE ASTROLOGY ELEMENT
- PSYCHIC INTERESTS IN SOCIETY
- SEIZING SUCCESS

IV IS THE FUTURE SOMEHOW CREATING US? 83

- CAN REAL INFORMATION ABOUT THE FUTURE PENETRATE OUR INTELLECTS?
- FUTURE-SEEING, OR, PERCEIVING THE FUTURE
- A SUCCESS IN ACKNOWLEDGING FUTURE-SEEING
- ABRAHAM LINCOLN FUTURE-SEES HIS OWN DEATH
- A GLUT OF FUTURE-SEEING REPORTS
- A FUTURE-SEEING THAT SAVED MY LIFE
- A MAJOR PURPOSE OF FUTURE-SEEING
- THE FUTURE MUST EXIST IN ORDER TO BE "SEEN"

V THE DIFFERENCE BETWEEN PSYCHIC FACTORS AND PSYCHIC ABILITIES 97

- THE FOUR SEASONS EVENT
- PSYCHIC FACTORS
- PSYCHIC ABILITY
- PSYCHIC ATTRIBUTES

VI OUR PSYCHIC ATTRIBUTES AND THE BASIC PURPOSES THEY SERVE 111

- OUR DIRECT-SENSING SYSTEMS GATHER HIDDEN INFORMATION
- BELIEF IS NOT ENOUGH

VII COMMUNAL PSYCHIC CAPABILITIES AND PSYCHIC NETWORKS 126

- PSYCHIC NETWORKING OF THE ANCIENTS
- COMMUNAL PSYCHIC CAPABILITIES
- ABERFAN, 1966
- THE *TITANIC*

VIII A LOOK AT PSYCHIC EXCELLENCE 145

- THREE KNOWN TYPES OF PSYCHIC ACTIVITY
- GREAT EVENTS ARE PRECEDED BY PSYCHIC ALERTS
- SEPHARIAL AND CHEIRO
- EVANGELINE ADAMS
- JEANE DIXON

IX MIRACULOUS HEALING   173

- OUR BRAINS
- THE JOHN TRAYNOR EVENT
- HOW TO DEBUNK CURES AT LOURDES
- THE "FISH-SKIN" EVENT
- A SPECTRUM OF PSYCHIC POTENTIALS

PART TWO

X A NEW PSYCHIC SYNTHESIS   195

- THE FAILURE OF THE MODERN PSYCHIC SYNTHESIS
- WHAT ARE PSYCHIC POTENTIALS REALLY PART OF?

XI THE MEANINGFUL DIFFERENCE BETWEEN PSYCHIC ENERGIES AND PSYCHIC FORCES   202

- THE PSYCHIC OCEAN
- INTELLECTUAL DEFINITIONS OF "ENERGY" AND "FORCE"

XII THE CONSTRUCTIVE AND DESTRUCTIVE NATURE OF THE INVISIBLES   210

- HARMONY AND DISHARMONY
- TAKING ADVANTAGE OF CONSTRUCTIVE AND DESTRUCTIVE FORCES
- PSYCHIC CREATIVITY

XIII FATE AND DESTINY   221

- FATE AND DESTRUCTIVE FORCES
- DESTINY AND LIFE-GIVING ENERGIES

XIV OUR HIDDEN PSYCHIC AGENDAS   229

- OUR HIDDEN PSYCHIC AGENDAS
- SENSING ONE'S DESTINY
- CONSTRUCTIVE AND DESTRUCTIVE ELEMENTS IN HIDDEN PSYCHIC AGENDAS

XV PSYCHIC LINKAGES   247

- TRACKING DOWN THE ESSENTIAL PURPOSE OF PSYCHIC STUFF

XVI WHAT IS PSYCHIC PERCEPTION, ANYWAY? 257
- PSYCHIC APPERCEPTION
- THE FUNDAMENTAL SECRET OF PSYCHIC PROFICIENCY

XVII THE PSYCHIC ARTS AND CRAFTS 267
- KNOWLEDGE IS POWER
- THE CRUX OF UNDERSTANDING
- THE PSYCHIC ARTS AND CRAFTS
- WHAT THE PSYCHIC CRAFTS ACTUALLY DO
- THE ASTROLOGY OF A MASS MURDERER
- THE ASTROLOGY OF FORTUNE
- SPONTANEOUS SOOTHSAYING
- OMEN READING

XVIII THE ELECTROMAGNETIC FUTURE 288
- MEET THE GEOMAGNETOSPHERE

XIX THE BIOELECTRIC HUMAN 296
- BEYOND TIME AND SPACE
- THE NEW SCIENCE OF THE ELECTRONIC BIOPSYCHIC HUMAN

XX SCIENTIFIC ASTROLOGY 304
- SYNCHRONICITY AND COSMIC "ARRANGEMENTS"
- THE ASTROLOGICAL CONNECTIONS
- THE ASTROLOGY OF CYCLES
- WHY WE NEED TO KNOW ABOUT ASTROLOGY AND CYCLES
- THE INESCAPABLE CONCLUSION

CONCLUSION 322

AFTERWORD 326

GLOSSARY 332

BIBLIOGRAPHY 342

BEHIND EVERY VISIBLE, MORE IMMEDIATE ENERGY AND
FORCE ARE, SO TO SPEAK, TEN THAT ARE INVISIBLE.

Editor's Preface

This manuscript was discovered during processing of the Ingo Swann papers, which are held in Special Collections at the University of West Georgia Library. Contained in this collection are all the notes, manuscripts, correspondence, and research materials that make up Ingo Swann's personal research. This work represents the perfect storm of psi research: Ingo was naturally talented as a laboratory-proven psychic, he developed methods to increase his psychic accuracy, he received significant institutional support and funding, he completed literally millions of experimental trials, and he performed an enormous amount of scholarly research.

Ingo was a pioneer. He did not shy away from our deepest and most difficult questions about human consciousness, nor did he fall into the many rhetorical and conceptual traps that surround these concepts. As he states in this book, he was a fact-gatherer first and a theorist second. This ruthlessly empirical approach likely aided him in his achievements in the development of remote viewing because he was concerned with authentic experience more than intellectual explanation. For Ingo, psychic phenomena were a lived reality. They were not statistical data, a collection of anecdotes, or a curious anomaly. Instead, they were part of his everyday life.

Psychic Literacy is Ingo's attempt to translate that set of experiences into a common language. It is written for the everyday person, with the idea that psychic phenomena are much more natural and ordinary than we think. We only lack the "literacy" to know how to recognize them and utilize their potentials. There is a lucid simplicity to the way Ingo lays out this idea as one that is eminently present and relevant throughout all of human history.

Originally written in 1989, this book takes on problems that still impede our general societal advancement — things like institutional dogmatism, the scientific limitations of reductive materialism, and the common cultural censorship of unconventional experience and ideas. It does not hold back in its criticisms of "scientism," the failures of parapsychology, or the larger culture of skepticism, nor is it afraid to address scientifically taboo subjects like astrology and prophecy. In a way, *Psychic Literacy* itself is a prophecy. It blazes past all these obstacles to offer a grand vision of a "coming psychic renaissance" in which science and culture are no longer at odds with the reality of psychic phenomena.

When I first encountered this manuscript in his collection of materials, I was taken aback by its bold approach. Why he never published it was something of a mystery. However, after working through more of his material in the archives, it became clear how he had toiled for two decades to write *the* book on all things psychic. There are other unfinished manuscripts in the collection with titles like "The Hidden Greatness of Human Consciousness," "Panoramic Consciousness," "The Emerald Kingdom," and "Psychic Secrets of the Human Nature Environment." All of them take slightly different approaches in searching for a way to address the big question of innate human psychic potentials. Of these, *Psychic Literacy* was only Ingo's first attempt, but it was also his most complete draft.

What does "psychic" even mean? What is the true extent of our real human potential? How can we harness those latent abilities? These types of questions were the driving core of Ingo's work. A close reading of *Psychic Literacy* reveals the incredible challenge of addressing these questions honestly. The fact that even Ingo Swann, "father of remote viewing," struggled to define what "psychic" means reveals the magnitude of these enigmas.

The reader is encouraged to approach this text as a daring attempt to envision the full landscape of our innate psychic potential, not as a final word on the subject. In total, it represents a remarkable contribution to our understanding of the nature of consciousness.

Minor editing has been performed on the manuscript for the sake of clarity and grammatical correctness.

BRIAN LORD, 2018
UNIVERSITY OF WEST GEORGIA

Introduction

Colin Wilson, 1989

I read the typescript of this book with steadily increasing excitement. At the time he asked me to write this introduction, I was aware of Ingo Swann as one of the most interesting and gifted psychics in the world. What I had not realized is that he is also one of the most intelligent and articulate, and that he has an amazing ability to express complex ideas in simple terms. Very few writers on "the paranormal" have this gift, and of those few — such as William James, Frederick Myers, and G.N.M. Tyrrell — none have been practicing "psychics." That makes the present work virtually unique.

It is an interesting coincidence that Ingo Swann and I both became involved in "the paranormal" in the year 1969. He describes in this book how a chance meeting with Cleve Backster — the "secret life of plants" man — led him to begin testing his own psychic abilities in the laboratory, and to the discovery that his gifts in that direction were of a high order. I became involved just as casually when an American publisher asked me if I would be interested in writing a book on "the occult," and I took on the commission merely for the sake of keeping my bank manager happy. At that time, I was not exactly a skeptic about the "paranormal," but I certainly took it for granted that it would turn out to be 90% wishful thinking and self-deception. That autumn, I was staying in a village in Majorca, and I asked the advice of Robert Graves about writing the book; he gave it in a single world: "Don't." Yet in later conversations, it became clear that Graves took the subject very seriously. And as I embarked on the study of the evidence for "psychic" faculties, I began to see why. It is so plentiful and so powerful that, if it concerned any other subject in the world, it would be taken for granted by every educated person. Instead of which, it actually seems to repel a large number of intelligent and educated people, as if there were something vaguely indecent or nasty about it.

Ingo Swann goes to the heart of the problem in the fifteenth chapter of the present book. He had persuaded backers to finance a three-year study project on psychic abilities. "At the beginning of this project, I and the others involved actually believed that when all the facts were in, they would fall naturally into place and we could then provide the sense so far missing. But, by the middle of the second year, a dismal realization had set in. All the facts taken together were not going to make sense. You could take history, the occult, the spiritual, general science, consciousness studies, and even religions...and still the whole of them would not fit together into a unifying picture..."

It took me some time to reach the same disconcerting conclusion. In fact, to begin with, I was convinced I could see a simple unifying pattern. It is, quite simply, that we all possess strange unconscious powers of which we are unaware. These include telepathy, clairvoyance, the ability to "dowse" and — probably — the ability to induce "out-of-body" experiences. So-called poltergeist phenomena could be explained by the power of psychokinesis, or mind-over-matter. And the odd things that take place at seances can often be explained in terms of these same powers of telepathy and clairvoyance. I did not actually rule out the possibility of life after death, but it seemed to me that was not of pressing importance.

When it appeared in 1971, *The Occult* did more than make my bank manager happy: it reached a wider audience than anything I had written since my first book *The Outsider*. Yet I must admit that although I had written the book with enormous pleasure, I had no intention of continuing to write about the paranormal. The real question at the heart of all my work is the question of why we are alive and what we are supposed to do now we are here. It is no answer to say, "we possess paranormal powers," or, "we shall continue to exist after death." That is neither here nor there. Which is why I had no intention of writing more books on "the occult;" the subject didn't interest me enough. The success of *The Occult* forced me to rethink my attitude. Readers drew all kinds of fascinating cases to my attention; publishers expressed interest in further books. And I realized that if I turned my back on the subject at this point, I would have left the major question unanswered: what does it all *mean*? If, for example, human beings can really see into the future, what does this mean for our normal view of time as a "one-way street?" Surely it overturns our deepest assumption about reality? Like Ingo Swann and his colleagues, I found myself brooding on the question of how to fit a mass of bewildering facts into a unified picture.

It was incredibly frustrating. Even the simplest subjects proved to be far more complicated than I had assumed. I was fascinated, for example, by the strange faculty known as psychometry — the ability of a psychic to "read" the history of an object by holding in his hands. It was "discovered" in the 1840s by a professor named Joseph Rodes Buchanan, whose pupils showed an astonishing ability to identify various substances that were wrapped up in thick brown paper packages. One of his followers, William Denton — a professor of geology — discovered that these pupils could "see" prehistoric panoramas when presented with dinosaur teeth or fragments of pterodactyl, even though these specimens were wrapped in paper and "shuffled" among a dozen other similar packages so that even the experimenter had no idea of which was which. Buchanan and Denton assumed that, in some strange sense, all objects "record" their history — particularly if they are associated with strong emotions — and that a "sensitive" is able to "play back" the recording. In other words, a psychometrist is simply a kind of "psychic bloodhound." It all seemed marvelously straightforward, and eminently scientific — until I began writing a book about it and learned that many "sensitives" had good reason to believe that they were obtaining their information from "spirits," and that all the evidence suggested they were correct...

I have still not given up my attempt to discover a "unifying theory" of the paranormal — a bulky volume called *Beyond the Occult* represents my most strenuous attempt so far. But as soon as I began to Ingo Swann's marvelously clear and simply book, I realized that *he* has come up with some fundamental answers with an enviable lack of effort. Because he is a born psychic, he can go straight to the heart of the matter with the certainty of one who knows exactly what he is talking about, and the problems seem to dissolve away.

But his major achievement in this remarkable book is to present it all in such a direct and logical manner that even skeptics will have to agree that it makes sense. Moreover, the logic is reinforced by his accounts of his own experiences, which possess an air of quiet authenticity. The result is that, as you progress from the "psychic revolution" in the Soviet Union, through descriptions of clairvoyance, precognition, and healing, it is possible to feel that this is how it *must* be, and that the "anti-psychic lobby" consists of bigots who are too lazy to study the facts. A reader who opened the book halfway through, and began reading his views on "the invisibles," on synchronicity, on "hidden psychic agendas" and on fate and destiny, might well conclude that he was being asked to believe a dozen impossible things before breakfast. But when these questions are considered in their proper sequence, it is hard to disagree that they follow logically from the premises laid down in the first hundred pages, and that no intelligent person need feel ashamed of taking them seriously.

I have never met Ingo Swann, but he emerges in this book as a delightful and intelligent man with a rare gift of self-expression. I was familiar with his early autobiographical book *To Kiss Earth Goodbye*, as well as with his "do-it-yourself" guide to "natural ESP," and a remarkably accomplished novel called *Star Fire*. But it is obvious that *Psychic Literacy* is the book he has always intended to write, the result of more than fifty years personal experience (he had his first "out-of-body" experience in 1936, at the age of three, under dental anesthetic) and twenty years of scientific study and investigation. If I wished to introduce a beginner to the whole complex panorama of modern "occultism and parapsychology," this is the book I would present him with.

Preface

An evolutionary leap is taking place regarding psychic matters — surprisingly not because of any special breakthroughs in the familiar field of parapsychology, but because of advances in areas outside it. Many new factors, completely unimagined only fifteen years ago, now need to be considered as we try to comprehend the meanings and functions of our extremely valuable psychic potentials.

This evolutionary leap will require a new level of psychic literacy — a broader spectrum of the background information we use to make sense of psychic matters and how they interact with our daily lives. In any event, *one thing is certain*: the whole of society, including science, is verging on recognizing not only the existence of psychic stuff but the role it plays in human life.

As you read this book, you might keep the following in mind. In many ways our society is coming apart and going down the tubes. One of the obvious reasons for this decomposition is that people cannot foresee the *real* outcomes of activities they set in motion.

Real foresight is always psychic in nature, and it is interesting to note that we are the inheritors of dominant social forces which skeptically denied the importance of human psychic potentials. These potentials thus have not been developed and *used*, and social outcomes have trended toward disaster as a result. Additionally, the unexpected can *never* be foreseen save through psychic foresight, and thus our modern society many times has blundered into the unexpected only to be surprised or dismayed by it.

The Psychic Renaissance must occur during this time in which it is generally recognized that new visions and ideas must be developed. In this book I've tried to align many of the new and old factors which are converging to form what future historians looking back are very likely to call the "Psychic Age."

Between 1972 and the present I've been invited to work on more than three dozen research projects exploring psychic matters. Many of these projects were interconnected, involved hundreds of people, and altogether constituted the largest organized and sustained effort ever undertaken in the United States or the West to understand psychic topics and their meanings to our culture.

A large part of this work of course involved "laboratory experiments" and hundreds of thousands of dollar/man hours resulted in millions of bits of scientifically-gathered information regarding our "powers of mind." Early on, this experimentation conformed to standard parapsychology approaches, but accumulating data gave good grounds for beginning to step outside the parapsychological paradigm and explore new ways and methods.

It is, I think, essential to point out that this vast, combined effort enjoyed a situation not typical of many other parapsychological research programs.

The combined effort was sponsored by individuals, organizations, and enterprises which felt it was time to move beyond the occult, beyond parapsychology, and beyond skepticism, and which did not question or debate the "real" existence of psychic phenomena. Thus, the burden of having to prove anything to entrenched skeptics was lifted, and the scientific mission was to ensure that the statistical data was gathered and protected as reliably as possible.

A design for "protecting the data" was worked out quite early. At no time was control of the precautions allowed to rest with the researchers or subjects. A long string of independent "oversight" committees was brought into existence, often composed of some of the most respected scientists in the nation. These approved protocols and ensured precautions, and often many members of these oversight committees observed research "on site."

...

[Ed. note: a page of the typed manuscript is missing. Its content herein is omitted.]

...

client-proprietary conditions which were uncomfortable to many and for which there has been criticism in the more open communities. The primary reason for the confidentiality hinged on several particular matters, but in general resulted from the American mainstream's prejudiced against psychic research and ridicule those professionals interested in it. In any event, there was nothing I could do to change the prevailing status of confidentiality, my choice being to work within it or not. Life is filled with compromises of this kind.

The confidentiality was undertaken to protect the who's involved and not so much the substance of what was being investigated. Contracts can be made to work both ways, and for the most part the substance of my share of the work remained proprietary to me.

Throughout the twenty years involved, I took, and still do, all aspects of my contributions very seriously, but especially those having to do with projecting where psychic things were headed. I was much of the opinion that projecting the future needed to be approached with great care, rather than making gross speculations that could result in pseudo-futuristic "realities" closer to cultural fads than any relationship to facts. But it was also true that psychic matters represented unknown and unrealized factors the nature of which were really quite hard to determine with any clarity, much less any certainty. Thus, there was to be some risk involved in trying to determine where things were headed.

One of the first tasks I accepted in this regard was to try to help determine whether the scientific approach was the best way to go about understanding psychic matters, and if it was not what were the other ways. This was no small undertaking, since our American mainstream thought had long viewed the scientific approach to things as the only legitimate one. But this also meant that our culture's literacy concerning psychic matters basically depended on science's attitudes to them.

It was my feeling that as long as science proper continued to stereotype psychic matters as irrational they could not be seen other than through the screen of the irrational. It was not that psychic matters were incapable of being rendered sensible via scientific methods. They most certainly can be. But as long as science holds them to be unscientific, unreal, unprovable, or superstitious, then the *overall* value of the scientific approach is in question.

In this way, then, there came into view the topic of this book — *Psychic Literacy*. In the larger perspective, it seemed very important not only to determine what American psychic literacy consisted of, but of what it *should* consist. The best way to study anything is first to achieve a literacy concerning it. Every particular topic or issue demands a particular form of literacy. After all, if one is very literate regarding orange trees, one can hardly use that same form of literacy to conclude anything about skunks.

There appear to be two fundamental requirements for achieving literacy. The first is that one needs to have an overall picture of what one is dealing with, and the larger and more accurate that picture the better. Second, one needs to feel able, in a social sense, openly to *discuss* what the picture might imply. With the exception of a few knowledgeable individuals, American psychic literacy was, and largely still is, in a terrible state of affairs. Professional people could hardly admit even to having an interest in psychic matters without being thought of by their peers as being kooky. Essentially, we had at least five generations of Americans who had been trained by the System to believe psychic matters were also irrational matters and hence the mainstream aversion to them was, although not justifiable, at least understandable.

Regarding a definition of *literacy*, I follow the one set forth by E.D. Hirsch, Jr. in his best-selling opus *Cultural Literacy*, published in 1987, and which might be read in conjunction with this book. Literacy consists of a network of background information that enables one to read or observe with adequate levels of comprehension, get the point of what is seen or read, grasp the implications, and, especially, understand more than just the apparent surface meanings.

Hirsh speaks of grasping the "unspoken contexts" of what is seen or learned as fundamental to literacy in general. But to grasp unspoken contexts we have to have a great deal of information already stored in our minds that can be recombined in new or different forms to produce new understandings not only about what is obvious, but about what is not so obvious. This book seeks to provide an assortment of background information that is large enough to provoke a new general understanding regarding the meaning and significance of experienced psychic phenomena.

Although Hirsh does not so stipulate, in a certain sense he is talking about *recombinant literacy* and, in the case of grasping unspoken contexts, about forms of *intuition*. In any event, grasping unspoken contexts is experienced as a form of intuition by most people and usually described as such. Literacy in any form then seems to require a certain intuitive grasping and, in this sense, brings the problems of literacy quite near the arenas of other psychic matters.

Psychic literacy involves much more than just acknowledging that certain people are psychically gifted. Gifted psychics have been present in all societies, although social tolerance of them has varied. However, the individual who is *seen* as being psychic is the *product* of many background processes and factors that culminate in his or her psychicness — processes and factors which are present, to some degree, in all of us.

Grasping what some of these background processes are and how they appear to be working is fundamental to establishing any viable form of psychic literacy.

Psychic individuals come and go, but the processes remain active, so to speak, and manifest in others.

If we focus solely on psychic individuals who come to public notice and do not achieve some grasp of the background processes involved, then we cannot really think of ourselves as being psychically literate.

Becoming aware of new information being discovered and confirmed regarding these processes and factors must, of course, take precedence over past beliefs, assumptions, and myths and not only enhance our psychic literacy levels, but alter our expectations, too.

This book assumes that the reader already understands that the human organism possesses the powers of deduction, induction, introspection, and memory — which will be referred to as powers or modes of our *waking intellects*. It also assumes that, in the "visceral" category, we understand we possess those difficult attributes identified as emotions, sensations, feelings, sentiments, and instincts, and that these interact with our intellectual processes.

We have no real way of identifying how many people understand that the human organism also possesses powers of intuition, extrasensory perceptions, attunement to "wavelengths" of the future, the past, other "dimensions," and memory older than ourselves. It seems clear enough that with regard to their personal experiences many people are aware of these attributes, but it is also clear that in the absence of an in-depth literacy regarding them that these attributes can be "fulfilled" only in a minimal or sporadic way.

We need not only achieve information about these psychic attributes, but the information must be interpreted as to its *significance* also — a sort of information-plus-significance type of thing.

Further, we need to know that these strange attributes are not unique to a given few individuals, a mistaken idea which serves to alienate others from these attributes on personal, human levels, but to know that these attributes are *commonly shared* among the larger population in general. In this regard, I've opted for a narrative form that includes my personal experiences and viewpoints alongside those of many others whose experiences are found in the literature or which have been narrated to me.

I have a somewhat sardonic nature which I fear I can't conceal altogether. In spite of an occasional sardonic lapse, the tone of this book is, I hope, positive. We all know there is a lot wrong with the world, but I think conscious efforts should be made to support positivistic attitudes. It is far easier to point out and inveigh against what is wrong than it is to point out and enhance what is good and constructive in the world.

Except for the things that are most obviously destructive, few other things are completely so. American "consciousness" is presently undergoing a phase in which denouncing "wrongnesses" is so fashionable, even in the arts, that it has become endemic, and our attention is hardly ever directed to what is good, positive, beautiful, or wonderful about ourselves and our conditions. Rather than denounce wrongs, it seems more important to understand how and why they have occurred, and then get on with things.

As it happens, a psychic renaissance is getting up steam amid this endemic focusing on negativities, but not because this "neg-focusing" is itself creating a better world — it most certainly is not. Recent discoveries in psychic matters have begun to confirm the fact that we are all interconnected, and the whole we constitute is influenced by negativity as well as positivity. If true, this is reason enough to "convert" to positivity.

Regarding the psychic terminology used in this book, we are at a point where past, familiar terms are being dumped and new ones coming into existence. Rather than define them throughout the text, I've included an extensive glossary (which the reader might wish to scan before reading the bulk of this book).

This is not a "how-to" book, *per se*. But at the end of each chapter I'll summarize the important information it contains and give suggested exercises that will promote the reader's increasing contact with either observational or direct psychic experience.

I've adopted a narrative style which incorporates my encounters with new phenomena which are very important to our understanding of psychic matters overall. I've also incorporated many of my own psychic experiences which, I think, many readers will recognize as analogous to their own.

As will be seen, raw psychic experiences and grasping their real meaning to our lives is going to play an increasingly important role as we enlarge our understanding of psychic matters. While psychic matters today *are* of increasing interest, still we are somewhat removed from identifying a workable "psychic technology."

A basic form of psychic literacy must come first: one that is built not upon past myths and science-fiction expectations, but one that correlates with real human psychic experience and new discoveries, one that is completely sharable and gets everyone working on the same wavelengths, so to speak.

INGO SWANN
NEW YORK, 1989

PART ONE

Background Information

I

The Psychic Renaissance Begins

In 1923, in the newly-formed Soviet Union, a psychic Event took place in a most unlikely situation. Yet, insofar as anything that affects human affairs can be said to have beginnings, it commenced a new epoch regarding what we in the United States call psychical or parapsychological research.

For forty-six years the meaning of this Event remained almost completely unappreciated in the United States — until, in 1969, its implications began to be grasped within an aura of disbelief. What this Event was, along with its enormous impact, takes some explaining. But in a precise sense, it cracked open a special door to a different kind of future — a door whose existence had long been suspected by some, but hotly debated by the many.

This first Event, and others analogous to it that were to follow, eventually came to have what we like to call "great implications." The vista of these implications is now widening. They have begun to change our human image, our conception of our collective potential, and the nature of our immediate and distant future.

In retrospect, why the 1923 Soviet Event remained cloaked in obscurity as far as American comprehensions are concerned is understandable. Frankly speaking, Americans were not at all prepared to expect that psychic matters would ever take on anything other than fringe meaning. Thus, at the time, it certainly would not have been possible to assess this obscure Event as one that was destined to aim world society toward a future in which psychic matters would take on fundamental importance. But unquestionably it did so, and thus it is of great interest to understand the how and why.

THE TIFLIS EVENT

In 1919, in the city of Tiflis (later called Tbilisi) in the Georgian S.S.R., there lived a man named Bernard Bernardovich Kazhinski. During August of that year, his best friend fell ill of a fatal disease diagnosed as typhus. One night during the death crisis Kazhinski, was suddenly awakened out of a deep sleep by a noise that sounded like a silver spoon striking glass. In vain he looked for what might have caused this sound.

The next afternoon, he learned his friend had died during the night. Arriving at the dead man's house to pay his respects he noticed a glass with a silver spoon in it on the night table next to the bed in which the corpse was laid out. Seeing him studying these objects the dead man's mother burst anew into tears. She explained that she had been about to give her son his medicine, but at the very moment she put the spoon to his lips he died, and she had dropped the spoon into the empty glass. When the mother demonstrated just how she had done this Kazhinski heard the exact sound that had awakened him at the very moment his friend had died — even though their mutual homes were a mile apart.

Kazhinski was very moved and excited. How was it possible that the tone had communicated itself to him across such a distance and awakened him from a deep sleep? Kazhinski, a confirmed materialist, had no time for "superstition," but, apparently, he was a man who could acknowledge a strange fact drawn from his own experience. So, on that August day he vowed he would solve the mystery of what had linked his own mind with that of the mother and the dying friend.

In order to fulfill his vow, Kazhinski began to study the human nervous system under the famous scientist Alexander Vassilievitch Leontivich and became an electro-technologist specializing in studying the electrical nature of the human nervous system. By 1923 he had collected facts and had concluded that the human nervous system can react, by means unknown, to stimuli not accessible to the normal five senses. In 1923 he published his findings in a book entitled *Thought Transference*. The book interested a number of Soviet scientists — and, in this way, a new epoch in psychic research began.

Now, it is not so much that Kazhinski delved into telepathy or noted the existence of invisible means of communication that made an Event of all this. Such psychic stuff had been noted throughout history and, in what we refer to as our modern times, similar effects were being researched by various scientists and organizations set up to do so.

To understand what made Kazhinski's work particularly significant, we are obliged to consider the social and political context and *auspices* within which it occurred.

In 1919 the Russian Revolution was barely two years old, and by 1923 all activities in the Soviet Union, including scientific research, were under state control. Research could not be pursued except by government permission, and no research reports could be published unless their content and conclusions likewise had official approval. This system was considerably different from the way things were done in the United States or Europe, where research may be pursued outside of mainstream governmental supervision by any who are prepared to do so. Thus, in our West, psychic-type research can go on as it may in the total absence of any form of mainstream approval or official governmental approval.

In approving Kazhinski's research and the eventual publication of his book, then, the Soviet state was the first society and government *officially to endorse* the existence of unknown, invisible factors that affect human interactions — which is to say, the first officially to approve and sponsor any form of psychic research. Thus, a form of psychic research became appended to a major political entity. This endorsement constituted an Event of no mean magnitude, all the more remarkable if the ideological precepts of the premier Marxist-Leninist State are considered.

Under the State-approval system in the U.S.S.R., the publishing of a document that sought to establish any kind of psychic phenomenon as valid and real was a serious business. After all, the Soviet government had been founded upon concepts of trenchant materialism whose ideology was adamantly antagonistic to any kind of "superstition," within which term psychic matters were included. The new Soviet government had proposed to eradicate all forms of superstition, and this particular aspect of its ideology had been broadly announced world-wide.

It is hardly conceivable, therefore, that Kazhinski or any other Soviet scientist could hope to publish a document reporting on any form of psychic research *unless* the evidence offered was absolutely beyond dispute.

We can hardly imagine the extent of the scientific, ideological, and political committees needed to sift through Kazhinski's evidence and conclusions before his book *Thought Transference* was permitted into print.

In fact, the Soviet apparatus of censorship was already enormous and immeasurably powerful, and, logically speaking, since psychic stuff was "ideologically unsound," it would have been far easier for the governmental system simply to refuse approval for this kind of research. It is meaningful to understand why it probably did not do so in this case.

If superstition was to have no place in the New Soviet Society, on the other hand it had been broadly advertised that the New Society was to be completely *scientific*. Its ideology was to be built upon scientific factors and modified in ways those factors demanded. Hence, wherever scientific evidence justified it should direct effort, effort *would* be directed, and the society would follow.

There can be little doubt that the decision-makers of Soviet scientific, ideological, and political machinery found themselves "surprised" when solid statistical evidence for the existence of unknown invisible, intangible "energies" was presented to them. The problem the evidence presented was clear. Should the evidence be suppressed in favor of maintaining ideological purity? If such a tactic was to be seized upon, clearly it defeated the *other* purity by which the Soviets proposed to guide their destiny — scientific purity.

In any event, from the new Soviet view, suppression of inconvenient evidence was characteristic of bourgeois, capitalistic societies which guided their destinies mostly with regard to vested interests. If the new Soviets were also to adopt this tactic, in effect the meaning of the Revolution would be lost having barely got going.

Considering the harsh nature of the nascent Soviet program regarding many other areas of activity, their decision doubtlessly was made less based upon scientific altruism than upon practical considerations. After all, if all scientists who uncovered inconvenient evidence were to be rounded up and sequestered in Siberia it was easy enough to see that shortly all Soviet scientific efforts might grind to a halt. The goal of science was to uncover and understand the new, and if the new *was* discovered and verified, then in some form the new had to be incorporated into what the state saw and did.

Much to the honor of the basic scientific hypothesis, then, and to its own credit, the Soviet system made the decision not to suppress inconvenient scientific evidence nor, in fact, quibble with it based on philosophical objections to its nature. The Soviet state machinery moved to endorse the strange, new frontier suggested by thought-transference, i.e., telepathy. Obviously, this decision was to have great meaning for the destiny of humanity, although nearly five decades were to pass before this fact began to be understood outside the Soviet Union.

THE PSYCHIC RENAISSANCE GETS UP STEAM IN THE U.S.S.R.

Thus, Kazhinski continued his research, of course under state auspices and with state funding. Eventually, in 1967 his principal opus, entitled *Biological Radio Communication*, was published by the Ukrainian Academy of Sciences in Kiev. This large document outlined in excruciating detail the clear evidence that there exist invisible biological "energies" that act as carriers of information, that these energies act independently of the recognized physical senses, and that they "extend" contact between biological organisms in ways far exceeding those attributed to the same five senses.

In 1923 Kazhinski's first book, *Thought Transference*, stimulated great interest among other Soviet researchers. As it happened, one of these was the most famous animal tamers of the time, one Vladimir Leonidovitch Durov. Durov's experiences with animals had convinced him that it was possible to communicate thoughts to them. Under the supervision of scientists and other experts, he conducted ten thousand experiments between 1923 and 1924, succeeding, for example, in communicating "orders" to animals by getting them to pick up some object and bring it to him.

When these experiments were evaluated statistically, it was calculated that the probability of a success being attributed to chance alone was sixteen out of ten million. This statistical outcome convinced, as it should, even the most skeptical Soviet critics and scientists. In explanation of the "effect," again the existence of some unknown form of invisible "energy" was postulated as the "carrier" of the telepathic impulses.

Among other things, Durov was convinced that the eyes of humans and animals emit or radiate "rays." Many of the ancients also had believed this, and so the concept, although unusual, was not unfamiliar. Durov began to run experiments in which he fixed his gaze immovably upon the back of peoples' necks who had no idea what he was up to. In one hundred percent of the cases the persons so stared at turned their heads to look at him — and, indeed, here we encounter a "psychic" effect well within the boundaries of *average human experience*. In fact, millions have experienced something like this. But the effect is so legion and is taken so much for granted that it is not even included in the list of topics of the more usual parapsychological research conducted in the West.

The reason for this disinterest in Western psychical research circles has to do with the reluctance of Western researchers to begin dealing with the probable existence of what the Soviet researchers came to call "invisible biological energies." In our Western scientific system, nothing can legitimately be researched until it has been proven to exist, and up until the 1980s, American science attitudes in general were antipathetic to "energies" that could not be registered with existing equipment or explained by accepted theory. That the early Soviets made the speculative jump across this conceptual barrier and began thinking in terms of the existence of invisible and intangible biological energies is precisely what separated Soviet efforts from Western scientific research methods and expectations.

In 1959, at a physiologists' congress in Buenos Aires, a Soviet scientist read a report giving evidence that electrical stimulation of a human subject's pineal gland had generated subjective impressions of "light." One hypothesis that could be drawn from this evidence involved telepathy — in that *if* telepathy could be associated with some kind of electromagnetic "rays," then such rays might also impact upon the pineal gland arousing subjective impressions of the information the rays "carried."

The distinction between the American and the Soviet conception of telepathy might not at first be clear. In the American mode of psychic understanding it had long been assumed that telepathy, in keeping with the mind/body dualism favored by Westerners, was primarily a *mental* effect, not a *biological* or an *electromagnetic* one. While American parapsychologists did sometimes refer to mental "radio," still this term was used more as a descriptive reference for some aspect of "mind waves" operating independently of the rest of the bio-organism. The actual existence of subtle electromagnetic biological waves was not generally acknowledged, and thus not really anticipated.

The Soviets, however, made this connection, and consequently did not feel they were dealing with mental or psychological phenomena *per se*, but primarily with unknown, but easily demonstrable, forms of biological electromagnetism, or at least something analogous to it. It was not until the mid-1970s that American researchers began to acknowledge the probable existence of biological electromagnetism, and then the acknowledgement occurred not in parapsychology but in other fields not primarily concerned with psychic phenomena.

In any event, the Soviets concentrated on "biologically unknown energetic factors," and, for example, began to assume that if electromagnetic impulses did impact upon the pineal gland and arouse subjective impressions, then (as Kazhinski rightly pointed out) physiologists and brain specialists were obliged to take long-distance causes and effects into consideration. After all, the entire universe is filled with electromagnetic "radiations," both known and unknown, and our biological systems *must* be interacting with them.

It is extremely important here to realize that the direct transmission from bio-organism to bio-organism (i.e., from person to person) of information over long distances constitutes the phenomenon that has been the central subject of research of Western *psychical* researchers and parapsychologists. There should remain no confusion here about whether or not psychic research and biological radio research are concerned with different phenomena. They are not. But the basic assumptions underlying the approaches *are* different, and thus the expectations as to how the problems are to be explored and are to find resolution and understanding are also different.

It is exactly these long-distance causes and effects that are the substance of what we, in America, have referred to as ESP, or ESP-like — but without coupling ESP with the concept of biological electromagnetic sub-strata inherent in the human organism as a whole. In other words, we have conceived of ESP as powers of the mind, not as *functions* of an indwelling electromagnetic "body."

Between 1923 and 1960 the Soviet researchers referred to the hypothesized biological electromagnetism as "transference rays." In Leningrad, in 1942, a certain professor, S.J. Turlugin, published a paper in which he showed that the effect of the "rays" of the human gaze was *nullified* when an ultra-fine mesh of wire was placed between the "transmitter" of the rays and the "receiver" of them, but *not nullified* by metal mirrors.

On the one hand, this complicated attempts at understanding of what might be happening; but on the other hand, the fact that a physical net of wire could stop or deflect the effect of the gaze clearly demonstrated that some kind of electromagnetic radiation was at issue, or at least a type of radiation that somewhat "obeyed" the usual understanding of electromagnetism. In other words, it was now clear that at least certain kinds of psychic effects probably did have electromagnetic explanations.

A member of the Soviet Academy of Sciences, one P.O. Lazareff, subjected Turlungin's research to extreme procedures. It was concluded that Turlugin's research was correct, and that radiations emanating from the human eye must be made up of electromagnetic-like waves of extremely short duration, high-frequency waves of millimeter length. The great Russian physiologist, Ivan Pavlov, had already established the probable relationship of similar electromagnetic phenomena in relationship to telepathy and, by inference, to clairvoyance. If special kinds of electromagnetic radiations *were* carriers of "information," and such radiations impacted upon the human biological systems arousing subjective impressions of the *meaning* of the information, then the only possible conclusion was that telepathy and clairvoyance indeed *must* exist as had been claimed historically.

Taking this line of research a step further, F.P. Petrov of the Pavlov Institute discovered in 1952 that low-frequency electromagnetic fields also have effects on higher nervous system activity, and in 1959 he reported that magnetic fields of high frequency also affect the higher nervous system, alter reflex action, cause feelings of pain, and, sometimes, stimulate the arousal of subjective impressions.

At first, American researchers, who by now had begun to learn of this line of research, were dubious. But it is now known that long-term exposure to high-tension wires can, for example, apparently cause leukemia among other effects. Today we refer to this as electromagnetic pollution.

With regard to consistency of expectation, then, if electromagnetic frequencies affect the higher nervous system over even a distance of a hundred yards, then biological communication over longer distances *must* be accepted, providing it can be demonstrated that human biological systems themselves contain electromagnetic principles. As we shall see later, there is no longer any question that this is the case.

In the early 1960s, W.A. Kosak of the Pavlov Institute took the position that the electro-biological transmission of thought or emotions (both being "psychic" phenomena universally experienced in the population) generated across large distances may be affected by "fields of energy" that may not necessarily be only electromagnetic in nature. For example, it was demonstrated at the Pavlov Institute that many kinds of unknown "energy fields" and "energy waves" probably exist, and that these probably affect human biosystems. Indeed, some of these "fields" or "waves" bypass conscious perception and impact on the subconscious.

One of the methods by which this was explored experimentally might seem rather cruel: human volunteers, positioned near metal stepladders, got electrical shocks accompanied by an inaudible high-frequency sound signal each time they touched the ladders. After the volunteers had "learned" they would get shocked each time they touched the ladders, they were asked to touch them at times no electrical current was present. There was no response. But when the inaudible high-frequency sound (not registering on the human ear) alone was given, the subconscious (presumably) reacted as if it had received the electric shock, and the volunteers jerked their hands away. Their conscious perceptions could not perceive the sound signal, but something beneath their consciousness *could associate the inaudible signal with danger.*

From experiments like these, it has definitively been established that human biological systems are being subjected all the time to "radiations," "fields," and "waves" to which primary consciousness does not respond, but to which other sub-levels do. The meaning of this is clear, but it is somewhat shocking. Our Western concept of ourselves is that we are individuals characterized by conscious intelligence, and that this conscious intelligence is and as well "governs" us. In other words, *we are* our conscious mind. We have acknowledged a mind-body dualism, but we have not attributed to the body-half of this dualism a "mind" which is independent of our conscious mind. In other words, we believe that we have only *one* mind, and this mind is closely identified with our mental apparatus.

The Soviet research indicated the existence of a "*biological* mind" which possesses characteristics quite different from our "mental mind," and, further, that this biological mind is electromagnetic in nature.

In this context then, once the scientist knows the biological mind can receive signals that have not passed through or impacted upon any of the five recognized senses that support our conscious mind, yet are demonstrably substantial in nature, the existence of invisible factors *must* be acknowledged. Once it is understood *how* these invisible factors interact with the human bioenergetic system as a whole, then phenomena such as telepathy, clairvoyance, and even psychokinesis will be understood as expansions of human faculties of perception *into the unknown.*

There are, of course, many other interesting details of the Soviet effort, some of which we'll encounter ahead. But by 1965 in the Soviet Union, the emerging field of biological communication, sometimes also referred to as bioenergetic or psychotronic research, had become very large and was considered an important aspect of the government-sponsored scientific worldview. The literature had become so large that in 1971 two Soviet scientists, E.K. Naumov and L.V. Vilenskaya, issued in Moscow a short bibliography of eighty-two of the most important references dealing with biological communication research.

As they explained, extensive experimental material had been accumulated by Soviet and foreign scientists on biological communication and related phenomena. The accumulated reports left "no doubt of the existence of the phenomena." However, the eminent Soviet scientist, A.S. Presman of the Department of Biophysics, Moscow University, had already published a book which was rendered into English in 1971, entitled *Electromagnetic Fields and Life*. This book gave nearly seven hundred references, including references to American, British, French, and Italian research in biological electromagnetism — but Soviet work accounts for seventy percent of Presman's bibliographical references, which underscored the vitality of the Soviet effort.

It is probably meaningful to point out that I've been talking only about reports of Soviet bio-communication research that have become *available* in the West. During the period under review here (1923-1973), the Soviet Union was an ultra-secretive society, and there can be little doubt that what reports have become available probably are evidential of only a small portion of an effort that was and remains considerably larger.

For example, as early as 1973, it became known that extensive psychic-related research was being carried out in at least fourteen *major* Soviet facilities: among others, at Science City in western Siberia, at the Institute of Clinical and Experimental Medicine and the Institute of Automation and Electrometry at Novosibirsk, at the Institute of Bio-Communication, the Popov Scientific and Technical Society of Radio Communication, and the Laboratory for Bio-Information in Moscow.

But the size of the Soviet effort can be better grasped by getting some idea of the budgets and personnel involved. Western estimates of annual Soviet State expenditures for bio-communications research ranged between $60 million and $100 million, both estimates being feasible but probably also conservative. Thousands of scientists, technologists, and human subjects had become involved.

In rumor-ridden Moscow, gossip circulated that all school children, college students, and even the entire Soviet Army and Navy were being "tested" in an effort to discover individuals with pronounced psychic "gifts." Siberian shamans were airlifted to important bio-communication research centers; Tibetan monks were imported for study. Some part of these rumors was certainly true. But if only twenty-five percent of the estimates and rumors were true, still we would be talking about an effort much larger than all psychic research efforts of all the Western nations *combined.*

By 1967, in any event, whether or not the Soviets had really confirmed the existence of invisible, unknown forms of information exchange was no longer arguable. They had, but they were still occupied with determining which general hypotheses might account for them the best. Apparently, there were two camps regarding this, one whose partisans attempted to place the phenomena in the framework of existing physical concepts, and another whose adherents pointed out the incongruities between the experimental data and the acknowledged physical concepts of the universe, and who proposed radical revisions of those concepts.

THE INITIAL AMERICAN RESPONSE

Naturally, reports of Soviet bio-communication research and "related phenomena" had in various ways begun to filter into Europe and the United States. As might be expected, the true import and meaning of the reports was at first not exactly understood, and those few that probably did comprehend the facts understandably were reluctant to be among the first to proclaim them openly. This would have required them to go before leading governmental officials, scientists, academics, and, even more significantly, the American media, and announce something to the effect that "the Russians are conducting a very large effort in psychic research."

But between 1967 and 1971 it began to dawn on American analysts that the Soviet biological communication and "related phenomena" actually *did* refer to phenomena we Americans conceive of as psychic or parapsychological — which is to say, phenomena that neither the American government nor American science had yet accepted as legitimate or scientifically demonstrable. Needless to say, this realization began to cause not a little confusion in important circles of the government bureaucracy which were responsible for attempting accurately to analyze Soviet activity overall.

In large part, leading American scientists and specialists, whom American strategists and analysts normally depend on for informed opinion, were, in general, implacably opposed to accepting the real existence of psychic phenomena. The result was that American analysts had to try to interpret the Soviet bio-communication effort through a psychic literacy gap on the American end. This gap quickly became referred to as the "psi gap." The nomenclature somewhat reflects, I think, the sense of "crisis" which had emerged.

Since the United States did not, at the time, possess any recognized discipline (and still really does not recognize one) akin to Soviet biological communication, American perceptions of what the Soviets were doing necessarily were filtered through our American concepts of parapsychology on the one hand and through science-fiction concepts on the other — concepts clearly inadequate to allow much accurate interpretation to take place. For example, telepathy as a *special* mental power of mind, as American parapsychologists would define it, and telepathy as a *general* manifestation of bio-physical electromagnetic communication, as the Soviets were defining it, were two definitions that are not very compatible or mutually interchangeable.

Thus, a crisis of confusion built up, and a sense of incredibility prevailed for quite some time — which is somewhat ironic. None of the available reports of Soviet biological communications research, openly published between 1923 and 1971 ever minced words, and the reports clearly stated that "related phenomena" referred to psychic phenomena and/or information transmission *outside* the limits of the five physical senses.

In trying to make sense out of what was happening in the U.S.S.R. in this regard, American analysts at first were hampered to two generally accepted opinions: that psychic phenomena had never been scientifically demonstrated and were therefore not real; and that the Soviet ideology could not possibly have permitted any, much less a vast, psychic research program to come into existence in the Marxist-Leninist State. Therefore, many of the early official interpretations, some of which I was eventually able to read, concluded that the "alleged" Soviet bio-communication-psychic program was in reality a misinformation program designed to "confuse American analysts."

At any rate, it was near this juncture, which is to say 1969, that I entered American parapsychological research and, at the ripening age of thirty-seven, began a surprising new career as a so-called laboratory "guinea pig," which has now lasted nearly twenty years, parts of which will unfold narratively in the pages ahead. At the time, I had no idea at all that any of what I've just reviewed above had been taking place, and when I began to hear rumors that the Soviets were "light years ahead of us" in psychical research, such a possibility seemed very dim to me.

THE WORLD LEARNS OF SOVIET PSYCHIC RESEARCH

However, if American officialdom was reluctant to undertake a more correct analysis of Soviet psychic facts, two intrepid women were not. In 1970, Sheila Ostrander and Lynn Schroeder, after a tour of Moscow and other stops in the Soviet Union, published their best-selling bombshell under the title *Psychic Discoveries Behind the Iron Curtain*. Thereafter, American awareness began settling into the shock of the idea that the world's premiere Marxist-Leninist state, and much against any rational expectation, probably had become the world's premiere state in researching psychic matters — in fact was the only nation officially endorsing such research.

It was clear that psychical research was here to stay, that it now had acquired political, sociological, and scientific implications far in excess of American interpretations, and that such research thus had tremendous future implications.

I, myself, made some haste to accumulate my "Soviet library" in this regard to try to bring my literacy and understanding up to speed. It took me about a year to track down, read, digest, and build up an overview from the available literature on Soviet psychic research. In Washington, and in various other sectors of the American Establishment, similar efforts were underway, I daresay on a scale far larger than my own, as the idea sunk in that the Soviets had been pursuing "strange forms" of psychic research for *fifty years* — and presumably had made breakthroughs that justified the five-decade effort.

The implications of this on the American side centered on the fact that American mainstream scientific attitudes held psychic matters in disrepute and ridicule and attributed them to nothing more than pathological irrationality. Political assessment of psychic matters thus had followed the scientific attitudes, which is to say that no governmental or scientific procedures existed which could be seen as literate enough to cope with the real meanings and implications of this Soviet development. Further, the vast and powerful American scientific community was likely to remain antagonistic with regard to psychic matters for some time to come. By 1973 this situation was being referred to as "Washington's psychic dilemma."

WASHINGTON'S PSYCHIC DILEMMA

It must be remembered that all this was taking place some fifteen years before *glasnost* and the "thaw" in U.S.-Soviet relations were to commence, and when the Soviets were still seen by American analysts as aggressors with the goal of world dominion. The implications of the idea that psychic powers might some way be utilized by the "evil empire" to further its own ends certainly served to place psychic matters in a mainstream perspective they had not thereto enjoyed. And, in my own mind at least, this development served irrevocably to place psychic matters in a limelight that future generations should try never to lose sight of.

A note of explanation is appropriate in this regard. The concerns of American analysts regarding the possibilities of *using* psychic powers for "warfare" purposes consisted of much more than "hawkish paranoia." Certainly, any nation which developed practical uses for psychic powers probably *would* use them for political, military, and intelligence-gathering purposes. After all, not a few science-fiction writers had prepared American consciousness for this probability, had they not?

But, if these fictional expectations served to constitute a "special reality" in this regard, still there was the matter of human nature itself. It is part and parcel of the human problem that men and women *will use* whatever they can to further their own ends, even those of crass opportunism. Thus, outside the political-military complex, for example, competitive industries and businesses might, like the Soviets, utilize psychic powers to try to gain advantages. It is certainly naive to think otherwise. Indeed, there is much evidence that entrepreneurs of various kinds have indeed utilized psychic powers, real or imagined, as we shall see ahead. I've *met* many of them, and discussed the issues involved, and the implications of all this should, I think, be carried in mind as each of us begins to construct our new platforms of psychic literacy.

In any event, the concern over the possibilities of "psychic warfare" in general served to lift psychic matters out of the American pro-and-con diatribes with which we are familiar. It was hardly profitable to insist that psychic phenomena did not exist or were illusory in the face of the fact that the Soviet Empire was seriously researching them. The Soviets certainly were researching *something*, and the vastness of their effort indicated the presence of breakthroughs which justified the vastness.

Thus, to help resolve Washington's dilemma and to get thinking about psychic matters on a new track, the Central Intelligence Agency commissioned the AiResearch Manufacturing Company of Torrance, California to study the new situation and prepared a report on its findings. This report, four years in preparation, was issued on January 14, 1976. Among other things, the report suggested that Soviet researchers probably had discovered electronic means for boosting telepathic communications, and it recommended the government should initiate interest in "Novel Biophysical Information Transfer Mechanisms (NBIT)" which "may have no relationship" to common parapsychological phenomena or parapsychological methodologies.

The report went on to indicate that if the Soviets had made breakthroughs in biophysical, electromagnetic psi, then they could have developed sensitive instruments to detect, monitor, and analyze very low frequency (VLF) and extremely low frequency (ELF) biological radiations. Study of the human body's electric and magnetic fields may have yielded valid observations concerning the psychic properties of "bio-organic molecules."

THE PSYCHIC RENAISSANCE EMERGES
IN THE UNITED STATES

When the CIA accepted the AiResearch report, the "psi race" heated up. In this rather roundabout way the United States government became the *second* governmental entity to begin to take psychic matters with a seriousness they thereto had not enjoyed in the cultural West. If, then, the Soviet psychic renaissance had begun in 1923, it now commenced in the United States some five decades later under the euphemistic heading of the "psi race."

Thus, American analysts found themselves "ready" to listen to the pro side of the argument as well as the skeptical side. In fact, they were willing to listen to *anyone* who might help them sort out the implications. Soon anybody who was anyone in American psychic matters was being "interviewed."

When the first of these information-gatherers came, as it were, knocking at my door, I was grateful not only for my life-long interest in psychic matters, but also for my collegiate background in biology and my long tenure at the United Nations. Indeed, what the Soviets were saying was not that psychic powers were special mental powers, powers of the mind *per se*, but that psychic phenomena fundamentally were *biological* in nature — hence the Soviet term *biological communication.*

Further, the Soviet research was stipulating that on many levels beneath or outside of the conscious, intellectual mind, living organisms radiated and/or exchanged information via electrical or magnetic "fields." What we in the West call "gifted psychics" are only so gifted because they have acquired more *conscious participation* with what essentially is a psychic-biological heritage inherent in our bio-genetic makeup.

Along with others, I was able to point out that if this was indeed the case, then psychic powers were *not* a special problem of psychology or parapsychology, as Americans tended to believe, but represented issues that more properly belonged in the scientific sense to physics, biology, physiology, and bio-electrical technology. In other words, pursuing psychic matters via the American hypothesis that they constituted problems special only to psychology, or parapsychology, would not result in any equivalent understanding of the Soviet effort. The American hypothesis was too limited and limiting.

PREDICTING A NEW SOVIET VITALISM

One of the results of this train of thought (which was, of course, not unique to myself) was that I was one of many who began to be invited to give briefings to decision makers, whose mandates required them to chart courses of action and responses "relevant to the situation." It is customary to conclude these types of "briefings" with projections or estimations of where things are headed.

Normally such projections must be in accord with observable facts and the evidence supporting them. But in the case of psychic matters few facts existed. And where facts regarding an "urgent" situation are in short supply, even decision-makers are prone to giving intuitions a hearing.

In 1974 I began startling not a few with an "intuition" which was more or less based on the following rationale. One of the aspects quite characteristic of psychic awareness, and which is historically demonstrable, is that it often acts as a catalyst of some kind that initiates a special sense of the vitality of life and the interconnectedness of its separate factors. In other words, psychic awareness initiates a sense of holism. This sense has often been expressed as "higher awareness," "all is one," or "cosmic awareness," and in better examples of it a sense of kinship with all life is obtained.

This sense can be acquired, as it has, either via a moment of "mystical ecstasy," "psychic insight," or through plodding study, but the resulting effects seem to be the same. A catharsis is obtained, one which traditionally has been exemplified by a sense of purification and which brings about "spiritual" renewal and release from tensions. That a "psychology" goes with this catharsis is undeniable, but the basis for it appears to be much deeper and more fundamental than anything that can be described only as psychological. A sense of "communion with all that is" is more intuitively serviceable, although it is intellectually difficult to describe what that consists of.

This catharsis is more familiarly initiated by some form of "religious, psychic-like ecstasy" but nonetheless can also be found among those who become "biologically aware" — in other words, among people who possess no special spiritual or religious outlook, but who somehow began to sense the real nature of biological existence.

These people seem to break through the constraints of personalized, intellectualized ego identities and the social armoring that endorses their maintenance to establish a sense of the beauty and miraculous nature of biological life itself. Biological awareness of this kind is completely analogous to mystical, spiritual, or psychic awareness arrived at by other means. In the next chapter, we will review some confirmed *evidence* regarding this.

In any event, *one* of the results of all this is that people who do achieve bio-psychic awareness become (among other things) pacifists and humanitarians sometimes of no mean reputation. It appears they no longer "wish" to function as ego-centered competitors do, and the dictum of "survival of the fittest" has little vital meaning for them.

Based upon thoughts like this, it was entirely possible to foresee that *if* the Soviets had begun scientifically to confirm that biocommunication exists and that it electromagnetically interconnects all biological organisms, then their scientific overview would come to contain catharsis-like biological awareness.

If this did occur, and on a national level, and *if* the Soviets were to respond in a fashion that acknowledged their own biocommunication discoveries, then they would not be able to maintain their Communist ideology, at least insofar as its totalitarian aspects required. In other words, the catharsis would occur, and the Soviets would begin to dismantle their alienating Marxist-Leninist ideology — no small or insignificant result of "psychic" research, to be sure.

In 1974 such a projection was met with not a few blank stares, and more than once I was advised that if the Soviet ideology did fall it would more likely be the result of other internal reasons — a declining economy and resulting internal mass discontent. Now, if I had gotten up the nerve to project this outcome via briefings to "concerned officials," naturally I should not be willing to back down from it. I countered with the observation that the economic explanation would be the one Americans would be more comfortable in accepting because it would not require any revision on their part regarding *psychic* reasons for such a monumental historical shift on the Soviet part.

Further, I pointed out that a totalitarian state can persist as long as it is willing to sacrifice actual "expendable" human lives and creativity to do so. If the Soviets actually were achieving a national form of biological awareness, and if the historically demonstrable catharsis was to hold true for them, then the sacrifice of life would cease to be a *rational* option for them: some such sentiments played a role, for example, in the establishment of Gandhi's India. In fact, as I insisted, all intellectually designed ideologies that do not take into account the interconnectedness of all life must fall if biological awareness is *accepted* for what it implies.

In fact, the acceptance of *scientifically-achieved* psychic-biological awareness and the catharsis it implies is *not* out of keeping with essential Leninist doctrines, although it is at great variance with the Marxist doctrines of trenchant materialism. After all, Lenin projected that the Soviet State should be prepared to *evolve* in accord with scientific certainty — no matter where that certainty led. To do otherwise was to defeat the essential purposes of the Revolution.

Although the methods Lenin proposed to utilize to achieve this evolution are difficult to justify, still the Revolution was based only in part on the destruction of "bourgeois" elements that (Lenin thought) imprisoned human potentials overall. According to Lenin, the Revolution would not be complete until a New Society had been achieved, a Society based on the merits of true, all-encompassing scientific discovery.

In any event, Lenin was in full possession of the Soviet state and its censorship apparatus until he died in 1924. The Georgian S.S.R., where Kazhinski first lived and worked, had been subsumed into the Soviet Union in 1922. Kazhinski's first book, *Thought Transference*, redolent as it was of "superstition and psychic nonsense," must have constituted a special problem for the ideological machinery of the new Communist state. It is very unlikely, therefore, that such an ideologically difficult book could have been published in 1923 within the Soviet system of ideological propaganda control without Lenin's direct knowledge and approval.

At the time my opinions in this regard were, in some quarters, regarded as kooky, but being considered kooky is part of the cross anyone deeply identified with psychic research must bear in the United States. In retrospect, however, many had intuitive feelings that the Soviets would have to alter their own overview eventually. My "prophecy" was not incompatible with these generally-shared intuitions, and the more daring analysts began to study the "implications" bearing this possibility in mind.

As we all now know, with the advent of Chairman Gorbachev, the Soviet Union began to undergo reorientations which Westerners were happy and relieved to witness. The actual reasons for these reorientations are probably many. The economic vitality of the Soviet Union is clearly one of them. But this alone cannot account for other changes which are distinctly cultural and even spiritual in nature and primarily consist of a humanitarian renewal of some kind, personified by the catharsis-like behavior of Mr. Gorbachev himself.

If this catharsis, as described above, is a product of biological awareness or psychic awareness, the terminology used to describe it is irrelevant. As the saying goes, psychic phenomena by any other names are still psychic phenomena. We should, however, be able to discover the verifiable existence of this same catharsis-like product in, for example, the American scene. If we can, then we may be able to witness, for the first time, a very meaningful reason for increasing research into psychic matters, a reason that far outweighs any skeptical objections for doing so. I'll incorporate observations relevant to this into the next chapter.

THE SECOND AMERICAN RESPONSE

In this way, then, an obscure, psychic-related Event in 1923, more or less dragged psychic matters out of the fringes and served to place them in new sociological, scientific, and political contexts. In the United States, the state of affairs cooked along until, in June 1981, the Committee on Science and Technology of the House of Representatives issued a staff report that called for a serious assessment of parapsychological research.

This report was somewhat flawed in its overview, but nonetheless indicated that psychic matters were on the way to achieving an unanticipated importance for the future. The report wondered if funding for such research was sufficient, what the Federal role should be, and what agencies should be involved.

But the report also took a step that is very meaningful for the future. It established the probability that psychic matters had not only scientific, but religious, humanitarian, and sociological ramifications, and it suggested that it should be determined how the public perceives psychic matters both from subjective and objective points of view.

This was an extraordinary suggestion. Up until this time, in the mainstream sense psychic matters were perceived only as being of scientific concern, and science had identified them as part and parcel of "irrationality." However, the public might view them was irrelevant. As we shall see ahead, isolating psychic matters this way in the framework of science gave rise to some very serious misunderstandings about them. This extraordinary suggestion and subsequent responses to it has already begun to change the way we think of psychic matters and has launched the American psychic renaissance.

THE PSYCHIC RENAISSANCE BEGINS

- It is important to note that when the Soviets, in 1923, accepted the existence of "invisible" energies and forces as valid, psychic research was destined to take on a different meaning for the world as a whole. No other government had officially endorsed the existence of invisibles. The Soviet initiative, therefore, launched the phenomenon which I'm calling a "psychic renaissance."

- Since the American mainstream had generally disregarded psychic matters, it was little prepared to deal with the Soviet developments when, beginning in 1969, it learned of them.

- American psychic literacy certainly did not contain many expectations that psychic matters had meaningful political, sociological, military, or cultural significance.

- With the exception of a few independent researchers who had proposed the existence of human electromagnetic potentials, in general the American public had no information that certain psychic phenomena could be associated with invisible electromagnetic "radiations."

SUGGESTED PRACTICAL EXERCISES THAT WILL HELP IN EXPANDING PSYCHIC LITERACY

- There are several ways to enhance overall literacy, one of which is to locate gaps in it, acknowledge these gaps, and try to fill them in with background information. Review the information contained in this chapter and compare it to your own pool of stored information. Bear in mind that some of the information in this chapter consists of my personal opinions, and you need not accept them as valid.

- Another very important way to expand your own psychic literacy is to compare yours to that of others. For example, ask others if they have ever heard of or can conceive of biological communication, or find out if they can conceive of such a special form of literacy as psychic literacy. Except for those who reject psychic possibilities altogether, I've found many people like to, or are even eager to, discuss the issues involved. It is actually more meaningful to gather information from them rather than to try to compel yours on them. Literacy of any form is enhanced by listening and observing what's what, so to speak.

II

American Psychic Literacy

The title of this chapter implies that there is a kind of psychic literacy that is peculiarly or uniquely American. This cannot be completely true, of course, since Americans are part of the human race and it is not unreasonable to assume that fundamental psychic experience, psychic functions, and psychic needs are similar throughout the genus *Homo sapiens* to which we all belong.

However, it is clear that psychic matters are not *understood* the same way by the various nationalities, social units, intellectual levels, and mindsets that otherwise characterize our species. In this sense, then, we can probably identify types of psychic literacy that are distinctly American in orientation.

Indeed, if literacy is based primarily upon the information it contains, then the information Americans have used to build what psychic literacy they have must, so to speak, bear the American "stamp."

Other authors before me have identified, for example, an *American mind*, or an *American psyche*, characterized by the presence of certain boundaries of attitude and understanding that differ from, say, the German, British, or Russian psyche. We do, of course, speak of our American culture, and that it differs greatly from other cultural attitudes is undeniable.

To some degree, we can speak of an *American mainstream*. I don't like the term very much, mostly because it seems to me that the United States is too large, too polymorphous, to manifest the single mainstream the term implies.

Rather it is composed of several attitude "streams" which interlock, and which are identified, in some quarters, as *the* American mainstream.

But American mainstream is a handy term of reference insofar as it is in common usage, if we understand it to refer to ever-changing, somewhat unstable, sets of major attitudes that typify the American mind at any given time.

MAINSTREAM ATTITUDES REGARDING PSYCHIC MATTERS

Prior to 1963, I had always assumed that psychic matters and psychic phenomena were valid events of personal experience or awareness, and that these constituted in turn special problems for scientific study and/or psychological or religious evaluation. I knew that many people viewed psychic stuff in a negative way. But I assumed that inspired thinkers and innovators at the cutting edges of science and philosophy must somehow be working toward incorporating the implications of psychic matters into the advancing understanding of human nature overall.

I was thirty years old before I fully understood that this was not the case at all, and that the dominant attitudes of the modern scientific American mainstream really did hold psychic-mystical matters in such low esteem that it denied the validity of their existence altogether. Indeed, when I later undertook an organized study of the development of mainstream science and philosophy in the modern age (from circa 1875 to 1969), it was possible to see in them the adamant consistency of the rejection of psychic matters *in toto*.

In the postmodern times we are living in now this adamant rejection is no longer completely the case. But clearly, this negative attitude accordingly colored what passed for American mainstream psychic literacy — and was perpetuated into the mainstream public via the various kinds of educative machinery used to instill what was considered appropriate scientific and academic thinking. In this sense, then, the fundamental information package underlying American psychic literacy had to do with ideas that psychic matters were unscientific and irrational and, even, a threat to sanity.

The only other national psyche or mind that had achieved this attitude was the French one, whose modernist mainstream also held psychic matters in such low regard that it could justify having no official scientific or cultural interest in them. No other national mainstream attitudes had become so detached from psychic-mystical matters that it could abandon interest in them altogether.

It is of course quite true that other national cultures were overlaid with similar modernist scientific criteria that brought the *value* of psychic matters into question. But these cultural mainstreams, in general, never were completely willing to relinquish interest in them altogether — and in fact were usually quite astonished to discover that the American psyche was prepared to do so and even to label belief in them as superstitious foolishness.

For example, Americans foolishly thought they could go into Islamic countries and say, as they did, that human destiny was to be completely governed and "humanized" by modern scientific intellects and not by the will of Allah and simultaneously hope to achieve profitable rapprochements with the Islamic world. Several insightful cultural analysts, among them George Kennan, warned of the negative outcomes, but these warnings went unheeded. (Only recently have Americans become completely aware of the intensity with which the Islamic world all along intended to defend their psychic-mystic religious construct.) Likewise, psychic ignorance had Americans of official status going into India and announcing that reincarnation, karma, and astrology were bunk superstitions; the Indians of course considered the American officials completely insensitive to life's basic values.

Indeed, these American mainstream anti-psychic attitudes were part-and-parcel of the "Ugly American" psyche which began to be openly dissected in the 1950s and 1960s. What modernist and ethnocentric Americans failed to realize is that in many other traditions psychic matters were always identified, not with irrationality, but with the achieving or manifesting of "higher forms of consciousness" and psychological well-being. And that other national-cultural mainstreams were not prepared to abandon this understanding *just because* the Americans had!

On the other hand, other nations probably failed completely in understanding why scientifically minded Americans had detached themselves from psychic-cum-higher-understanding matters. The reason for this is, I think, not hard to identify — and it is, in fact, an important reason. The United States (excluding its indigenous Indian populations) is the only nation that does not possess a unique and unified traditional psyche based upon an historical past. Our national identity is, in fact, poly-psychic, as the founding fathers intended it to be. But to "be American" requires a certain levelling of this poly-psychicness — not only in order to achieve a necessary American identity, but to reduce the likelihood of internal conflicts that can be the result of the essential psychic differences imported from other nations.

This psychic levelling (not always successful) has been in process since the success of the American Revolution associated it with the "manifest destiny" of the United States. In other words, ethnic psychic differences present problems to achieving a unified American psyche. Modernist Americans, like their counterparts the modernist Soviets and Europeans, saw science as sort of an alchemical furnace that could distill the real facts of life and existence into a unifying whole. In this sense, the scientific way has represented for Americans not only a way to reveal the secrets of the cosmos and existence, but a way to achieve a higher consciousness founded on scientifically discovered facts.

The essential truth of this postulate can hardly be denied. But a good part of its workability thence depended on how science was conceived and defined. In the American version, the American "melting-pot" identity was to transcend the essential psychic differences that made up its populations.

Since it was felt that these psychic differences *needed* to be levelled to achieve scientific transcendence, many early scientific hard-liners envisioning the scientific utopia felt there was no obvious reason why psychic-based "superstitions" should be considered in the first place. One of the goals of science was to transcend superstition, and there was no reason any longer to pander to it or any of its alleged elements.

What modernist scientists and philosophers looked for was common experience which could be shared by the majority and scientifically demonstrated as "real," which was completely independent of special experiences identifiable only by their psychic differences. Scientific methods and scientific statistics were seen as the only processes that could identify these majority qualities and certify their real existence by repeatable verification. The expectation was that scientific certainty could replace contrasting worldviews and manifest a single new frame of reality all could rationally subscribe to. Indeed, between 1880 and 1945, it was widely believed that scientific certainty could and would unify the entire world.

In other words, if something could be seen to exist by virtue of being repeatably "tested," then the American scientific psyche would accept it as "real." Any phenomena that did not offer themselves up to these processes on a repeating or repeatable basis became marginal and uncertain and, of course, quite suspect.

The enthusiasm for this paradigm is not hard to understand. After all, it *does* constitute the bridge that allows mainstream American consciousness to transcend the philosophical, theological, and spiritual differences that otherwise characterize its diverse populations. Unity based on scientific "realities" was conceived of as benefitting the whole American organism.

Something like this is still completely logical. But there are attendant problems, not the least of which is the fact that certain American populations are reluctant to give up their special psychic identities and traditions, or reluctant to deny personal psychic-mystic experiences. For example, certain cultural-religious sectors in the United States do not wish to abandon their psychic sense of God as universal creator in favor of the Big Bang theory taken on so enthusiastically by the scientific-cultural American mainstream only three decades ago.

Still another problem is that scientists continually revise and sometimes *reverse* their interpretation of "facts," and they also not infrequently discover completely new scientific "realities" which are at odds with former theories.

In the United States, then, the achievement of higher forms of consciousness and scientific research were considered by the modernist American mainstream to equate to the same thing. This, in fact, is not impossible, providing scientific expectations are revised. There can be little doubt that scientifically isolating and confirming the facts of human existence and of the cosmos contributes to a higher form of consciousness that can base its fundamental precepts on the facts. But at the same time, science is not a perfected eternal verity-in-itself, as many mistakenly think it to be. Rather it is a *method* of inquiry which, to fulfill its human-service functions, *must evolve*. Scientists, of course, realize this: but *how* science is to evolve is a matter of some debate and intra-science warfare beyond the scope of this book.

On the whole, modern-age scientists viewed themselves as belonging to a brotherhood of higher consciousness facilitators dedicated to factual discovery and rational interpretation of what was discovered. Naturally the brotherhood wanted to present a unified front, which it sometimes could. That scientists, having dug their professions out of the ephemeral psychic differences that characterize any non-scientific society, should plunge their sense of hard-won evolution back into psychic matters obviously is a matter of some concern to them. This concern has long characterized the "barrier" between scientific research and psychic research.

After all, psychic researchers "deal" in phenomena that cannot at all be seen to have the same qualities of *repeatability* demanded by American scientists in general. Even where psychic researchers can offer up statistical data, still the data cannot be seen (by most scientists) to be supported by any *theoretical* basis that remotely fits in with accepted theories of the world or mind that more easily integrate with established facts.

From the viewpoint of the larger prevailing scientific attitudes, then, psychical research cannot be acknowledged as technically valid until it fulfills *both* requirements, i.e., repeatability of occurrence and compatibility with prevailing theories. But behind these technical reasons for rejecting psychic matters lies the traditional anti-psychic philosophy that has characterized science for many decades and which has deeply colored American psychic literacy.

When the American mainstream began to become aware, circa 1969, that the Soviets were doing serious psychic research on a vast scale, its own attitude that psychic phenomena of any kind were not scientific and merely irrational prevailed in science, academia, the media, and government. Since one ideational element (i.e., that psychic stuff is irrational and not scientific) does not a literacy make, it can be said that in 1969 the American mainstream in general did not possess any real sense of psychic literacy, and in the absence of this its perceptions of psychic matters were quite likely to be fueled more by science-fiction expectations than by any psychic facts.

That such was the case became apparent to me when, in its April 23, 1973 issue, *Time* magazine published a feature essay entitled "Reaching Beyond the Rational." *Time* was, and is, generally accepted as reflecting standard American mainstream literacy and intelligence. In this essay, the pitfalls inherent in the American scientific overview were pointed out, and it was stipulated that science's "alleged objectivity and its attendant evils have denatured man's personal experience and taken the mystery and sacredness out of his life." Somewhat more aggressively, the essay also declared, "One of the most pernicious falsehoods ever to be almost universally accepted is that the scientific method is the only reliable way to truth," and, referring to an article that had recently appeared in *Scientific American*, the idea that some "new revolutionary paradigm" was needed "to explain what now seems to be a complete breach of elementary physical laws" was given an airing.

However, the essay, in addition to accurately conveying the sense of cultural crisis building up, published a photo of me somewhat in juxtaposition to an exploding nuclear bomb, implying that mysterious and terrifying powers lurk inside gifted subjects.

One of the outcomes of this essay was a media flurry preoccupied with the "threat" of psychic powers, in which it was wondered (among other speculations) whether psychic powers like I and others had demonstrated might be used for espionage or to detonate nuclear stockpiles.

In reality, I had demonstrated nothing of the kind. I had, however, taken part in several kinds of parapsychological experiments in which it was demonstrated for the first time in any American laboratory, to the satisfaction of the scientists conducting the experiments, that certain psychic phenomena could be achieved on a repeatable statistical basis and over long periods of time. Presumably, this repeatability was analogous, for example, to phenomena Kazhinski had observed which had launched the Soviet Union into large-scale psychic-type research.

It is the repeatability of phenomena that is normally considered *scientific* in the American framework, and it was dismaying that this exact meaning *never* was conveyed in any of the popular media's excursions into the nature of the psychic phenomena looked at in the laboratory. Rather, "superpsychics" were imaginatively portrayed as being able to melt steel doors with their powers and read secret documents stored in Kremlin vaults — activities that are never seen outside of fiction or myth. I'm not, of course, challenging the value of myth or fiction, since everything in our world has some element of truth in it. But a literacy based *primarily* in myth and fiction can hardly be a workable one, leading as it probably will to false expectations and erroneous interpretation of meaningful factors.

AN ASTONISHING GAP IN AMERICAN PSYCHIC LITERACY

But the true, and deplorable, extent of American psychic literacy dawned on me in a more personal way.

In the winter of 1973, I was invited to join a seminar and give a lecture on any psychic topic of my choice to an important group of decision-makers in the Washington, D.C. area. During one of the social functions that always accompany such seminars, a very high-ranking general came up to me with a question he felt was important.

"Could you tell me," he asked, "what the word 'psychic' means in terms I can understand?" At first, I stared at him in some bewilderment. Didn't everyone know what "psychic" meant? As if picking up on this telepathically, the general explained, "I've asked dozens of people. And, so far as I can tell, no one seems to know. No two people have agreed on what it means." He went on, "You people are urging funds be committed to something no one can define. I don't want to tell you your business, of course, but there is a problem here."

I was absolutely flabbergasted. Trying to comport myself with as much élan as possible, I said: "I'll certainly be glad to send you a written definition in a very short time."

It took me four months to supply him with a definition that he might understand. But in struggling to get this definition down on paper, an awful truth began to dawn on me. If those of us working in the psychic fields can't even define our most basic terms, then we were actually...psychic illiterates, and the implications were just terrible. The main theme of this book began to develop at that time — i.e., what is the basic information people should have stored in their minds to form a workable psychic literacy?

Now, I realize that one of the most boring things one can do, except if one is a lexicographer (one who compiles dictionaries), is to dissect word definitions. Few get really turned on by the chore. Yet, if we are to activate higher levels of psychic literacy we ought at least to be able to go to an average dictionary, find out what the term "psychic" means, and come away with relatively precise, workable understandings that are *applicable* to the practical aspects of our lives.

I somewhat regret having to be the one to point it out, but nothing of the kind is possible at the moment — although we do find the term "psychic" in the dictionary, and although we use it *as if* we understand what it means, a deeper examination proves otherwise.

Webster's indicates the word comes from the Greek *psyche*, meaning soul, and otherwise means:

> Of or relating to the psyche, i.e., originating in the mind or emotional conflict;
> Lying outside the sphere of physical science or knowledge;
> Immaterial, moral, or spiritual in origin or force;
> Sensitive to nonphysical or supernatural forces and influences.

We are so much in the intellectual habit of using the term within the scope of these "definitions" that we have lost sight of the fact that we don't actually know what they mean. For example:

We don't really know what "soul" means, and we certainly don't know for sure what originates "in the mind" or what originates elsewhere;

We do not know what, if anything, lies outside the sphere of the physical sciences, since, excepting quantum physics, modernist scientific thinking has long assumed that nothing does;

We do not know what is immaterial and what is not, for sure, and we do not at all understand the origins of things spiritual;

Certain people do accept the real existence of nonphysical forces and influences (as I do in this book), but the term "supernatural" is a vast non-term, since outside of pure fiction nothing that exists can be anything other than natural.

If you consider these definitions carefully, you can see that the term "psychic" is vaguely defined by four definitions that are themselves vague.

But this particular difficulty is compounded even more. If, in seeking a definition for "psychic," we turn to special, authoritative sources, we shall have no better luck. For example, such an authoritative text as *Parapsychology: Sources of Information*, published in 1973 under the auspices of the august American Society for Psychical Research, does not contain a definition of "psychic" at all.

We do learn, however, on page 13 that "parapsychology does *not* [emphasis in text] deal with astrology, numerology, Tarot cards, Theosophy, witchcraft, or other occult systems of practices." This disclaimer only further confuses the issues since what is being disclaimed are traditional and historical psychic arts and crafts dealing with invisible energies and forces.

The *Encyclopedia of Occultism and Parapsychology* contains no less than fifty-two entries beginning with the word *psychic*, but for the term itself it is merely described as: (1) denoting, as an adjective, the supernormal character of certain phenomena, (2) meaning, as a noun, a medium. Beyond that, the Encyclopedia merely notes that Flammarion (1852-1925), the famous astronomer and early psychical researcher, was the first to use it as a French term, and that one Serjeant Cox (?-1879) was the first to suggest it (c. 1872) in England.

Apparently, the adjectives "supernatural," "supernormal," and, later, "paranormal," were enough to establish the unspoken context of what was meant by the term "psychic," in that whatever "psychic" referred to, it was beyond or above so-called "normal" or natural human activity. However, the terms "supernatural," "supernormal," and "paranormal" in reality are most certainly fallacious in that anything that exists must have a natural status in the scheme of things and bear normal relationships to all other things. Anything that can be perceived to exist can only be something that is some kind of a manifestation of the whole organization or interplay of the interconnected universe.

It is of little wonder, then, why the Soviet psychic researchers abandoned the term psychic and replaced it with a series of terms more explicitly comprehensible. The words "biological" and "communication" both possess extensively unambiguous definitions that at least allow people in general to comprehend and agree about what is being referred to.

In working my way through the "problem" the general had pointed out, it soon enough became clear why, other than on a very superficial level, he could not understand what "psychic" meant. At that point, I couldn't either. But, in our American mainstream context, "psychic" is usually taken to refer to mental phenomena that can't be fitted into accepted scientific theories.

That science has not been able to fit psychic matters into its basic precepts may well have preserved the integrity of those scientific precepts, but in sociological terms it has insinuated a deep division in our communal American psyche, and hence in our psychic literacy potential. The 1973 essay in *Time* noted the existence of this division as a "current disenchantment rooted in the growing gulf between scientists and laymen" which exists because "in the name of knowledge" science is "screening out of our experience" our experiential reservoir of "spiritual knowledge and power."

No form of literacy can be stable if the information upon which it is based itself contains conflicting data which defeat the effort of trying to arrive intellectually at workable conclusions. A psychologist might say that data that is internally contradictory or that conflicts with experience is prone to arousing schizoid-like episodes in those who are unable to surmount or resolve the conflict. Thus, if our general American perception of psychic matters considers them unscientific, then the implication is that they must also be abnormal. In fact, this has been the premise of American psychiatry all along.

PSYCHIC PHENOMENA AS ABNORMAL PHENOMENA

Almost from its inception, American psychiatry and psychology labeled psychic phenomena as historically *abnormal* or specifically as irrational. While it is true, now, that certain psychological therapies have begun to view psychic phenomena more constructively, American psychiatry continues to identify psychic phenomena with abnormality.

For example, the *Diagnostic and Statistical Manual of Mental Disorders* (known as the DSM-III for its 1987 revised edition and compiled by nearly four hundred leading psychiatrists) serves as the "bible" of psych students, college teachers, doctors, clinicians, counselors, psychologists and psychiatrists, and even law enforcement specialists. On page 187 of the *DSM-III*, the illness long called schizophrenia is described as some phase of mental derangement always involving delusions, hallucinations, or certain characteristic disturbances. Such diagnosis is made only when it cannot be established that an organic factor initiated and maintained the disturbance.

Then, on pages 194-195, under "Diagnostic Criteria for Schizophrenia," are listed several categories the reader can consult which typify certain behavior as schizophrenic. Included in this list are "beliefs or magical thinking influencing behavior and inconsistent with cultural norms, e.g., superstitiousness, belief in clairvoyance, telepathy, a 'sixth sense,' 'others can feel my feelings,' overvalued ideas, ideas of reference."

It is understandable, then, why our American concepts of what constitutes psychic literacy contain elements antipathetic to accumulating such a type of literacy in the first place. The average person, at least in any professional sense, would not wish to expend time and effort in studying a topic whose nature might serve to bring down on him or her the label of abnormality. The extent and quality of American psychic literacy is thus much influenced by professional antipathies to the subject itself, and this situation certainly in large part accounts for the American failure to construct a coherent form of psychic literacy.

But since this *is* the situation, obviously powerful reasons would be needed to override these antipathies. One has not been forthcoming until just very recently, as we shall review shortly.

Another factor that plays an important role in the extent and quality of American psychic literacy is a simple numbers game. The first scientific psychical research societies were launched beginning in 1882. Between then and 1973 the total of all individuals who undertook scientific-like inquiry into psychic matters was exceedingly small, even miniscule, when compared to the numbers of individuals who undertook other kinds of scientific careers during the same period.

I've tried to arrive at some idea of the near-exact numbers involved, but these are quite difficult to compile. However, the ratio of 1 to 500,000 plus is completely feasible, i.e., for each single person who entered into psychical research or parapsychology, five hundred thousand others undertook more standard scientific careers.

Between 1882, and the present, then, but excluding the Soviet Union, there have certainly been less than two thousand committed psychic researchers in Europe and the United States while scientists in other specialties have numbered in the hundreds of thousands. The rule of the majority, and thus the *opinions* of the majority, are factors that must be taken into consideration.

It is also important to consider another factor. The majority *not* researching psychic phenomena was always on far better grounds than the miniscule minority of psychical researchers it overshadowed. Scientists of all other waters have been able to establish demonstrable practical uses for the results of their research, whereas psychical researchers and parapsychologists have not been able to do so — at least with the certainty typical of other sciences.

But these gigantic statistical and practical-applications differences only reveal another imponderable mystery in a starker light: *why* have psychic matters always retained the high popular interest and hence cultural visibility they have in spite of the scorn and hostility of the undeniably powerful scientific majority?

Under the circumstances outlined just above, it might have seemed that psychic matters should have faded into history and cultural oblivion.

In fact, just the opposite is true. They have not at any time during the last one hundred years faded into oblivion, and interest in them today is as pronounced as ever, and even more so, now that the split between science and human experience has been acknowledged. Reasons for this sustained interest can in no way be attributed to anything achieved in psychical research or contemporary parapsychology (the latter of which, after its brilliant start-up in the 1930s, indeed is more or less now considered as having failed its mission).

THE AMERICAN BREAKTHROUGH

No feasible explanation for this split between public interest and scientific opinion was forthcoming until just recently.

The basis for identifying psychic experience as mental phenomena "suffered" only by minor segments of the population appears to rest on a hundred-year-old British survey which sought to determine the percentages of British, American, Russian, Brazilian, and European populations which experienced "hallucinations" of various kinds. This survey was published in 1897 by Edmund Parish under the title *Hallucinations and Illusions: A Study of the Fallacies of Perception*, as a volume in the Contemporary Science Series. Substantive parts of the survey were presented in 1889 in Paris at the International Congress of Psychology and again in a similar Congress convened in London in 1892.

The study was styled as an "international census of waking hallucinations in the sane," but in fact its statistics and conclusions are somewhat intermixed with clinical studies of the insane — which leads to difficulties of interpretation. As does the definition of "hallucination" which, then and today, according to the *Psychiatric Dictionary*, refers to "an apparent perception of an external object when no such object is present...a sense perception to which there is no external stimulus." Since people are always calling up from memory perceptions of objects and even events that are not present, the implication of this definition is that our memories are hallucinations. We can even, for example, re-smell our favorite flowers or grandmother's roasts even though they are long gone as "present" objects. Few of us, and rightly so, would agree that these experienced phenomena should bear the stigma attached to the term "hallucination."

The census determined that 7 to 10 percent of the sane experienced hallucinations in such categories as telepathic hallucinations, hallucinations of memory, hallucinations of death-coincidences (knowing someone had died at a distance), exaggeration of coincidences, false perceptions of distant objects and events, and so forth. In other words, it was estimated that one-tenth of the sane and mentally healthy experienced hallucinations at various times or that one-tenth of the sane suffered abnormal episodes some of the time. It was probably felt safe to assume that this relatively small percentage did not reflect psychic-type experiences as being typical of the mentally healthy *majority*.

In retrospect, the census could not possibly have reflected actual conditions, since 1897 was also the peak of the wave of Spiritualism that engulfed the Western hemisphere and Russia and was making large media headlines analogous to those of the so-called "New Age" movement during the 1980s. It is more likely that the census reflected the numbers of those who were willing to admit, in writing, they had experienced such a socially unacceptable thing as a hallucination.

But the 10 percent statistic caught on and prevailed as a professional standard of adjudication until 1973. In that year the National Opinion Research Council of the University of Chicago undertook a poll to try to establish how many Americans experienced some form of psychic phenomena. The results of the first poll were so significant that another was mounted whose results were published in 1987.

The latter poll revealed that 67 percent of Americans have experienced some form of ESP and *déjà vu*, 29 percent had visions, an average of 54 percent had experienced contact with the dead, 31 percent had experienced clairvoyance, and that a "small minority, maybe under 20 million" had undergone profoundly religious moments of ecstasy. Further, the statistical increase of the 1987 poll over the 1973 poll (an average of 20 percent) was taken to mean that the number of Americans who had experienced some form of psychic phenomena was probably not greater but that more had become comfortable with admitting to them.

These polls established that nearly three-fourths of all Americans experience some kind of psychic phenomena, at least at intervals.

If *majority* experience of any given phenomena is taken also to constitute cultural norms regarding them, then these statistics reveal a situation regarding psychic experience that stands in stark contrast to the psychiatric interpretation of them as outlined in the *DSM-III*.

But there was a further development, a very significant one. The Americans interviewed for the polls were for the most part ordinary Americans, somewhat above the norm in education and intelligence and somewhat less than average in religious involvement. People who had some of the deeper mystical and psychic experiences were tested against the Affect Balance Scale of psychological well-being, accepted as a standard measure of the healthy personality.

Those who had undergone some kind of "profound" psychic and/or mystical experience scored at the top of the Affect Balance Scale. Norman Bradburn of the University of Chicago, who had developed the Scale, was quoted as saying that no other factor has ever "correlated so highly" with psychological healthiness as measured by the ABS.[1]

These statistics and correlations arrived at by accepted scientific methods certainly bring a new light to psychic-type phenomena and to the scope of psychic matters as a whole. In fact, the implications are not only startling, but enormous. After all, it is commonly acknowledged that we are living today amid a cultural malaise and ecological ambience characterized as being overly-mechanized and overly-scientific and in which any sense of psychological well-being is becoming increasingly difficult to achieve and maintain. The Chicago polls consulted not science opinion or parapsychological expertise, but wide human experience (as recommended by the Congressional report of 1981). These tests and polls of people who had experienced deeply moving psychic states revealed that psychic experience *does* play a significant role in achieving psychological well-being — and in this sense psychic experience for the first time in the United States was seen to be linked to something that has undeniable value: psychological well-being. An American breakthrough, at last!

THE HISTORICAL CONTINUITY OF PSYCHIC EXPERIENCE

The results of the University of Chicago polls and Affect Balance Scale of testing for psychological well-being are extremely important to the future growth and development of the American mind or American psyche and to American psychic literacy in general.

Beyond establishing that psychic phenomena are widely experienced and have important psychological values, the polls and

---

1 Greeley, Andrew, "Mysticism Goes Mainstream," American Health, January/February 1982, p. 47-49.

tests demonstrate that human psychic experience has *survived* the terrible dehumanizing philosophies characteristic of the twentieth century. In 1978, as part of the psychic research in which I was involved, I was asked to compile a report listing and outlining the anti-psychic nature of these philosophies. Since they are by now receding into history and are not the direct subject of this book, I'll not go into them.

But, in general, they all assumed psychic perceptions did not exist and hence were illusory and abnormal. As Andrew Greeley put it in his important essay *Mysticism Goes Mainstream*: "To pretend that such perceptions do not occur to ordinary people in everyday life is like a Victorian novelist pretending that sexual intercourse does not occur. [This] sham is, to say the least, nonscientific — if not inhuman."[2]

In a significant way, then, the Chicago polls serve to reconnect the American psyche to the historical human heritage from which many of the fashionable twentieth-century, anti-psychic philosophies disconnected it. From ancient times through modern times people have experienced ESP, *déjà vu*, clairvoyance, telepathy, contact with the dead, and visions which led to practical inventions and poignant works of art, as well as the establishment of sacred rituals to restore or enhance renewing psychological well-being.

As the classical historian Walter Burkert emphasized (during his Carl Newell Jackson Lectures at Harvard University in April 1982), the initiation rituals of the ancient sacred mystery cults between 600 B.C. and 350 A.D. were aimed at achieving a renewing sense of psychological well-being via ritualized experience of the "sacred," which is to say via ritualized access to psychic states in which the sacred *became apparent*.[3]

The knowledge that experienced psychic states do enhance the sense of psychological well-being has always been one of the most fundamental precepts of sacred, religious, spiritualistic, and occult doctrines, and it is really only this aspect that can account for the perpetual human interest in such matters. It is completely feasible to assume that the human organism at all levels is "interested" in achieving and maintaining states of well-being, since well-being is

---

2 Ibid., p. 48.
3 Burkert, Walter, Ancient Mystery Cults, Harvard University Press, Cambridge, 1987, p. 21-26.

perceived as having something to do with survival — even if the intellectual apparatus of the organism cannot articulate the perceptions involved.

Indeed, as Robert C. Fuller, professor of religious studies at Bradley University, has pointed out in his 1982 book *Mesmerism and the American Cure of Souls*, between the 1830s and circa the 1920s the American Mind-Cure movement and New Thought Movement were deeply rooted in psychic phenomena obtained via various kinds of induced trances. These trances resulted not only in increases of psychological well-being by perceiving "man's unity with the Almighty," but also in distinct clairvoyant and telepathic phenomena often quite remarkable in nature.

More precisely, extraordinary psychic states separated individuals from their accustomed identity and then temporarily induced a "paranormal" state of consciousness understood to be one which imparts a vivid insight into ontological truths otherwise beyond human comprehension. As a result, the individual, now experientially invigorated, was afterward returned to everyday reality armed with new insights into the nature of life.[4]

These results, as described, sound like the effects obtained via the ancient sacred mystery initiations as they are described in what remains of ancient literature and artifacts. And, as well, they are quite similar, if not identical, to the results reflected via the Affect Balance Scale testing in the 1980s.

It isn't difficult at all to recognize the clarion call of the so-called New Age movement — to expand consciousness — as the most recent upsurge of the organismic need to achieve psychological well-being via the psychic methodologies modern science tried to skirt around in *its* quest for higher awareness.

This new (rather, regained) understanding shows why psychic phenomena have always maintained a high interest and have never faded into oblivion. The new statistics show that psychic phenomena are forms of general and *majority* experience, and that there exists some kind of intuitive sense regarding them that has to do with "therapeutically" achieving psychological well-being.

In fact, the Chicago "breakthrough" establishes the first practical demonstration of the "uses" of psychic experience, a breakthrough which did not occur either in science proper or via

---

4 Fuller, Robert C., Mesmerism and the American Cure of Souls, University of Pennsylvania Press, Philadelphia, 1982, p. 69-74.

historical psychic research and parapsychology. Anything that helps enhance psychological well-being really cannot be dismissed on any rational grounds whatsoever. *An increase in our overall understanding of psychic experiences, and hence an elevation in general psychic literacy, could change the very nature of our society for the better.*

Our old form of American psychic literacy more or less consisted of assuming that psychic phenomena and psychic matters were unscientific and, in the psychological sense, abnormal. Thus, if Americans did experience some kind of psychic phenomenon, it was likely that they, themselves, interpreted it — or that it was interpreted for them — through the intellectual assumption that it was unscientific and abnormal.

This constituted a literacy situation in which disbelief in psychic matters was paramount. In other words, it was a situation that *could not* lead to any accurate assessment of the function or meaning of psychic experiences — which, in turn, of course led to an inferior form of overall psychic literacy. In the absence of a valid form of American psychic literacy, what then passed for that literacy in the United States was fueled by the science-fiction expectations generated by imaginative authors, movie-makers, media hype — and, all too often, by opportunistic mystagogues preying upon popular needs to acknowledge and benefit from psychic experiences.

REWORKING OUR CONCEPTS OF DISCOVERY

A major change is taking place in, so to speak, trying to find out what's what. Numerous analysts of the human situation have begun to realize that our hopes, outlooks, and expectations have been shaped far too much by theories rather than by facts, and that by following where the theories were supposed to lead they have led, instead, into impractical dead ends and sometimes dismal situations.

We need theories as well as facts, of course, but excessive theory-following has led to what is being referred to as "the intellectual crisis" which is given detailed and grueling exposé in, for example, Allan Bloom's best-selling book *The Closing of the American Mind*. E. D. Hirsch, Jr., points out in *Cultural Literacy* that our educational and literacy standards are declining well below acceptable limits because educationalists have tried to model learning standards in accord with educational theories rather than in accord with factual needs of students. Historian Paul Johnson, in his lively book *Intellectuals*, dissects and illuminates the fallacies in popular theories of various intellectuals since the French Revolution that have had tremendous impact on shaping our outlooks, ideas, and expectations.

Behind the scenes in science, sociology, and philosophy battles have long been waged between fact gatherers and theorists who work to make the facts fit together. It stands to reason that a theory is only as good as the facts that support it; but in the way things work human-wise, theories can be more glamorous and hopeful than facts and attract much more enthusiasm. This has often led to an over-dependence on or an over-allegiance to theories by themselves.

In the stress of our present times, it can be seen that many past popular theories are not working the way they should, and so there is a renewed enthusiasm for fact gathering. Scientists who once governed their outlooks by theories are showing an increasing willingness to look for facts. This shift actually represents a great change in methods overall and has already led to a few myth-offsetting discoveries.

For example, as reported in *The New York Times* on October 10, 1989, psychologists have discovered that many children cannot interpret nonverbal cues in the physical expressions of people which leads to severe problems, as might be expected. Studies of more than one thousand children aged 9 to 11 showed that those who could not read nonverbal facial cues scored lowest on these and tended to be among the least popular in their class.

The willingness of investigators to work with such a large number of children served to uncover this fact. Prior to this discovery, whether or not children could read nonverbal cues was not even considered. I don't know why, really. Reading nonverbal facial cues is a key feature in many professions, for example, in sports competition, business, ballet, the martial arts, and, even, in love affairs, sexual encounters, and on the streets among the street wise. Yet up until this fact was gathered there was no theory that considered it as important.

Fact gatherers have also discovered (as reported in *The New York Times*, August 8, 1989) that some of the widespread beliefs in psychology and psychiatry about mourning are largely myths. Numerous interviews revealed that although people do grieve upon the loss of a loved one, many do not have the protracted mourning period which had been assumed as normal, and even perhaps abnormal if it was absent.

In another areas, researchers working with large numbers of guinea pigs and volunteers have discovered that the most certain way to catch a common cold is to shake hands with or touch someone with a cold. The viruses migrate up the arm and into the nasal passages. Prior to this factual discovery, theory had it that colds were air borne.

The presence of theories seems to result in a failure among people to get out and find out what is really what. As we have already seen, up until the Chicago polls were taken in 1987, theory had it that only a small percentage of people experienced psychic phenomena. The poll showed differently and, in fact, revealed that the majority of people do experience various kinds of the phenomena.

I tend to be a fact gatherer *first* and a theorist *second*.

The facts of psychic phenomena are really not that hard to gather. For example, in one project I was part of we asked two hundred and fifty people to try three simple ESP tests. The only qualification we used to select these people was that they were sure they had no psychic gifts at all and didn't believe in psychic stuff. Thirty-five percent of these non-believers (in spite of themselves) scored very high on the tests and 85 percent of the rest showed *some* psychic processes were at work in them.

Prevailing theories about psychic stuff has long held either that only a few experience psychic phenomena or that such experiences are abnormal. Yet when researchers start consulting raw human experience, a different picture begins to emerge. This suggests that if we interview and test more people about important factors regarding our psychic nature (as it is alleged the Soviets have done with their military forces), our picture of psychic potentials might become quite different.

As in many other areas, the presence of prevailing theories regarding the supposed nonexistence of psychic "stuff" is preventing large-scale fact-gathering regarding the actual presence of psychic phenomena in people in general. In my mind, there is no reason at all why facts shouldn't be gathered from large resources of people, and there seems to be very little reason to continue to guide our destinies or fates predominantly by theories.

A large part of this book is devoted to portraying typical psychic experiences of the kind that have happened to many people, from antiquity to the present. Raw human experience constitutes a fundamental aspect of any kind of literacy. Human experience is, after all, our most sharable form of reality. The trend of scientists to expand their inquiries from laboratory enterprises governed by theories to fact-gathering from the population as a whole almost assuredly will radically change our image of ourselves, and thus our certainties, hopes, and expectations.

PSYCHIC MATTERS AND THEIR SURVIVAL VALUE

The foregoing constitutes but a rough summary of the state of what I've elected to term our general American mainstream form of psychic (il)literacy. During the last decade this literacy has been undergoing swift modification, fueled principally by new scientific interests and by a plethora of so-called New Age literature tackling the issues from other than their scientific aspects. Indeed, it is possible to say that we now possess two forms of psychic literacy: (1) a mainstream type still somewhat locked into past anti-psychic attitudes, and (2) a counter-mainstream type breaking away from those attitudes and which will likely rise in prominence in the future.

In general, the new form of psychic literacy focuses on holistic consciousness, the holistic bio-organism, and the regaining of a more holistic view of existence. Principally this reflects an attempt to fill in the gaps of human experience that "in the bleak mindscape of scientific rationality" have been screened "out of our experience in the name of what we call knowledge."[5]

In large part the new American form of psychic literacy is going to be based on accepting the validity of experienced psychic phenomena and establishing their import and meaning to human welfare and creativity.

It is beginning to appear that identifying human psychic experiences and grasping their survival meanings will be fundamental. In other words, ways and means need to be figured out to reveal not only why and how humans experience psychic phenomena, but what *purposes* those phenomena serve. As mentioned earlier, the willingness to enhance a given form of

---

5 "Reaching Beyond the Rational," Time, April 23, 1973, p. 84.

literacy greatly depends upon perceiving reasons why it should be enhanced in the first place. It is on some of those reasons that the remainder of this book will now focus.

TOWARD A "WORKING" PSYCHIC LITERACY

A working literacy does not demand the existence of final knowledge before acquisition and use of it can be undertaken. Literacy rather is a series of processes whereby we balance ourselves knowledgeably and/or intuitively against what we must deal with — even though we don't understand what we are dealing with completely and finally.

It is doubtful that forms of literacy acquired only intellectually — i.e., "armchair" literacy — can be as effective as forms of literacy which are additionally supported by raw human experience. Raw, but real, experience brings a vitality to literacy that may be absent from the book-learned forms of it.

It has been my experience, as I shall show, that many people do experience psychic phenomena of many different kinds, but they are unable to "digest" their meaning and see their value because they have no background information to aid in doing so. The swiftest way to gain such a background is to "program in" a store of background information by observing directly or indirectly how others have experienced psychic phenomena and how such phenomena have impacted on their lives.

It is entirely appropriate to begin to get a wider picture of psychic phenomena, not from strictly scientific, skeptical, parapsychological, or even philosophical points of view, but rather from the human *experiential* angle. It is not fruitful to study psychic phenomena as phenomena detached or detachable from our whole-life experience, problems, and goals — our sense of purpose in life.

AMERICAN PSYCHIC LITERACY

- American mainstream appreciation of psychic matters more or less has hinged on scientific attitudes which held that psychic stuff was irrational and abnormal. These attitudes were perpetuated into the public via educational materials which led to a general intellectual belief that psychic matters should be avoided.

- If scientific attitudes were in error in this regard, still it must be observed that scientific methods do represent a way to achieve more certainty about the world, and even higher forms of consciousness.

- The first real American breakthrough regarding psychic matters occurred as a result of polls which ascertained that there is a large percentage of people who have experienced some form of them, and that these profound psychic-mystical experiences are strongly linked with a sense of psychological well-being.

- The polls and tests suggest that efforts to understand personal psychic experiences and their value to psychological well-being should now constitute a valid area of inquiry.

SUGGESTED PRACTICAL EXERCISES THAT WILL HELP IN EXPANDING PSYCHIC LITERACY

- Locate gaps in your own psychic literacy by comparing your background knowledge to the information contained in this chapter. Obviously, some of this information consists of opinions that are mine, and you need not accept them. But certain facts presented are stable, and you can verify them through other sources.

- If you wish, begin asking other people if they have had profound psychic or mystical experiences, and try to discover if these have contributed to an increased sense of psychological well-being for them. But try not to be judgmental. You may find some people take all this very seriously. Remember that such conversations can become very lively!

- Ask others for *their* definition of psychic. See how their views differ from your own.

- If you are up to it, make a list of anti-psychic programming you have been exposed to. Be sure to write your impressions down and then study them. Doing so will give your intellect a chance to correct its confusions. If we try to do everything in our heads, we soon begin to experience mental states akin to washing machines in which everything just tumbles around together. Your intellect possesses a very important attribute — commonly called its "ability to use common sense." It can fall back on common sense if you take active steps to help organize, in written form, what it is trying to cope with. Many successful people are always making notes of their thoughts and observations, reviewing them from time to time, and watching fuller comprehensions emerge as a result.

III

Profiting from Psychic Information

Generally speaking, people are more interested in themselves, their success, and their money problems than anything else. Largely, these are generally conceived to be affairs of the material world. So, at first sight a book about what I'm calling "psychic stuff" might not seem really pertinent to these three serious and quite valid interests. I'm going to use this first chapter to show that psychic information has a direct, positive relationship to ourselves, our potential successes, and to our supply of money.

The single biggest difficulty most people encounter is a lack of money. We work and slave away using the so-called "normal" procedures we have all been taught in order to earn money. Yet, as everyone somehow knows, we seldom can get much money using only "normal" means. True, hard work often pays off. But in order to really prosper somehow you also have to beat the odds.

How is this done?

Only rarely can you beat the odds by intellect and reason alone. Successful people talk about playing on hunches, gut feelings, intuitions, prophetic insights, future-seeing — all historically accepted as psychic sources of information. For that matter, we need hunches, gut feelings, intuitions, and prophetic insights to succeed at *anything*, sometimes even our most basic necessities.

Essentially, in all things from small to great, and whether you consciously realize it or not, you need a certain amount of psychic information to *foresee* where you are going, how you might get there, and what will happen once you have arrived. And you need to know you have chances to succeed in order to bolster your sense of self-esteem, without which your image of yourself gets rather swampy and counter-productive — even to the point that you might begin to dislike yourself.

If you want to make your life a real challenge, just try living it with nothing more than your non-psychic attributes, that is, with only intellect, reason, logic, and rationalism. It won't be long before you've made a mess of things both for yourself and for others. Intellect, reason, logic, and rationalism unaided by psychic factors are capable of making many silly and most abysmal mistakes (as we will see via several hot examples given ahead).

Our Modernist System (which came into existence in about 1850 and is fading into its well-deserved oblivion today) taught us to ignore psychic factors, asserting the belief that they were superstitious nonsense. In this book, if nothing else, we are going to see that not only are they *not* nonsense but that we *must* resurrect them from the cellars to which modernist scientisms relegated them. We must dust them off by reinstituting a higher level of psychic literacy. We are also going to see that psychic factors weave through our lives like links of good fortune. The stupid ignore these links. The wise seek to understand and use them to their advantage — as have a great many of those who have *become* super-successful.

SUCCESSFUL PEOPLE USE PSYCHIC INFORMATION

If you want to become successful, there are, I suppose, many ways to do so. A straight-forward way is to get down out of the intellectualizing armchair and actually begin to talk to successful people and get them to "confess" their deepest feelings as to why success came their way. All too often people trying to make it (but who don't really know how) spend a lot of time talking to others trying to make it (who also don't know how). Or worse, failures talk with failures in order to try to conceive of new plans for making it.

Normally, successful people don't want to say how they made it if *their* psychic factors had a hand in it. But they will, if you have something they want. In my case, having achieved a reputation as a so-called "superpsychic," many successful people have come to me to discuss the psychic aspects of success. So, in the twenty years I've been working in psychic research, I've had many opportunities to talk with dozens of highly-achieved, money-making people who have gotten where they did because they were able to use some psychic aspect to point them in the right direction or to seize some unlikely opportunity that paid off for them.

For example, one was a man who made it big in real estate management and development. His base corporation eventually came to possess more than four hundred subsidiary corporations. He had accumulated a vast amount of money. Another had built from scratch one of America's largest aerodynamic corporations, employing thousands of people. Another had built a life insurance company which profited him personally to the tune of more than $100 million a year.

All these men wanted to talk about psychic things. I said they probably knew more about them than I did, considering their very visible successes. As their stories unfolded, all were very certain they owed their success primarily to psychic factors. They wanted nothing more from me than an opportunity to talk about psychic stuff they really could not discuss elsewhere without provoking ridicule.

So, we talked...about something that had helped make spectacular fortunes for each of these men yet could not be openly discussed in our society. All of these men asserted that they had based some of the biggest decisions of their lives on some kind of psychic information which usually ran counter to the opinions of their advisors.

Another was a young man, only thirty-one. I met him in 1975, at one of those opulent movie colony parties held in lawn tents in Beverly Hills. He said he wanted to consult with me. I said I only did research and never gave psychic consultations. "Can you bend your principles for $5,000?" he asked as he pulled out of his pocket a wallet that was stuffed thick with $100 bills. Since he had my attention, I bargained him down to a good dinner at a fancy restaurant in Los Angeles.

It turned out he was a drug smuggler who flew the stuff from Mexico across the Texas border in a low-flying plane beneath radar scrutiny. I was absolutely terrified that the Feds would burst into the restaurant, and I'd have a lot of explaining to do. Not to worry, said he. "I own the place, and it is well guarded."

The scene — which included two bottles of $400 wine (the only really expensive wine I've ever drunk) was right out of the movies. The talk wasn't. "I have this knack," he said. "I psych out the Feds, the Texas Border Patrol, and know where their choppers are going to be. It's easy. What do you think of that?"

"I think it's all terribly illegal and very immoral," I said, moving into my "drugs kill" lecture. But — I'm interested in life, and here was a real drug smuggler, so I asked him to explain his philosophy, why he had become one. "I know drugs kill, but it's a dirty life, anyway. Money is the only game in town. No one cares about anything else. I just went with the flow. After all, some of the biggest fortunes in the world started out with drug smuggling from China. Nothing changes, and that's a fact."

I pointed out that many fortunes had been made without coming near drug smuggling, and then asked, "don't you think drugs are ruining our country?"

"Sure, but it's not the drugs that are doing it. It's where our heads are at. They are nowhere, man. That's the problem. No one has anything else to live for but to get money. It's our ideas that are ruining us, not the drugs themselves. Besides, if I don't do it, others will."

So, there I was — dining with a drug smuggler, and I had to decide whether or not I should walk out or treat the situation as a research project. Well, here was someone *using* his psychic abilities on more or less a daily basis. Research won. I asked him how he had discovered his abilities: "In Vietnam. Shit, man, you had to be psychic to survive there. Before 'Nam, I was going to be an accountant. I had no interest in psychic stuff. But in 'Nam, well, if you weren't psychic, you were going to go down. Nothing special happened, no zap of psychic light or anything like that. I just started getting feelings not to go there or not to do that. The strange thing was that it wasn't just me. Guys sized each other up sort of psychically. We didn't call it that, of course. We said, 'that dude is with it' or that 'asshole ain't.' No one wanted to do a mission with one of the assholes. Even asshole squad leaders started looking for guys with the sixth sense to be point leaders."

"But why the drug thing?" I asked.

"Well, for one thing, when I got back to the States, I couldn't find a job. The drug scene was really big, you know — turn on and zap to the stars. So I went to Mexico and made a few deals. Then I leased a small plane and just let my ESP do the rest. I fly mostly at night with lights out and near the ground. Shit, you just have to be psychic to do that."

"How much do you make," I asked, no longer able to curtail my curiosity.

"I average a million every month or two, sometimes more, sometimes less. But what I want to talk about is that I've been getting this flash. I see my plane crashing and I'm dead. What do you think? This is always a rational possibility, of course. Do you think this is a real psychic warning?"

"Well," I replied. "I think you have psychic insight, and if I were you I'd definitely not get into a plane for a while." As I learned some months later, he did, and he's dead — having ignored his *own* inner psychic information. Shortly, we will encounter some other people who are dead because they ignored their *own* psychic insights, too — not the least of whom were Abraham Lincoln and John F. Kennedy, as we shall see.

Among the psychic types I've met who *used* their psychic factors were two men I met by chance at New York art and furniture auctions. These two used *their* psychic abilities to prowl around junky auctions with the express purpose of buying for a few dollars cracked, dirty, musty old paintings no one else wanted — and then trotting them up to Sotheby's to sell them, now properly identified, of course, for five or six figures. Both were, of course, highly trained art experts, but when in doubt they fell back on psychic factors to help them out.

In 1975, in Houston, I met one of those human specimens called an oil field "wild-catter." This guy specialized in buying up leases from major oil companies after they had failed to find oil on them. The wild-catter drilled a new well and three times out of four brought up the oil or gas. As he told me, "I don't depend on geological surveys. I psych out the lease. If I get this special feeling, I walk around until I know I'm standing on top of it. I put the marker down and get in a drilling rig." By the time I met this wild-catter, he owned a large corporation — and a football team, to boot.

With the exception of the two art speculators, all these men had sought me out — not to tell me they were psychic, nor to consult my own psychic capabilities, but just to talk about the psychic factor and the potentials involved. Generally, they had no one else to talk to because in our present culture psychic factors are highly ridiculed. Even if you become wealthy, you are still sensitive to public ridicule. As successful as they were, these men could not openly talk about psychic stuff, or they would be laughed at by their peers, employees, and, in two cases I know of, even by their wives.

One of these women, absolutely beautiful and completely charming, had no interest at all in psychic matters, while at the same time living in the enormous mansion and enjoying the very enviable social and financial status her husband's ESP (combined with his business acumen) had provided her. You can't really blame her. She was sensitive to her peer and leadership status; any positive reference to psychic stuff would have been damaging to it. She really couldn't go public with the statement, "Well, *my* husband made it with his ESP." (You see: it *does* sound silly, doesn't it?) She would have been laughed out of town.

I've given these few beginning examples to illustrate how closely linked psychic information is to money-making and thus to self-esteem and success. While many successful types are reluctant to go too public about their psychic proficiencies, if you search the literature you will find there are, in print, thousands upon thousands of testimonials from greater or lesser money-makers, all of whom declare without reservation that they owe a great deal to some aspect of psychic reality. And many of them state, unequivocally, that without their being able to benefit from psychic information they probably would have remained in lower class employment status and not have succeeded on their own.

Now, you can trace testimonials like these back through the ages. There is a psychic history here. Thus, one would have thought by now that psychic stuff like this would have gained some serious recognition as an important aspect of our human development. Quite the contrary. Nothing of the kind has happened. Psychic stuff is largely considered to be irrational nonsense and is laughed at. Now really, I ask you. What is going on here?

If you want success and to make extraordinary amounts of money, it seems the better part of common sense to talk with those who, judged by their visible achievements, have succeeded in doing so. If these people by the hundreds say their psychic factors are very important *keys* to achieving success, and you turn away, giggle, and assume these achievers have taken leave of their sanity — well, this means *you*, not they, are not hooked up right. It's a little bit like asking God how He created the universe. And when He tells you thus and so, and you find this does not jibe with *your* understanding of things, you laugh and say, "No, this can't be. You must have done it some other way." What kind of sense does that make?

Now, I am certainly not the first writer to try to bring this news to public attention. Many others have already done so. Here we come to another mysterious phenomenon. Books that truly explain some important aspect of our psychic factors always become best sellers. For example, in 1948, one Claude M. Bristol published, through Prentice-Hall, Inc., a book entitled *The Magic of Believing*. This book might more aptly have been entitled *The Efficacy and Practice of Psychic Magic in Making Money*, but, as Bristol explained, he avoided the term "psychic" because it aroused too much antagonism. He substituted the term "mind stuff." At any rate, within only four years his book, with its dozens of testimonials, had undergone no less than nineteen printings, indicating there was a large, large, large audience interested in finding out more about how "mind stuff" (psychic stuff) operates.

Success Through a Positive Mental Attitude by Napoleon Hill and W. Clement Stone came out in 1960 and underwent no less than thirty printings by 1970. These two daring authors openly used the term "psychic" and left little doubt that psychic factors were extraordinarily important in all human affairs, but especially so in becoming successful in business. There have been many other similar books since then — like Shakti Gawain's *Creative Visualization* which has sold over a million copies since it was released in 1979.

Here, then, we have a society which on the one hand ridicules psychic stuff, but on the other hand gobbles up relevant insights regarding it.

Many wise, aggressive people, of course, keep their own counsel, transcend this discrepancy, and quietly use their psychic proficiencies, to merge their psychic activities with the winds of success. But this discrepancy has a negative impact on the attitudes of the population as a whole in that the meanings and values of our psychic experiences remain illegitimate and thus unincorporated in our educational outlooks.

We Americans, in particular, have a hard time dealing with the realities of psychic stuff. But people from other nations apparently do not. I found this out in a strange way while I was working at the United Nations in New York, long before I began working actively in experimental psychic research.

THE ASTROLOGY ELEMENT

The famous and powerful financier, John Pierpont Morgan, is alleged to have said that mere millionaires might not need astrology, but billionaires do. It is not unlikely that Morgan did say this, since he did consult astrologers, especially Evangeline Adams, the first astrologer in modern times to win a legal action brought against her as a fortune-teller. If you actually talk to successful people about psychic matters, it soon will be discovered that wherever successful people are there is always some interest in the possibilities of astrology. I uncovered this fact in the strangest of ways.

When I was working in the United Nations Secretariat in the 1960s, I had no idea at all that *anyone* really tried to use psychic factors for anything practical. I was a product of our culture, too, and in the U.N. especially the attitude among Westerners toward psychic things was very much anti — or so it appeared.

In the Secretariat building, office space is jealously guarded like tribal territory. I was working in the Office of Public Information (OPI), which was housed on the third floor of the Secretariat. OPI office space had long been the preserves of strident press veterans, who were immovable other than through retirement or death. Not long after U Thant became Secretary-General, suddenly one of these immovable fixtures was ejected from his office upon orders on high, to the great alarm of all, and relegated to a cubicle in the basement. A buxom blonde woman promptly moved into the vacated office, closed the door, and began some mysterious work.

Shortly, various diplomatic types began visiting her — Africans, Asians, Europeans, Arabs, Indians, etc. Each would stay for an hour or so, quickly to be followed by another. Sometimes there was even a *line* waiting. We were all utterly dying of curiosity.

This situation persisted this way for over a month. One afternoon, one of the office managers dashed up to my desk, a woman whose eyes were wide and whose face was flushed, and who I knew had no time for psychic stuff since she referred to it as "bullshit."

"Ingo," she said, "you know something about this psychic garbage, don't you? Well, we finally know what is going on in *that* office. *That woman* is an astrologer! She is giving astrology readings right here in the middle of OPI. This is absolutely horrible, and something has to be done about it. How did she get in here, anyway?"

Now, I was absolutely stunned and, frankly, didn't believe her. But when this gossip hit the fan, shortly it was alleged that *that woman* was no less than U Thant's personal astrologer (and more) who moonlighted giving astrological readings to other diplomats. Subsequently, we all became cognizant of the fact that Far Easterners don't make a move without consulting an astrologer -- and judging from traffic in and out that "horrible" woman's door, it was not just Easterners who consult.

Eventually, such a ruckus arose over this untenable situation in the middle of OPI's offices that the woman was moved "upstairs" to a luxurious office nearer the Secretary-General himself where her "work" allegedly went on for some years.

So, we know at least that many of our world's diplomats try to use the advice, psychic or otherwise, of astrologers — astrology being, in proper hands, one of the psychic tools par excellence. Which, in a roundabout way, brings us to Mrs. Reagan. When news of *her* astrological bent leaked out not long ago, the media and press tried to make a scandal of it (in, ironically, many of the same tabloids that print daily astrological columns).

My phone rang off the hook during this "White House Astrological Crisis." People wanted to know what I thought about it. Well, frankly, I think Mrs. Reagan was a smart cookie in this regard — and we'll see why later.

In any event, there is no evidence that Mrs. Reagan or the President *used or depended upon* astrological stuff in complete disregard for other important issues. Also, it has to be admitted that many, many people consult astrologers — and that millions read the daily astrological columns in newspapers. In our concept of democracy, all citizens have a right to do so. Mrs. Reagan did not give up her civil rights by virtue of becoming First Lady. It is really too bad that the press, in its lust for scandal, should have challenged Mrs. Reagan's legitimate rights as a citizen. This is a bad omen for all of us.

Do I "believe" in astrology? I don't think that belief is the proper issue involved. The proper question is whether or not astrology, or any psychic-type techniques, can help out. People who use astrology do so toward attaining some goal, or, at least, in helping to attain it. My question was: what *were* those goals and what role could astrology play in achieving them?

The U.N. astrology scandal inspired me to study astrology — which up to that time I thought was only gobbledygook fortune-telling. It was not long before a few astrological facts became clearer — number one of which was that there are good astrologers and fools who call themselves astrologers. Number two was that, whatever else astrology may or may not be, it is a psychic tool that *can* pierce behind the veil of the visible and perceive what the invisible energies and forces are up to. And, number three, people who have no interest in finding out what the invisible energies and forces are up to probably should not study astrology, because it is very, very complex, involved, time-consuming, and full of pitfalls which tyro enthusiasts fall into all the time.

At any rate, I can definitely, and with good knowledge, now say that many Wall Street types and financiers often use it, and I know that some even keep astrologers and psychics on retainer, like they do their lawyers.

We also know that Hollywood denizens use psychics and astrologers, etc. Rising to the top in the Hollywood movie business is a very deadly and competitive affair in which one really needs to beat the odds to succeed. Since there reside more astrologers and psychics in the Los Angeles area than anywhere else, we must assume that there are also more consumers of their services there than anywhere else.

PSYCHIC INTERESTS IN SOCIETY

Who else uses psychic stuff? Well, get a load of this one. During the 1970s, after I had become an "acclaimed psychic," the group of people who visited me the most were what used to be called futurologists. Futurology was advertised as the gathering and study of statistics deep enough and broad enough so that future trends could be projected. In the 1960s and 1970s, futurology was big business. It had great éclat. There was the powerful and influential Club of Rome at which world political and financial leaders met to discuss the futurological future. The Rand Corporation had its futurologists, as did SRI and many other think tanks, and oil companies and manufacturers were diverting large grants into futurology studies believing they could correctly predict where things would be at, say, in two years, five years, ten years, at the year 2000, and so on.

As early as 1973, however, futurologists found they had several ponderable problems, for their statistical extrapolations could not predict important "vagaries" or "anomalies" of human behavior or Acts of God, to say nothing of unpredictable political trends, or the emergence of new phenomena such as international terrorism, or moods in fashion, or inexplicable turns on the stock market. Energies and forces emanating from these unpredictable sources made messes of their finely diagrammed statistical extrapolations.

Shortly thereafter, various rather nervous futurologists were calling in at my office at Stanford Research Institute, asking for luncheon dates during which I was asked how psychic stuff "might" be incorporated into the glittering future of futurology. A few pointed out there was lots of money available for psychic-futurology exploratory projects if only someone could conceive of a reasonable and convincing proposal — without using terms that might be embarrassing.

I'd know what to do about all this now, but in 1973-74, I really didn't — and so, eventually, I passed up working on the dilemmas of futurology. Anyway, these daring futurologists would have been subject to too much anti-psychic pressure, and I think the psychic-futurology effort would have gone down the tubes as did the whole of futurology anyway a few years later.

Among those who that have come to talk with me about psychic possibilities are racehorse breeders, miners, geologists, treasure-ship hunters, astronomers, policemen, archaeologists, physicists, and inventors. Typically, all these people often confront problems and situations that normal human senses or scientific instrumentation cannot penetrate.

The purpose of narrating all the above has been to establish the fact that although we do in our present culture have an anti-psychic myth that belittles psychic stuff, on the other hand beneath this myth the psychic pot is bubbling away — and in areas you would not normally suspect. In fact, the use or attempted use of psychic stuff is really rather widespread.

I like the way Dr. Nicholas Murray Butler (1862-1947) categorized people. Butler was known as an "insider" or a "behind-the-scenes man," and he was nominated to the presidency of Columbia University by J.P. Morgan. Dr. Butler observed that the world is divided into three kinds of people.

A relatively small group that makes things happen.

A somewhat larger group that watches things happen.

A great multitude that never knows what has happened.

In my way of looking at things and based upon my experience with all kinds of *living* real people (and not upon stereotyped ideas about them), those that make things happen are also those who are most likely to have the greatest constructive interest in trying to use their psychic potentials, in order, as it were, to seize success. I'd even go so far as to speculate that if your psychic factors are naturally operational, you will be one of those who probably do make things happen.

SEIZING SUCCESS

Now, before we continue into the deeper aspects of our psychic potentials, and since this book is, loosely, one of instruction on how to become more psychic by virtue of increasing our psychic literacy, we need to toss a few ideas around. One of the major questions we might ask is this: Why are some people more psychic, hence more successful, than others? We can ask this question with the proviso we understand what we *should* mean by "successful."

In our present culture, this has come to mean *only* getting to the top of the pile and/or getting your piece of the cake and the attainment of wealth, favor, or eminence. Certainly, all this is *one* of the definitions of success. But when it becomes the *only* definition, it sets standards that are unfortunate and can only create a society top heavy with success-androids — a society in which you are essentially a nobody if you can't make it to the top. Our popular American idea that success means just making it big, big, and bigger, is completely out of balance. This is just bullshit (and I don't know a better word for it).

I feel successful when I've managed to make it through the urine-perfumed New York subways unscathed. Last night, I watched a wonderful TV program about independent people who have taken it upon themselves with their own money and capabilities to save animals — turtles, birds, coyotes, and fish. There is no "top" to get to here. In fact, the most appropriate definition of "success" is "the favorable termination of a venture" — *any* venture. If we view success as meaning this, we can locate its potentials all around us — and not just on some far away ladder top.

With this in mind, then, let's turn to our psychic/not-psychic problem. One of the more important things I've discovered in life is that it is stupid and even dangerous to generalize about people too much — although it seems it is a permanent part of human nature to do so. But it is possible to say there are people who have not completely lost touch with sensory experience, and there are people who have.

The way this comes about, I think, is this. We group people into people-sectors and intellectually stereotype them with labels. But, once we start dealing too much with labels, we start living in a world where direct sensory experience is inferior to its intellectual symbolic representation. We substitute the stuff of our minds for the stuff of life. The stuff of our intellects detached from the stuff of life builds only empty, stereotyped (intellectual) empires for us — houses of cards, as the saying goes. When the stuff of our intellects is substituted for the stuff of life, all sorts of dooms will probably follow shortly. If you desire to fail in the short or long range at anything and everything, just join some empty, stereotyping intellectual empire.

Obviously, this is not a strategy by which the success-oriented can get very far. No one gets very far by just investing life's energies in intellectual symbolic representations (stereotypes). For reasons that are too long to go into here, our present culture is almost totally overwhelmed by stereotyping. I think almost everyone can recognize this is so. Therefore, the biggest problem most of us face today is how to dig ourselves out of the symbolic, stereotyping representations we have inherited from history and which are preserved like freeze-dried corpses in the intellectual equipment the cultural mainstream uses to service itself. This is a psychic-factor type of problem, pure and simple, both at the philosophical and *operative* levels.

Now, another thing I've learned in life, at great cost and wastage to myself, is that there really is a great difference between our intellectual functions and our direct-sensory operative functions. I'll give an embarrassing incident from my own life illustrating this shortly. We can, I think, understand what our intellects are — those parts of our minds that process ideas, calculate, compute, and make conscious decisions, etc. But we also possess a tremendous spectrum of senses and sensing "equipment." We are familiar enough with *some* of our physical senses — the most prominent ones like sight, hearing, etc. But we have extensions of these. Many of us can, for example, sense another's "vibes," and often talk about doing so. We can sense when a person is sad, or negative, or happy long before we can confirm such otherwise. We can sense when a situation is "not right" or "right." We can sense a change (or even a *coming* change) in situations, although our intellects can spot no obvious reason for the change.

All these sensings can be attributed to our direct-sensing operative systems. The point where these slide from what might be attributed to physical processes into what we would call psychic processes is very hard to determine. But it *is* clear that our direct-sensing systems incorporate both kinds of processes.

I think it is somewhat important to note that our educational systems actually teach us to confuse our intellects and our direct-sensing operative abilities as to their priority. Both *are* important, of course. But we tend to place our intellectual processes *above* our direct-sensory capabilities, so much so in some instances that many people have lost real touch with their direct-sensory operative functions. The result of this is that, as a cultural standard, we tend to place our intellectual-philosophical outlooks above our operational levels when actually it should be the other way around in many cases. We can build in our heads any intellectual outlook we want — and sometimes suffer greatly because of them.

As a painful example of this, in the mid-1960s, when I was still working at the United Nations, I had a dream three nights in a row which indicated I should buy Madison Square Garden stock.

Now, I had never had any real interest in stock speculating, probably because I never had any extra money with which to do the speculating. I had no idea at all that the Madison Square Garden Corporation issued stocks. I really didn't know how to go about investing, and my intellectual attitude held that more people lost their money than those who profited — which was, I thought, a totally valid reason for not getting involved in stock speculations.

But then came along these three dreams indicating I should buy Madison Square Garden stocks, which were trading, if memory serves me correctly, for something like thirty-three cents a share. Now, at the United Nations, one of my many supervisors was a woman called Aimee, somewhat a frump of a woman who did not strike one as a wiz in stock dealings. Yet she was. So, I told her of my dreams. She called her broker, who was of the opinion that Madison Square Garden had been inactive for years with no likelihood of a change in status.

Yet, I was tempted. But I had no money at all. At least I did not that what money I had should go into a stock speculation. To get extra money, as I saw it then, I would have had to take out a loan from the U.N. Co-operative Union. The Co-op did not loan money for stock speculations. I would have had to lie and claim I was going to buy a new camera and go on vacation — purposes for which the Co-op was happy to loan money.

Finally, all the factors involved in this project became so confusing that I *decided* (an intellectual function) to abandon it. Barely a week later, Madison Square Garden made headline news when it was announced that its board had decided to build a new Garden on Columbus Circle in New York. In three days, the stock went up to $15 a share, and two weeks later was trading at $36. Had I gone ahead, borrowed $330 from the Co-op (the cost of a relatively decent vacation in those days), and purchased a thousand shares, I would have been the proud possessor of $36,000 — not a bad profit from a *dream*.

As to Aimee, when I moaned over my misfortune, saying it was too bad we had not bought the stocks, she said (and I'll never forget her words): "Oh, but did. I always pay attention to dream tips, both my own and others." When I suggested she give me a commission for my tip, she replied: "No, all's fair in love and war and in making money." That was my first dream tip regarding stocks, and I've not experienced another since.

I think you can see, though, why this situation might make one sit up and take notice of one's psychic sensing apparatus, and it did contribute greatly to enhancing my longer-term interest in psychic stuff.

Eventually, I was able to see that my intellectual certitude contained "stereotyping" factors that had totally overwhelmed the information my psychic-sensing apparatus was trying to deliver up to it.

After all, sleep time (in which dreams occur) is also down time for the intellect. Apparently, while the intellect is sleeping, our more fundamental psychic sensing systems can take the opportunity to try to insert a valuable bit of information. We call this psychic.

People whose direct-sensing operative levels are healthy and vibrant are almost always the most successful and, I think, the most visibly psychic. They almost always have developed some kind of contact with the invisible, intangible factors that work behind visible and tangible forces. Those whose direct-sensing factors are overwhelmed by their intellectual-philosophical stereotyping "insights" almost always fail in many ways, and sometimes sooner rather than later.

People whose sensing levels are healthy have also retained a good sensory experience of Life. Philosophers deal in so-called "superior" symbolic representations, sometimes completely intellectual in nature, of what they imagine to be "life" — and lose sensory contact with Life. This difference may not become real to you until you begin checking it out yourself.

People who have retained a good sensory experience of life tend also to be more naturally psychic — as contrasted to those who deal in stereotyping symbolisms who have, as they say, "lost it" and don't seem to know what is happening in the real world.

Sensory-experience types of people tend to hang loose more. Intellectualizing stereotypists tend to condense into cement blocks. People who hang loose at the sensing levels can see opportunities and seize them better than those stereotypists who intellectually are very rigid in their decisions and activities.

To help you get the picture of this better, I've made an attempt to put it into a chart as follows. This chart is meant only as something you can begin to play around with. Perhaps you will be able to create a better one.

Psychic Literacy

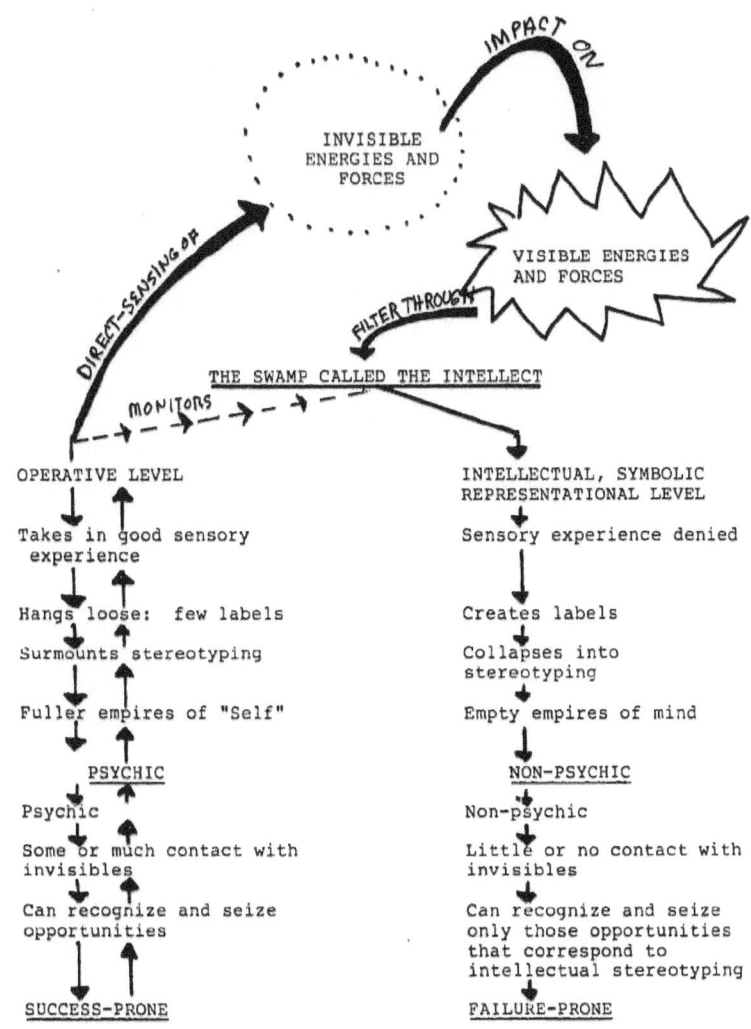

PROFITING FROM PSYCHIC INFORMATION

- We can observe that although psychic stuff is rejected by many anti-psychic individuals, groups, and echelons in our culture, there exists a sort of psychic underground composed of successful people who not only frequently depend on psychic inputs, but more or less covertly seek to extend their psychic literacy and knowledge. In all probability, this underground has always existed and always will, regardless of whether or not society "approves" of psychic stuff.

- We should also observe, I think, that the anti-psychic currents in our society exert undue influence regarding our overall educational processes, in that these processes do not seek to place, or teach us how to place, our psychic components in a proper perspective. The real issues involved thus become very confused and confusing — with the inevitable result that people who do experience some kind of psychic thing often feel guilty for having done so. If they do not intellectually reject their own psychic experiences altogether, they become, as it were, psychics in a closet.

- We can see that our intellects can do negate psychic information, with unfortunate results.

- We can also get a perspective on certain factors in regard to seizing success. Admittedly, the grasping of success is always a very elusive thing, but it is almost certain to elude intellects which cannot integrate information coming from our more basic direct-sensing systems.

SUGGESTED PRACTICAL EXERCISES THAT WILL HELP IN EXPANDING PSYCHIC LITERACY

o Find a quiet time, sit down with a pen and paper, and try to recall instances in which you have experienced some psychic prompting. Note the approximate date, write the prompting down, and then note whether you took advantage of it or not and what the outcome was. This will help your intellect become more aware of your personal psychic experience. Remember, the intellect learns by repeating things several times. Read your list every once in a while, adding to it upon occasion.

o Try to talk with people who you perceive as being successful in some way. With as much diplomacy as you can muster, lead the conversation to psychic matters and try to find out how much they have relied on psychic inputs or how they view sources of psychic information.

o Try to perceive people with reference to whether or not they seem to be open with regard to their direct-sensing capabilities or are imprisoned in intellectual psychic failure — but be sure not to tell people they are dwelling in psychic failure, for reasons that might be obvious. They will not appreciate this news at all. Just observe and learn — and keep your own counsel.

o In a sort of creative visualization mode, begin to ask your intellect to attune itself more and more, and in every way, to psychic pits of information it might perceive.

o Begin keeping a list of practical purposes you could use psychic clues for if you could learn to work with your psychic factors.

Now, all our psychic potentials are valuable, and have a reason for existing, as we shall see.

The overall hypothesis of this book is that there is nothing about us humans — no organ, no structure, no phenomenon — that does not exist for a purpose. Everything about us exists for some specific purpose and function. Therefore, our psychic factors exist for specific purposes and functions.

But certainly those that provide us (or try to provide us) with information about the future can be extraordinarily valuable, as we shall see in the next chapter.

IV

Is the Future Somehow Creating Us?

CAN REAL INFORMATION ABOUT THE FUTURE PENETRATE OUR INTELLECTS?

There is a prevailing idea which holds that since all human bodies are anatomically similar, at least as regards major, structural features, then all minds and intellects must share similar features, too, since the brains that presumably house them are also anatomically similar. Out of this prevailing idea comes another — that we can judge between normal and abnormal behavior by virtue of trying to find out which mental and intellectual similarities are shared by the greatest amounts of people.

Standing in direct contrast to these two prevailing ideas, human experience shows us very clearly, that even if minds and intellects may share similar physical features, they hardly ever develop or turn out the same behavior. Simply put, like snowflakes, behavior crystalizes in different ways, no two forms of it ever being exactly alike.

But we do know at least four things about *all* intellects:

1. They have to *learn* whatever it is they contain.
2. They are only as good as what they contain.
3. If a given intellect doesn't understand something very well, it is likely to be confused in *all* matters pertaining to it.
4. If a given intellect knows nothing at all about something, that something does not exist for it.

Intellects that work best are those which can grasp what is confusing them or what they don't know anything about, and, then, work themselves toward correcting the situation. But, intellects even have to learn to do *that*, and, in fact, how to do it — which is to say, intellects have to be taught the existence and importance of this vital self-improving factor.

When a given intellect encounters something which, as they say, "it can't relate to," it probably will not be able to accept, process, and store (learn) any information relating to that something. The usual, constructive way of coping with this failure-to-relate situation is by repeatedly exposing the intellect to what is involved until it does learn to accept, process, and store the pertinent information. What an intellect cannot learn, it cannot incorporate into its world view, and thus its world view becomes lopsided in a variety of ways. The whole of this is, of course, exceedingly more complex. But these basic considerations will serve our immediate purposes here.

If our intellects cannot recognize or relate to certain kinds of information being provided by our direct sensing equipment, then they will be unable accurately to incorporate the real meaning of these signals into their own processes. Two cases in point are my own Madison Square Garden fiasco and the deadly outcome of the drug-smuggling aviator narrated in the preceding chapter (and we'll review other cases throughout this book).

If our intellects contain ideas that information about the future is *not* accessible via our direct sensing equipment, then will they be able to recognize and constructively process such information if it does appear? Usually not, I think, and historical cases will bear me out.

Considering the fact that our intellects are learning-dependent, we are more or less obliged to undertake to *deliberately provide the necessary learning experiences* for them to function well — that is, to *increase* their overall literacy. Considering the fact that intellects learn best via repetition and repetitive exposure, providing them with such is demonstrably the best way to enhance literacy in any given area.

FUTURE-SEEING, OR, PERCEIVING THE FUTURE

All our psychic potentials are so astonishing (as we shall see ahead) that it is difficult to say which among them is the more important. But the *future* is important to us. After all, we are headed for it, for better or worse. So those psychic aptitudes that apparently can perceive some aspect of the future certainly have a very meaningful importance.

About the only way I can talk about future-seeing is by giving examples of it, of which many are to follow. I am quite satisfied that *all* the examples contained in this book happened more or less the way they were reported, and that the only explanation for them is a psychic explanation. If critics wish to argue them they are free to do so — and, at any rate, if they don't like some of these examples they can get down from their armchair observation posts and, with a little research of their own, discover similar and equivalent ones. The psychic archives are vast. Real-time human experience is even larger.

So, I'm going to begin by narrating four future-seeing events which will help you get the gist of future-seeing. The events speak for themselves. They are not "impossible" since they *did* occur.

As to how they can have occurred, there is really only one workable hypothesis. It is a staggering hypothesis. See if *you* can figure it out as you read.

As I was preparing on February 1, 1989, to apply fingers to word processor and begin this book, I wished I had a verified, widely-known, *current* example of someone who had future knowledge which came true. That very evening, the NBC TV program, "Unsolved Mysteries," aired one for all America to see. It's a sad, tragic tale. But our psychic factors concern themselves with the whole of life — not just with its gooey sweetness and light.

Living in Las Vegas with her mother and sister was a young girl named Catherine Hobbs. From about the age of eight, she began to be convinced she would not live past sixteen, an age she would reach late in 1988. Naturally, this premonition rather blighted her life. She talked about it often and gloomily noted the passing of each birthday. She wrote little letters to herself, to be found when she was gone, saying no one was to regret her passing, since, as far as she could make out, this was how things were to be. She was *fated* to die around the time of her sixteenth birthday. This was her future, and that was that.

It is hard to imagine a child and teenager living under this pall of premonition, and doubtless everyone involved thought it was all conceived as a result of some morbid imagination of her own — especially when her sixteenth birthday came, and she was sixteen plus one day. Cathy herself was astonished and overjoyed she was still alive at sixteen.

Three months after her sixteenth birthday, at 11:30 p.m., dressed in pink pants and white blouse, Cathy went to an all-night grocery store three blocks from her home to buy a new novel to read. Las Vegas streets are brilliantly lit at night, and she had made the same trip many times before. Cathy kissed her mother, saying goodbye. When her mother asked why the "goodbye," Cathy, a little confused, said she thought the mother would be asleep before she got back. The mother, indeed, went to bed.

At about 3:00 a.m., the mother woke up, having experienced a feeling like a hard blow to her head — followed by a feeling of extreme peace and "a gratefulness" that "it" was finally over. Being unable to make anything of this strange event, she went back to sleep. The next morning, she discovered Cathy had not come home.

Later evidence showed that someone, probably Cathy, had bought a novel in the all-night store, after which she disappeared. About nine days later, her stinking, bloated, decomposing corpse, still dressed in pink pants and white blouse, was found fifty miles out in the Nevada desert by a man searching for rock crystals.

It is easy enough for us to assume the utterly sad and sick reason for her awful demise. She was kidnapped, probably raped, then murdered by persons unknown, and dumped far out in the arid wastes to rot under the scorching desert sun.

What is not easy to explain at all is why, during her childhood and teenage years, the girl should have foretold her own death and been completely convinced she would not live past the age of sixteen. If she had died from any of the more natural reasons, skeptics of psychic precognition could joyfully say, as, damn them, they do, that she died from some morbid, psychological wish fulfillment which had little to do with actual future-seeing.

We cannot possibly think (and still call ourselves sane) that she died spontaneously of some morbid wish fulfillment and then dragged her mutilated body fifty miles into the arid wastes, leaving it to feed desert scavengers, ants, and insects.

Now, if we try to adopt the largest overview possible to try to explain Cathy's murder, we can see that many elements, or factors, had to come together to complete her own psychic prophecy of "not living past sixteen" — majorly, that she had to encounter, at some appointed time and place, with her killer or killers, and that death was to be the outcome of this baleful meeting. We will get more deeply into this larger overview shortly.

And what of the mother's obvious telepathic experience, in which she probably did "experience" the death blow — *and* what we might assume were Cathy's afterlife, out-of-body feelings of being relieved it was "all over?" Thousands of similar telepathic bonding experiences are on record.

A SUCCESS IN ACKNOWLEDGING FUTURE-SEEING

I've collected thousands of examples of future-seeing, some dating back to ten thousand years ago, showing that our future-seeing psychic potentials have long been with us. One of the more upbeat examples, which completely fascinated me many years ago when I came across it, concerned a boy named Adrian Christian who, in 1833 dreamed he was captain of a ship and that his family, on another ship, was in danger. He rescued them. He told his dream to his brother Thomas, and to his family, and in this way, the dream of the young Adrian Christian got into letters and notes.[1]

Forty-seven years later, Adrian Christian had indeed become captain of a ship, the *British India*, sailing from Sydney, Australia, for Rangoon and Burma. A few days after sailing, he dreamt of a ship in distress. At the end of the dream the word FAMILY appeared in flaming letters. Christian promptly doubled the lookout. The following night, again he dreamt of a sinking ship and gained the impression that it was due north of his own vessel.

Over protestations of his skeptical officers, he ordered the *British India's* course to be altered to due north. Two days later, a sinking hulk was sighted on the horizon. From this sinking hulk Adrian Christian rescued two hundred sixty-nine people — among whom, to his astonishment, was his *own* brother, Thomas, whom Adrian thought was still at home. The name of the doomed vessel was *The Family*. Put that one in your pipe and smoke it.

Just try to imagine all the lines-of-life factors that had to come together in order for the psychic dream-prophecy, experienced forty-seven years *earlier*, of the young Adrian Christian to be fulfilled. How is it possible that forty-seven years before all the elements of the actual physical sinking "arrangements" of *The Family* could come together that *anyone* could "see" *anything* in *any form* that would take place in the future? Unless...

ABRAHAM LINCOLN FUTURE-SEES HIS OWN DEATH

Here is another well-documented example. A few days before Abraham Lincoln was shot, he had a dreamt an out-of-body glimpse

---

1 Day, Harvey, Seeing Into the Future, Thorsons Publishers, Ltd., London, 1966, p. 157.

into his own future.[2] He confided to his wife and his friend, Ward Lamon, that he wandered from room to room in the White House. The building was empty, but from every room came the sound of sobbing. In the East Room, he saw a catafalque in which lay a corpse clothed in funeral vestments. Surrounding the soldiers on guard was a throng of weeping mourners. In this dream-like, out-of-body state, the President asked the soldiers: "Who lies dead in the White House?"

"The President," they answered. "He was assassinated."

The afternoon before he was shot in 1865, Lincoln's Cabinet entered the council room for a meeting to find the President seated at the table, his head buried in his hands. As they entered, he looked up.

"Gentlemen," he said, "before long you will have some important news."

"Have you had bad news, Mr. President?" one asked.

"I have heard nothing. But last night again I had a dream. I was in a boat, alone. I had no oars, no rudder. I was helpless in a boundless sea. Yes, gentlemen. Perhaps tomorrow, perhaps in a few hours, you will have important news."

Lincoln was assassinated five hours later.

A GLUT OF FUTURE-SEEING REPORTS

I could go very far back into history to dredge up thousands of examples of future-seeing. Back to Cicero, for example. Back to the oracle at Dodona. Alexander the Great never undertook a campaign without consulting future-seers, except once, and then he met his end. The Bible records a dozen or more instances of future-seeing. Future-seeing is taking place today, as the first example above shows.

Now, simply asked, if the future *can* be seen in any way by anyone at all, is this not an important implication? To say otherwise, to minimize this extraordinary potential, is, as the down-to-earth miners in the High Rockies where I was born would comment, some kind of "crap." What we, today, would give to peer into the next forty years, what with the greenhouse effect, over-population, and environmental destruction hanging over our heads.

---

2 Ibid., p. 174. Lincoln's dream is also reported in several of his biographies.

At this point, it is only fair to alert you, the readers, that I am not reporting on these things as merely a dispassionate, unbiased observer. My own psychic forewarnings have saved my life at least six times (thrice during childhood, twice in Korea, and once in New York). So I emote over the possibilities involved. I get angry when skeptics try to explain it all away by silly contrivances. I get even angrier when multitudes trained in the so-called reason and logic of science follow the skeptics like sheep. For chrissakes, information revealing the nature and specifics of our future-seeing psychic potentials is in evidence everywhere — in archives, in history, in occult books, in daily life, in the media (especially in the pages of *FATE* magazine[3]), in the Bible, in biographies, in police records.

Yet, a pompous, psychically illiterate, intellectual few can propose that the whole is nonsense — and not an inconsiderable amount of anti-psychic stereotyped fanatics actually *believe* them. Yes, I *am* angry! There should be anger about this subject — if one begins to realize the implications and the human capabilities that are being thwarted by such anti-psychic nonsense.

I am, of course, talking about getting a psychic revolution going. If we *are* psychic, all of us, then it is time to give our psychic potentials a real chance to see what they can do.

Why am I so emotional about all this? Well, my own psychic factors have saved *my* life several times. One *has* to be interested in things that save one's life, unless one's brain has devolved into a self-destructing slime.

A FUTURE-SEEING THAT SAVED MY LIFE

When I was six, my parents and I lived in a small, two-bedroom house next to my grandmother whose house was huge. My room was off the kitchen. One night when I was just going to sleep (I was not yet asleep), I "saw" a terrific wall of flame erupt in the kitchen and blast through the open door into my room. I remember it very, very well. Hot, yellow-like heat that seared the wallpaper off the boards and incinerated the skin off my little body.

---

3 Fate, bless its heart, is the only periodical in the world which invites the public to send in their psychic experiences. As such, its archives are extremely valuable, since they represent a voluminous cross-section of human experience in these matters.

I ran screaming into my parents' bedroom. There was, of course, no fire at all. My father checked the kitchen and everything else that he could. But I screamed and yelled and would not even stay in the house. I was quite a feisty little brat. I had no intention of ever sleeping in my little bed again, nor even allowing my parents to stay in the house. The sum of it all was that before I would agree to quiet down the three of us had to go next door to spend the night at grandmother's.

About midnight, our little house erupted into a towering inferno, and before the fire department, a mere three blocks away, could arrive, the kitchen, bedrooms and dining room were gone. My uncle, who was seventeen at the time, had been necking with some girl in his Model-T Ford in front of our house and witnessed the explosion. He said the house just suddenly incandesced in flame like a bomb had gone off. He got himself a little toasted trying to rescue us, for he had not known we had removed to grandmother's. We never really knew why the house burnt, except to suppose it was the result of one of those sudden combustions in the attic due to old faulty electrical wiring.

The first bottom line is that if my parents had been able intellectually to talk me into going to sleep in my bed, the future-seeing vision would have been fulfilled in some form. The second bottom line is that since we removed ourselves to my grandmother's, *we changed the part of the future that included us getting incinerated*, and the calamity was avoided. A psychic input saved us, not only because *it* occurred, but because I, in my tantrum, overwhelmed intellectual resistance toward acknowledging it. As I interpreted it many years later, it was its *purpose* to do just that.

A MAJOR PURPOSE OF FUTURE-SEEING

Let's have a longer look at this. What more could a psychic factor do than *show* you what is going to happen? I mean, consider... If we can *see* what is going to happen, we can take steps to avoid it or, in the business sense, perhaps take advantage of it as many people do. If you are too intellectually dense and too psychically illiterate to acknowledge the presence of your psychic factors, even when they do alert you to something, well, perhaps you deserve what happens. In my case, perhaps if I had been a little older and more intellectually programmed in the "superior importance" of reason and logic (as we presently tend to conceive them), then I would have accepted the idea that my vision was probably only my imagination — and would have been dead...like the drug smuggler, poor Cathy, and Abe Lincoln.

But poor Cathy! Try to look at her awful Event like this. Apparently, her psychic factors had been intermittently (for *eight years!*) trying to alert her that a point in time in the future had, somehow, to be avoided. I'm sure she did not know what to do about her psychic alerts. Nor did her family, her teachers, nor anyone else. After all, she was living in a rational, logical society, was she not?

Even if her psychic alerts were ambiguous, I know for a fact that one can go to a sympathetic hypnotist. A little light hypnosis might have filled in enough details to have allowed Cathy to change her habits and avoid going to the all-night store. Even this might have not been necessary. I am sure no one sat down with her, tried to relax her and get a better picture of what her premonition consisted. It is far more likely everyone retreated into their psychic illiteracy and *avoided* even talking about it. And so, she met her terrible point in time and was murdered.

I also know for a fact, as we shall see, that one can consult one's horoscope — that ancient psychic tool. In the horoscope, the points in time that are going to be inimical and even deadly (as well as fortunate and favorable) are usually clearly indicated — and, in the hands of a competent astrologer, often *more than just a general idea of what may happen* can be gained. In the pages ahead, I propose to show that this is unequivocally true.

Now, I want to say something very clearly and with much emphasis: if we remain psychically illiterate, we do not stand any hope of learning to use our psychic capabilities to some good advantages. It may be that some people will need to depend on psychic alerts only once or twice during their lives. But that once or twice may be of strategic survival importance. On the other hand, if one is totally unprepared, well, they easily could go poor Cathy's way.

Now, the really sad — yet really wonderful — part of this is that *none of this is very hard to do!* It takes a little specialized training in these matters, to be sure. But we already have enough understanding of psychic stuff to do quite well — if we can step out of our prevailing anti-psychic ideas long enough to put it together and get on with it. We can put intuitions and premonitions (however they are dumped into our consciousness) together with light hypnosis and astrology and other psychic tools to come up with a psychic package that will show direct correlations to things that are going to happen in the future. By the time you are finished with this book, this will be a little clearer to you.

What is much more difficult is to invent reasons why we should *not* learn to take advantage of our psychic potentials, and it is even *more* difficult to make inane attempts to explain it all away completely. When you do try to explain it away, all that usually happens is that you dig an intellectual hole and then fall into it.

At any rate, ever since my childhood experience in which my own psychic factors saved not only myself but my parents, clearly it has been impossible for me to accept the well-advertised skeptical idea that our psychic potentials are nonsense and cannot be proven. But I believe it is time to say one thing further: Those who do not believe in psychic phenomena, and especially those who actively fulminate against researching them, are retrogressive Life-*avoiders* of the worst sort and should be cast into the sewers, along with polluters, animal murderers, war-mongers, and their ilk.

This having been said, let me now briefly say something about *how* it seems to me that future-seeing can take place (although I'll go into the topic in more detail later).

THE FUTURE MUST EXIST IN ORDER TO BE "SEEN"

Our world has an in-depth and very long record of future-seeing that goes back into prehistoric times. I am well enough versed in this record and most of the major commentaries (scientific and otherwise) that have been made about it.

In this record, there is something missing — a glaring omission that can only be perceived if one has read, read, and read. Although it is clear that future-seeing *is* possible and *does* occur, no one has tried to figure out the elements that must be involved if it is to take place at all. The sole exception to this might be J.W. Dunne, in his best-selling but somewhat confusing book, *Experiment with Time*, first published in 1927.

It is unbelievable that parapsychologists have not set themselves the task of digging into probable mechanisms of future-seeing, or at least tried to develop a rationale for it. But they have done neither.

In my way of thinking about the issues involved, the question must turn on this: can anyone see something that does not actually *already* exist in some place or in some dimension? If we try to bring a smattering of logic into the computations, it is practicably unthinkable that anyone could see, even by psychic means, anything that truly does not exist *anywhere*. How can anyone see something that is not?

If you let this question ferment in your intellect a little, a rather awesome, if mind-boggling, possibility begins to emerge. If no one can see what is not existing and hence is not formed, then events that will take place in the future can be seen *only if they already exist* somewhere, somehow, in some psychic dimension. For over ten years, I've cooked this question every way to Sunday and back again. And all mental avenues loop back to this fundamental probability. Future events (or at least some parts of them) already exist "someplace," for if they did not, no one could see them...ever.

The most basic implication of this is that the future is at least partially creating us, in some strange way we cannot yet understand. The future feeds back to us through psychic "seeing," allowing us to change it, if we are smart enough to grasp the chances to do so. Clearly, this is *the* Key to the universe. We cannot change present time. By the time present time takes place, it is too late to change it. What we can change, apparently, is the future — if we can learn to "see" it or even parts of it.

Admittedly, this concept makes a mess of how we view the uniqueness of our present-time continuum as being the only real reality. But since our worldviews are much in a mess anyway (if we are honest with ourselves), I can't see that this new mess matters all that much!

In the examples given above, the drug smuggler, Cathy, Adrian Christian, Lincoln, and myself all "saw" a "future" event that *came to be enacted* in our "present time" continuum. The three that ignored their psychic signals are dead. By "obeying" his psychic signals, Adrian Christian saved several hundred people, including his brother. I obeyed mine, and I saved myself and my parents. That there was a direct correlation between the psychic sightings and the events that came to transpire can be of little doubt.

These future-seeing Events required that pertinent factors necessary for their enactment come together at the "appointed" time in our "present-time" continuum. The implication is this: present-time Events are somehow being formed by the future, and the future is somehow looping back into present time.

And, quite clearly, there is one further implication: the psychic potentials every one of us possess can and *do* at times perceive the information in the loops via several of the different psychic functions (dreams, precognition, astrology, consulting seers, etc.), all of which, apparently, exist for that special purpose.

With all this in mind, several momentous questions now raise their heads, not the least of which is the question of whether one can *change* the future if and when one can adequately perceive it through some mode of the psychic capabilities, i.e., via our direct-sensing links to it. The answer is yes, that is, *if* we can learn to accept the alerts our psychic sensing elements try to impress into our intellects. The meaning of all this will become clearer as we proceed.

IS THE FUTURE SOMEHOW CREATING US?

- We can observe that we *must* possess specific factors in our psychic sensing apparatus which are occupied with trying to alert us to future life-threatening interludes. The collected literature clearly establishes that, time and again throughout history and into the present, people do experience *exact* pre-visions of some approaching calamity.

- We can observe that if and when people do something constructive with regard to these approaching calamities, they can make intellectual decisions to avoid, mitigate, or transcend them. If their intellects are stumbling psychic illiterates, then they will not be able to take advantage of the psychic promptings.

- This kind of evidence clearly *must* indicate that, somehow, the future is already formed in order for its aspects to feed back into present-time consciousness, via certain psychic factors. Whether or not these future aspects are cast in irrevocable cement or not will be discussed later.

- We should also begin to consider, I think, that these observations have very important implications regarding our present image of humanity, in that our present image does not really incorporate the extraordinary possibilities the accumulated evidence represents.

SUGGESTED PRACTICAL EXERCISES THAT WILL HELP IN EXPANDING PSYCHIC LITERACY

- If you have ever experienced one or more times a psychic-type prompting that tried to alert you to some life-threatening or life-preserving event, take paper and pencil and record it and how it turned out. Sometimes, as we have seen, a longish period of time can transpire between the prompting and its fulfillment. Re-read your notes at intervals — until you begin to sense your intellect has begun to get the idea of the importance of these kinds of psychic promptings.

- If you have no direct experiences of your own to record, ask around among people you know for theirs — and record them. Be sure to find out three things: when the psychic prompting occurred, whether or not the person acted on it, and how it turned out. This indirect observation is better than none, and, at any rate, intellects seem to accept phenomena more easily when they begin to perceive those phenomena happening to others.

V

The Difference Between Psychic Factors and Psychic Abilities

In 1977 I began to become aware of that there is a difference between what we usually call "psychic abilities" and what I am calling "psychic factors" in this book. It is a very important difference, and grasping it is essential, I think, for anyone who wants to begin to work with their psychic potentials.

We identify an ability as some sort of a natural endowment we can train through practice and thence think we can manage with our willpower in order to achieve specific ends. In our cultural Western tradition, we esteem the concept of the individual very highly, and we have come to believe that the individual, properly motivated, can overcome all things by acts of individual will.

During the last two decades, I've met many who were determined to develop their ESP abilities by acts of will and who at first fully believed that the determination to do so logically would result in heightened sensitivity and increased ESP proficiency. Most of them went down in flames, as it is said, and in some cases were surprised when their ESP did not get better at all, but actually *got worse*. It is, I think, a matter of observing the obvious. If at the individual level willpower and practice were all that were necessary to increase psychic abilities, then many would have become psychic superstars by now. Obviously other things are involved, and I'll call them "factors."

A factor is defined as something that actively contributes to the production of a good or bad result. A psychic factor is a something that does likewise in a psychic sense. Psychic factors, then, are invisible somethings that contribute to the production of a positive or negative result.

Many invisible factors exist *outside our individual spheres* of willpower and self-determination, but our philosophy of intense individualism instills the belief we are so self-powerful that it more or less trains us to be insensitive to their existence. Most of us possess natural psychic powers at least in rudimentary form, but no one can develop them very much unless the factors "attached" to them are also taken into account — at which time, as it were, a horse of a different color becomes visible.

I discovered the existence of psychic factors in the strangest of strange ways. This experience is worth narrating in full for it gives some idea of what the color of the different horse is like.

THE FOUR SEASONS EVENT

In 1967 my interests in art and painting had led me to meet a wonderful, dynamic woman, who was quite elderly at the time, and whom I'll call Alice to save her family from embarrassment. Alice was not only a great person, but a reasonably great artist, whose major works were murals in important buildings here in the United States, South America, and Europe. She was deeply interested in psychic stuff and had an enormous circle of friends, all of whom, including myself, considered her something of a phenomenon.

Alice's story is thus. She came from a very rich Chicago family, numbered among that city's elite "four hundred." She had married an upcoming Wall Street type as was expected of someone of her class. However, her husband lost his fortune in the Crash of 1929 and died shortly thereafter, leaving her with three young children.

Rather than remarry someone her family was in a position to select for her, she insisted on remaining in New York, where she took up portrait painting to earn money. This scandalized her family, especially her elder brother who was in the process of making a great fortune of his own in the Midwest.

The brother's attitude was completely chauvinistic, and he treated Alice quite badly, vowing never to help her financially until she came "to her senses." The fact that she became successful as an artist and put her children through college never impressed him, which, in turn irritated Alice to no end. The brother and sister hardly spoke and carried this state of affairs over into their old age and, in fact, until Alice died in a nursing home near Chicago.

Each Christmas, however, Alice sent her brother a gift. As she got older, she could undertake fewer and fewer commissions due to advancing arthritis. And so money got tight, a situation ignored by her enormously wealthy brother, who, by then, had endowed a large Midwestern college, which was named after him. In 1973, unable to go shopping for the annual gift, she asked me to undertake buying it.

"My brother has everything," she explained. "His only real passion is women, even at his age, and Chinese art. He has an enormous collection. I can afford $40. Will you go around and see if you can find some small Chinese thing for that price?"

I explained something she already knew — that it was very unlikely one could find even the smallest piece of reasonably good Chinese art for $40. "Try," she begged. "You have a good eye, and somehow I know you will succeed."

Now, it was because I had a "good eye" that I thought this whole effort would be fruitless. But Alice had been so good to me when I needed help that I felt obliged to give it my best and then report back to her that I had failed. For several days I trudged around Chinese fine art stores in uptown Manhattan. I tried to invoke my ESP — to no avail. The impossibility of the task was readily confirmed, and I got nowhere fast, as they say. I reported to Alice daily. She said, "Keep trying. This is important to me. I refuse to give my brother the satisfaction of the fact that I can't afford to buy him something he likes."

Finally, having exhausted all the logical possibilities, I was at my wit's end. Then it happened. It was early on a Saturday morning. I was setting out to tell Alice, in person, that I had failed and to give back her $40. I got down to the stoop of my building. At that point, I decided to give it one more try. "Where," I asked myself, "could I find a good piece of Chinese art for $40?"

I suffered the briefest moment of blackness in which some images formed (commonly called an intuitive flash). I "saw" a small glass case with two small figurines in it, with the sense that I would find them in, of all places, Chinatown in downtown Manhattan. Now, I had earlier dismissed the idea of finding collectable Chinese art in Chinatown because it was my impression it was filled with tourist-type stuff (which it is) and clearly Alice's brother, since he was a collector of Chinese art, was not going to be fooled by some miserable tourist junk. At this point, and with no other clue of what to do, I trudged off towards Chinatown.

Once there, I wandered slowly down Mott Street (Chinatown's main drag), looking in windows, carefully perusing the garish stuff in them. I came to a certain store whose interior walls were lined with stacks of cheap Chinese porcelain. For no apparent reason at all, I was suddenly impressed with the fact that "this was the store." So, I went in and slowly walked to the back.

I didn't see them at first, but shortly I noticed two small figurines, about three inches high, in a glass case on the back wall amid all the other clutter. I went up to inspect them more closely. Carved of a beautiful, near-white jadeite, they were not ornate, in fact quite rough in execution, but obviously things of some quality.

The old, very old, Chinese woman tending the store came up and said, as impossible as it might seem: "Ah, you have a good eye. Most people don't even look at these." Goosebumps ran up my spine. "Do you know what they are?" she asked.

"Well, I think there should be four of these. One is a representation of Autumn and the other of Winter. There should also be a Spring and Summer." The four seasons have long been a favorite theme in oriental art, in painting, poetry, and sculpture — and at least I knew, intellectually, that much.

"Ah, yes," replied the Chinese woman, obviously impressed. "I've had these two for many years. I never had Spring and Summer. These two are wanting to be rejoined to them."

"How much are they?" I asked.

"Once I was asking $100 each. But they have been here for so long. I can give both of them to you for $100."

So, I decided to explain the nature of my mission, emphasizing the infirmities of the aging Alice.

The Chinese woman regarded me closely for a moment. Then: "OK, I sense they will find a good home through you. To me they are exquisite, and in a way, I'm glad no one has bought them. But I won't be around much longer, as old as I'm getting. Take them both for $40."

I was ever-so-pleased with my bargaining ability. But Alice surveyed the tiny sculptures with a dubious eye. "Well," she finally said, "perhaps he won't notice the set is incomplete."

Shortly after Christmas, my telephone rang. It was an overjoyed Alice. "My brother was absolutely staggered by your small carvings," she began. "He recognized them immediately as the work of a well-known artist of the last century. And you'll never guess. He has the other two, the Spring and Summer. He says he bought them over forty years ago in Hong Kong and knew that one day he would acquire the other two. So the set of four are now rejoined. I can't thank you enough. He was perfectly civil to me. He hasn't visited my studio for over ten years but says he will come and do so shortly."

Now, altogether this was an incredible Event. Normally, the theories of mere coincidences or chance happenings are used to explain away something like this. But how, or more importantly, *why* should so many "chance happenings" group themselves together to produce such a meaningful result? Admittedly, a seemingly unimportant result — but a result nonetheless.

I mulled this perfectly ridiculous situation in my mind tor a long time. I had never met the brother and never did. My sympathies were with Alice, and even if I had been her I might not have lifted a finger to try to please him at all.

At any rate, I considered it my duty to return to the Chinese woman to tell her that the set was rejoined — to find out she had already died. The exquisite Four Seasons are now housed in a museum — in a section named after the brother — where, I trust, they will remain together forevermore.

PSYCHIC FACTORS

To me, the unexplainable, nonsensical complexities of this event had absolutely awesome implications, although I could not figure out intellectually what these were — until I began to get the idea of the existence of psychic *factors* as things that contribute to the production of a result.

When we think of our psychic abilities, we think of them as just that — our abilities. Since our abilities obviously contribute to the production of results, admittedly the line is very thin between a factor and an ability. "Ability" is defined as natural talent or acquired proficiency, competence in doing (as in a skill), and the physical, mental, or other power to perform.

Now, there are hardly any natural talents that we know of that do not require active developing, which is to say, acquiring proficiency through practice, exercise, learning, understanding, and maintenance. For example, most of us have a natural talent for riding a bicycle, but it does take a given amount of practice to be able to do so, and the acquiring of even more proficiency to become a daring downhill racer. When we think of ability, we automatically and correctly link it to the acquiring of proficiency.

But what about things that impact on us and contribute to the production of a result that are *NOT* dependent on whether or not we possess a natural talent or an acquired proficiency? The point I'm trying to make is that apparently there exist *factors* that are independent of our personal collection of abilities, but which produce results involving us anyway.

Since this may be one of the most important points in this book, it is worth taking some time to enlarge upon it.

The bringing together of the exquisite and, as I take it, the *precious* Four Seasons and preserving them for posterity was the result of invisible factors which none of the human players, by themselves, had the ability to pull off, but in which each played a significant *role*. The result entire was dependent on a lot of "ifs." Just look at some of them. For example:

If Alice's brother had not collected Chinese art;

If she, herself, had not dutifully sent an annual present;

If she had not been incapacitated and been forced to ask me to do her shopping;

If she had not "known" I would succeed in finding something suitable "because I had a good eye;"

If I had not exhausted *all* my rational, intellectual possibilities regarding locating a reasonably good piece of Chinese art for $40 and decided to "give it one more go;"

If I had not experienced an intuitive "flash" which delivered its significant information to my struggling intellect;

If the Chinese woman had not sensed I "had a good eye;"

If she had not sensed she was going to die soon and, presumably, knew she had no further use for the figurines;

If she had not sensed that through me the figurines "would find a good home;"

If she had not sensed the four sculptures were "seeking to be rejoined;"

If the brother had not bought Spring and Summer over forty years ago;

If the set had not been separated in the first place;

And, if the brother had not been wealthy and influential enough to establish a wing for his collection in a museum (a good home).

Well, absent any one of the ifs above and the Four Seasons would not have ended up together in a museum. All these *factors came together* to produce the result-event they did — although it is certainly not clear why it "needed" to take place at all. The Four Seasons are beautiful enough to be sure, but there must be hundreds of thousands of artistic versions representing the four seasons, many of which are certainly more valuable and even, possibly, greater art.

The worst part of all this is that at first glance it seems completely nonsensical, and it stumps our intellects whose first line of duty is to try to make sense out of what is being experienced.

I found it very difficult to try to deal with all this in my head. But I was absolutely awestruck by the event, and I really wanted to try to understand it the best I could. I got nowhere until I decided to take a piece of paper and list all the factors that seemed to be contained it — list them and draw a map of their interconnectedness. While I was doing just so, I suddenly had the impression that my somewhat confused intellect could "see," for the first time, what I was trying to get at. Shortly, there occurred what many people call some "cognitions" — "cognition" being the act or process of knowing, including both awareness and judgment.

The foremost implication of all this was twofold: (1) there are invisible activities going on around us which involve us and are invisible *only* because our intellects may not be able to perceive them and their workings; (2) these invisible activities produce their results even when our intellects have no immediate knowledge of what is actually happening.

Which is to say that the whole of this is *psychic* (i.e., essentially invisible) and reflects the existence of invisible "method-plans" in that one of the definitions of "plan" is a method of carrying out a design or actualizing in a result. If and when these invisible method-plans impact on one's life in a noticeable way, they most certainly are bound to confuse our intellects if they possess little or no information about their existence in the first place.

It is very important for me to say the following: if I had not taken the time to get a piece of paper and pencil and begin literally to list the factors involved, I fully believe that I would not have grasped this picture to this day. Most of us try to resolve everything in our heads — where thoughts come and go, sometimes fading away altogether while we are trying to study them, and where our ideas and beliefs about things always color each other in an ever-changing way.

Making lists of factors on paper which will not come together in our heads often causes them to fall together in ways our intellects cannot at first see. I'm not exactly sure why this is so, but that it is so seems beyond doubt. Many of the practical suggestions in this book ask for listings in various categories — which, if undertaken, almost assuredly will culminate in new insights regarding your psychic understandings.

In any event, a great time ago it appears that man began to notice something, which is: when things visible or invisible come together in a certain way, a certain result not only must, but *does*, ensue. We can also express this as: when certain *factors* come together, a certain result *actualizes*. We may possess *abilities* to recognize these factors and thus even foresee how they will turn out, but the factors themselves are significantly *independent* of our psychic abilities.

This is an extremely important distinction, for the following reason. When in our present culture we do focus upon our "psychic abilities," we more or less do so under the theoretical idea that developing them is an end in itself. If we develop *them* — which is to say achieve proficiency in them — then we will have *added* new capabilities to our pool of awareness potentials.

This makes such good *theoretical* sense to our intellects as they are presently constituted that we are almost completely incapable of seeing that this makes no sense at all.

Let's slowly work our way through this. For example, we speak of developing our telepathy, our clairvoyance, our capabilities to foresee the future when, indeed, we do not know exactly what telepathy, clairvoyance, or precognition are, or in fact even if they exist as we define them. What we *do* perceive are *results* of phenomena which we then label as telepathic, clairvoyant, or prophetic.

But, (slowly, now) when we "see" something via some psychic ability, what we are looking at is the *result* of some processes that have produced what we "see." We cannot further develop something that is *already a RESULT* of some *other* factors that produced them.

This is such a subtle distinction that it might take some getting used to. But if you get the idea that one cannot further develop a cake that is already baked, you'll be getting your intellect into the right ballpark here. Mistakenly, we interpret telepathy, clairvoyance, or precognition as processes, when they are, in all instances, the *results* of processes and not the processes themselves. Look at it this way. If telepathy, clairvoyance, precognition, and, even, intuition, *were* processes that could be developed, then we, the clever things we are, would have achieved widespread development of them long ago. There has certainly been no lack of trying to do so. Yet the population of so-called "superpsychics" remains tiny and completely fortuitous as well.

Yet, our intellectual stance continues to "think" along these lines, to try to develop as "processes" phenomena that are already results of processes our intellects have no real knowledge of. We fail, and then we conclude that psychic abilities remain "elusive" or "mysterious." Yes, they do — and will, unless we shift the gears of our intellects and alter our theorizing about psychic stuff.

PSYCHIC ABILITY

If we begin thinking along these lines, the term "ability" becomes problematical. We have gotten into the habit of using the term "*an* ability" so much of the time that we tend to think an ability is a thing in itself. There is no ability I know of that is a thing in itself. Rather, abilities *are made up of* or *are the sum of* many factors that altogether produce them. Which is to say, an ability is an end product achieved only by mastering and/or taking advantage of those elements or factors that combine in some fashion to create a state of proficiency.

Sports people and performers of all kinds seem to understand this best of all because they realize that it hardly improves anything to focus on the final product, except as a goal to be reached by focusing on and gaining mastery of the different elements or factors necessary to reach it. Such people are constantly discovering, identifying, and, even, rediscovering subtle factors that "need to be worked on" and thence combined and recombined with their overall skills.

Also, we may as well note that ability is not a stable thing, but it is something that fluctuates according to factors that are influencing or impinging on it one way or another. Which is to say, *ability is always a conditional or relative thing* whose proficiency, at any given moment, can be judged only by its actual performance.

Clearly, then, we cannot hope to achieve proficiency over psychic ability by focusing our intellects chiefly on end products identified by labels such as telepathy, clairvoyance, or precognition. In fact, parapsychologists and psychical researchers *themselves* have enormous problems dealing in these labels. When they do get some kind of psychic result in an experimental situation, arguments quickly start up as to whether the result was "obtained" by clairvoyance, telepathy, precognition, out-of-body perception, or some other category of psychic process. The basis for this argumentation is that the researchers assume they have to attribute their psychic *products* (if and when they manage to cultivate some) to one of the available labels — when, in fact, the labels are neither necessary nor serviceable at all (which will become clearer and clearer as we proceed).

Needless to say, I'll not be using the term "*a* psychic ability" very much in the rest of this book. Rather, we'll direct our attention to the identifying the psychic factors that *culminate* in psychic proficiency of one kind or another. To do that, we have to try to discover those factors over which we should try to gain proficiency. Doing so may revolutionize the way we should construct (rather, reconstruct) our intellectual theories regarding psychic stuff.

PSYCHIC ATTRIBUTES

A capability is an ability that has undergone positive development which results in an enhancement of the ability. We are born with raw abilities, but we are not necessarily born with capabilities. If capabilities need to be developed actively in order to have them at all, obviously the idea that we are born with them is a misconception. But it is also obvious that different humans are from birth better predisposed, fortuitously so, toward gaining specific capabilities. If we are not born with these capabilities themselves already mastered, what then are we born with?

The word that fills the bill here is "attributes," which refers to an inherent characteristic — "inherent" meaning involved in the constitution or essential character of something. The term "endowment" also comes to mind, i.e., a natural capacity, power, or ability potential.

The idea that people are born with different attributes, inherent characteristics, and endowments is not in vogue as of this present writing, in that present trends are emphasizing the idea that we are all born with "equal opportunity." This is a good idea, I think, and there is certainly much truth in it. On the other hand, natural capacities, powers, ability potentials, and inherent characteristics *do* have a lot to do with survival and the seizing of success — but they appear to be very unequally distributed amongst the population.

The truth of the matter seems to be that while all people are and should be equal in certain areas of intra-social activity, our species is as busy now turning out geniuses and fools as it was in the past and, presumably, will be into the foreseeable future. I don't want to push this point too much here, since it involves the matter of choices. I only want to make the point that inherent characteristics and psychic attributes *are* factors that must be considered in learning to work with your psychic potentials. As we shall begin to see, not only do we all internally possess some mix of psychic attributes, but the psychic environments in which we find ourselves at any given time possess them too.

* * *

Regarding the Four Seasons event, then, had any of the "if" factors not been present, the situation would not have turned out as it did. All the factors involved had to get in a special *alignment* with each other in order to pop off. If you reread the "ifs" list, you will be able to observe that if one of them had been out of place, the whole of the event *would not have occurred* the exact way it did — although, of course, something else *might* have occurred. I should point out, however, that one can quickly get the eerie feeling that the *future* somehow laid a "plan" in which its "design" was actualized when all the factors were in the exact alignment.

At any rate, we shall see this "pattern" in almost all the events narrated in what follows. And we shall begin to see that if, via our direct-sensing faculties *properly* linked to our intellectual awareness capabilities, we can tune in to these plans and locate our position *in* them, or *relative to* them, we will be in the best possible place to "foresee" their outcomes.

THE DIFFERENCE BETWEEN PSYCHIC FACTORS AND PSYCHIC ABILITIES

- We should observe that our present intellectual theories regarding psychic stuff probably are mixed up and pretty thoroughly confused.

- If we began to question these intellectual theories with a view to making sense of them, we can see that we have focused on end products rather than on the *factor-processes* through which the end products manifest.

- We can agree that, undeniably, we cannot further develop a cake that has already been baked. Since what we experience as telepathy, clairvoyance, precognition, etc., are instances of end products, we really should realize that we cannot further develop them *per se* but must try to locate and seek to become proficient in managing the factors that have culminated in them.

- We can observe that all psychic events, as we experience them, are composed of many factors that have to be just right for them to occur.

- But we should also observe that many psychic events do occur even when we have absolutely no intellectual knowledge of their underlying factors — the implication then being that there exists an invisible psychic "universe" which is "doing its thing" regardless of whether or not we know of its existence.

SUGGESTED PRACTICAL EXERCISES THAT WILL HELP IN EXPANDING PSYCHIC LITERACY

o If you have not thoroughly understood this chapter, do feel free to read it again.

o Take a pencil and paper and make a diagram of all the factors present in the Four Seasons event. Study it until you can see that it would not have occurred at all or turned out the way it did if even one of the factors involved was not present.

o Earlier herein it was suggested you write out the details of one of your own psychic experiences (Events). Take some time and try to list all the "ifs" necessary for it to have occurred and to have turned out the way it did. If you do not have an Event of your own, get one from someone else, and, together, work out the "ifs." This is a very significant exercise. It will help your intellect "get the idea" of what is involved. Note down any cognitions you might experience.

* * *

TO BE REMEMBERED

o A *psychic factor* is something that actively contributes to the production of a result, *any* result. In the sense that it is psychic, it is always invisible to our physical senses and can only be perceived by other attributes of our direct-sensing capabilities.

o An *ability* is the sum of the mastering of the proficiencies necessary to produce it. Abilities are not stable conditions but fluctuate depending on what is influencing or impacting on them.

o *Psychic attributes* refer to our inherent and natural psychic capabilities, powers, and ability potentials. There is some reason to assume these are akin to physical genetic factors and as such presumably are shared in some fashion by the human species as a whole.

***

With all this preparation, we are now in a position to begin expanding our background information a little more. There's some amazing stuff ahead.

Let us first concentrate on some of the identifiable purposes our psychic potentials serve — which is to say, their practical aspects.

VI

Our Psychic Attributes and the Basic Purposes They Serve

If you observe people in general, including yourself, it seems there must be a reason or a desire for us to want to do something. Some of us feel we have purposes to fulfill. But unless we experience that condition called "motivation," something that causes us to act, we do not take conscious, active steps in any given directions other than those determined by our biological functions.

I've known thousands of people interested in psychic matters. No two of them have been exactly alike. But they all share one *factor*: in whatever way they have arrived at it, they all have come to sense that psychic stuff figures, sometimes powerfully so, in the living of life and that its purposes and functions need to be understood better. People who have not arrived at this sense cannot see any reason to interest themselves in psychic matters. They are missing, or have missed, the reason that would motivate them to take interest.

If there is no apparent reason to take interest in something, few will do so. However, if a reason does become apparent, then few will remain disinterested.

Thus, as in all things, there must be reasons for us to want to increase our psychic literacy. There is little doubt in my mind that these reasons will remain rather vague as long as we cannot perceive that our psychic attributes serve some specific purposes, purposes important enough to arouse something more than just curiosity, lukewarm motivation or cautious reserve. Further, any such reasons need to take on good definition, sharpness and, even, urgency.

Now, I could give you a one-liner here and leave it at that — which is that if you don't develop some psychic proficiency, the universe is going to dump all over you one way or another. Even if you are healthy and wealthy today, well, there's always the unknown tomorrow, full of "surprises" as history well shows.

The best known, traditionally observed function of our psychic attributes involves "seeing" that tomorrow, otherwise known as the future. In my own psychically-derived opinion, those who can sense-perceive something of the future are going to be grateful they can — even if it leads only to their getting out of the way of it.

As it happens, enhancing one's literacy level in *any* area serves also to enhance, in positive ways, the overall spectrum of one's *awareness and choices*. If the range of our volitional choices is limited by areas of illiteracy and ignorance, then it is reasonable to expect to encounter "surprises" with which it is hard to cope, or which grind us into mincemeat. In a way, we tend to ignore the fact that there are plenty who *do* get ground up, always harboring the small, secret hope we will not be one of them. But total destruction is always just one step away, sometimes literally so.

For example, several years ago the director of a famous museum in New York was a tall, elegant man of great social distinction who achieved his station, it would seem, on the merit of his own proficiencies. There is little doubt he was a success and, since he was relatively young, had more glories ahead of him. Since I had met him once or twice at art functions, and since we had exchanged a word or two about what I did, I knew he had no interest in psychic stuff.

I got to wondering. Here was a self-made man, eminently successful in his field. He had no interest in psychic stuff (hence, his psychic literacy may have been nonexistent), and presumably had "made it" not only because of his proficiencies in museum management, but by intellectually outwitting his competitors (of whom there are plenty in the art scene). What was the meaning here? What need did he have to cultivate his psychic awarenesses when he had apparently gotten along so well without them?

One sunny afternoon on the way to lunch, the museum director was taken out of life by a speeding taxi. New York's culturati mourned, and that was that. But this got me thinking, trying to isolate the issues involved.

Tragedies like this happen all the time, of course. But it also happens all the time that certain people are saved from instantaneous and sudden tragedy by their psychic attributes — if they are alert enough to them and their intellectual "reason" does not cancel them out. I soon found this out myself.

Again several years ago, when Walkmans had become all the rage and, blissfully, ghetto blasters were in decline, I got in the habit of walking about the streets of New York enveloped in music, volume up to the maximum. It was glorious. One could now walk about and enhance the most common scenes with music — just like being in a movie. I am a Wagner freak, and so almost everywhere I went my ears were filled with his majestic, soul-rending music — at top volume to be sure, since Wagner can hardly be listened to any other way. Street noises were completely inaudible, of course, but then this was part of the new pleasure, was it not?

Early one morning, my ears filled with Wagnerian delirium, I popped out of my building and headed to the grocery store. I got to the curb and was about to step off it when, in the middle of a Wagnerian crescendo, and *much louder than it*, I heard the word "STOP!" I was so astonished, I did stop, leg in air. In the next instant from behind me there flashed past a car going all out, and then a second one, a cop car, lights turning, sirens going. I realized two things very quickly. I couldn't hear the sirens even when they were right in front of me. And had I finished my step off the curb, I'd have been right under the left front wheel of the first car.

I quickly looked to see if anyone near could have yelled "stop." It was very early, and I was alone in the street. Then the reaction set in. My legs trembled as adrenaline pumped through my system. But my mind trembled, too — with the implications. I sat down on the curb and sat there for some time. Meekly I rewound the tape a little, replaying it to see if somehow the word "stop" was in the tape. It was not. That was the end of Wagner in the streets.

In my considered opinion, the thing that kept me from becoming an obscure fatality in New York statistics was not the word "stop" itself *per se*, but the fact that my intellect and my psychic direct-sensing systems were sufficiently linked to be able to work together.

I am absolutely convinced that everyone possesses similar psychic direct-sensing systems, and that they always try to alert one to danger. I am also absolutely convinced, as I have said earlier, that the breakdown in the communication links between direct-sensing systems and intellect occurs primarily when intellects have not been made sensitive enough to the psychic inputs. In such cases, the intellect cannot integrate the psychic signals into what we call our volitional choices, since it is resisting these signals. Sometimes these choices must be made in an unexpected, instantaneous second.

All this represents the lowest common denominator to which I can reduce psychic stuff to illustrate a reason for motivating interest in it. There exist thousands of recorded anecdotes in which people have managed to survive some completely sudden calamity. It has even been asked of many of these: "Good Lord, didn't your direct sensing systems alert you to the presence of sudden danger?" Answer: "Yes, but I was confused and ignored the warning." Other people wail: "God! If only I'd listened to my intuitive hunch, I'd still have my leg" — or "not be confined to a wheelchair for the rest of my life."

There are also thousands of recorded instances in which people *have* been able to avoid *death* and danger *because* their direct-sensing systems and their intellects were mutually psychically interactive. If these combined archives were sparse there might be reason enough to conclude that the theory of coincidence was all that was necessary to explain them. But they are *not* sparse. They are mountainous. And all these reports detail the presence of psychic stuff either accepted or ignored — as a matter of intellectual *choice*.

Intellectual rationalizations focus, when they do so at all, on the "inexplicable" nature of such events. But they are *not* inexplicable if we accept the obvious. In addition to our intellectual capabilities, we possess psychic attributes whose *major* apparent functions extend our self-preserving capabilities overall. Yet (and here is my complaint again), our culture has elected to trust only in intellect and its admittedly faulty capabilities at "reasoning" and to ignore and ridicule our psychic direct-sensing systems.

OUR DIRECT-SENSING SYSTEMS GATHER HIDDEN INFORMATION

From this point on, we'll begin to drift gradually into other larger and very important reasons for being motivated to increase our overall psychic literacy — and hence our proficiency in connecting up to psychic matters. Let me tackle another right away.

We need an increase in psychic literacy not only to serve ourselves and our goals, but to be able to aid *others*.

For example, consider the case of poor Cathy given earlier whose direct-sensing attributes began pumping into her conscious intellect some precognitive insights concerning her potential death around the age of sixteen. We have to ask if it is the purpose of some part of the universal plan to take glee in torturing Cathy with such "fatalistic" insights — or whether Cathy's psychic promptings had a purpose?

It seems to me a common-sense thing to suppose that all life and all its parts are interested not in its destruction but in its survival, and that the purpose of psychic insights overall is to aid in that survival. If this is so, as I believe it to be, these kinds of intuitive promptings have the intent of alerting individuals to future times and events that will be dangerous to survival. If the individual could accept these insights as *alerts* (and not as unalterable fatal predictions), then extra precautions might be taken during the times indicated. Otherwise, we would have to accept the unavoidable fatalism implied. Indeed, many students of the occult and psychic matters have accepted the idea of psychic fatalism. But, in my opinion, psychic fatalism is hogwash. It does not make any common sense at all that the psychic factors would tease certain people with forecasts of their own doom unless it was for some completely constructive reason — the avoidance of that doom.

Having studied these kinds of psychic alerts for over twenty years now, I can say with complete confidence that our psychic factors, with regard to psychic alerts of this kind, operate just like any intelligence gathering and intelligence forecasting system — not unlike the activity of the CIA, MI-5 or the KGB. The purpose of any intelligence system is to gather information so as to enable people to understand what is really going on, and then to predict likely events that might take place as a result of what is really going on. Intelligence systems undertake to interpret energies and forces, where they are being or are likely to be deployed, and what will be the outcomes.

In fact, our prophetic alerting systems remain completely unintelligible as long as we fail to understand them as intelligence systems. I certainly could not understand them until it dawned on me that they operated exactly like the intelligence systems used by the military, governments, industries, and diplomatic corps.

In fact, it is quite possible to say that all *these more mundane* intelligence systems somehow try to emulate the psychic prophetic alerting systems innate in our biopsychic selves. The mechanics of both are almost identical. If we accept this as the case, we can bring as much "science" to psychic alerting systems as experts have brought to our more mundane intelligence-gathering organizations. Naturally, the tools used by our psychic alerting systems are a little different than the tools used by intelligence agencies. But the principles are exactly the same in both. It is only that our psychic alerting systems can really "see" the future, whereas our more mundane organizations really cannot and are reduced to making volitional choices based only on statistical probability or outright speculation. It is ironic that even the best intelligence operatives not infrequently have to fall back on intuitive "gut feelings" and hunches. Are these not psychic capabilities?

Now, let's go a little deeper into this. Poor Cathy. She lived in a time and in a social environment in which the cultural mainstream had been dedicated to ignoring (and destroying) psychic impulses more or less since the days of early Christianity. The cultural results of this anti-psychic attitude reach even into the arid precincts of Las Vegas.

Therefore, when Cathy began telling others about her premonitions, no one at all knew what to do about it. Quite likely, the whole was attributed to what psychologists call a "morbid fantasy." Her family must have believed this. Psychologists would have said she was paranoid-schizoid (their stock phrase for psychic experiences), i.e., pathologically abnormal. Her friends probably scoffed.

So it probably did not dawn on anyone to make any effort to try to interpret her foreknowledge through, for example, waking-dream analysis. No one thought to consult professional psychics to see if they might peer into the future to locate the *avoidable* particulars involved. Yet, from age eight onward, her own psychic insights were divulging *specific* information in that they produced the approximate *date* of great danger for her — around her sixteenth birthday. Normal intelligence services would give half their kingdom to have even the merest inklings of approximate dates of future events. Cathy's psychic alerting systems gave such a date.

Nothing was done, or could be done, about it — in our present cultural stance. Cathy was left to suffer the threat of the impending doom and ultimately encounter the culmination of the invisible energies and forces that would bring it into fact.

Her tragic death was probably avoidable. Her psychic alerting systems were operating so as to alert her to the need to exercise great caution around the time of her sixteenth birthday. If the purpose of such alerts were *understood for what they are*, then there are several constructive approaches available.

For example, hypnosis. After all, it is generally known in the hypnosis disciplines that light trances can be induced for the purpose of obtaining information from one's "subconscious" that is not readily available to intellectual consciousness. Look at it this way. If Cathy's direct sensing systems managed to push up into her intellectual awareness the approximate future date of her "death," it is entirely credible that they also "knew" about the other *factors* that would be involved.

In all likelihood if only *one* additional factor could have been "dug up," such as "it's going to happen after you leave a bookstore at night," then when the "fatal" time neared she might have changed her habits. She might have stayed in watching TV instead of making her habitual night trip to the bookstore. There is little doubt she would have been accused of fleeing before imaginary shadows in her mind — but she would still be alive.

And then there are the avenues that open up via *astrology*. Competent astrologers can, with relative ease, spot periods of great threat by studying one's horoscope and even get the gist of the factors that will be involved. Some astrologers are, as we shall say from now on, *psychically aligned*, and can even "get" images of those factors. I don't have Cathy's natal chart, so I can't say for sure if her horoscope would indicate what I've been talking about. But I'd bet money that it would.

At any rate, Cathy's own direct-sensing systems began to alert her beginning at the age of eight. Which is to say that she had *eight years to work on the situation* and change at least *one* of the factors involved. In her case, in the society in which she lived there was no psychic initiative anywhere for her to appeal to. So she eventually encountered the doom that her psychic attributes had been trying to alert her to, and that was that.

But we have, I think, every right to believe that we *can* change the outcomes of these kinds of situations — *by changing the factors involved in them*. To illustrate this point, earlier I gave the long description of the Four Seasons event — to illustrate that had even one of the factors involved been altered, even in the smallest way, the event would not have "come off."

Although I am missing Cathy's horoscope, in the case of Abraham Lincoln, I am not, and we are in a better place to see the overall picture. We have his recorded dream, which specifically told him the President had been assassinated, and that the event that would take place almost immediately. We also have his horoscope. If the noble President, or some astrologer, had been keeping track of his horoscope, he would have been able to see beyond a shadow of a doubt that the five days surrounding the fatal day of April 14, 1865, would probably be inimical to his life.

Get ready to have your mind boggled here. The normal interpretation of the horoscope is that it shows what the stars *decree*. This is absolute nonsense. What the horoscope does show is the "arrangement" of personal and environmental psychic energies and forces the individual will have to deal with during his or her life. Far from being merely what the stars decree, it is life's "game plan" for that individual. As such, one's horoscope interlocks (is interconnected) with the psychic energies and forces of others and the environment.

Our difficulty in dealing with the idea arises not from the idea itself, but from the difficulties our anti-psychic culture has against acknowledging that there is any life plan of this kind, especially one that transcends the individual will and its intellect and is connected to the future. If this anti-psychic resistance is overcome, it is easy enough to see that such game plans *do* exist. There are mountains of evidence available in support of this reality, as we shall see.

Mr. Lincoln's horoscope[1] shows Mars at 29 degrees Libra in the eighth house. What this means in plain English briefly is this: among other factors, Mars represents the energies and forces of calamity and danger, murder and assassination. The eighth house, among other things, is the house of death, dissolution, and danger, and is connected with public affairs and public places. Libra is the sign of democracy, justice, and equality. The sum of all this is that Mr. Lincoln, at various times during the course of his life, would be in danger of assassination in a public place, most precisely because of public affairs and his public policies relating to democracy, justice, and equality.

When would these "various times" be? Since ancient times, astrological lore has held that they are activated when, during the course of the life, one of the malefic planets comes into some hard aspect with the natal Mars. In Mr. Lincoln's case, the most baleful planetary aspect of all, Saturn, joined his Mars in direct conjunction on April 14, 1865. We all can recognize the symbolic meaning of Saturn through the many artful renderings of him as a skeleton carrying a scythe. Saturn is the planet of death.

Clearly, in astrological language, the transit of Saturn across Lincoln's natal Mars implies the activation of energies and forces that lead to assassination in a public place. Any competent astrologer would have pointed this out for him. April 14 was a day Mr. Lincoln should have stayed in bed and not thought of going into

---

[1] See Abraham Lincoln's nativity chart as given in Lois M. Rodden's The American Book of Charts, Astro Computing Services, San Diego, 1980.

public places. As it was, his *own* dream also tried to alert him to this fact.

But there is more that can be gleaned from his horoscope. His natal Neptune, in the ninth house, is at 6 degrees Sagittarius while his natal Saturn is at 3 degrees in the same sign. Both are on what is called the horoscope's mid-heaven — which is to say they have great astrological importance. Among other factors, Neptune represents psychic capabilities while, as we have seen, Saturn represents death. But the ninth house, among other things, is the house of dreams. Now, the Moon symbolically is the dream-planet. On the night of 13-14 April 1865, the Moon crossed Lincoln's natal Saturn and Neptune.

The sum of all this implies that Mr. Lincoln was psychic — a fact that hardly can be denied, since there is much recorded evidence that says so — and that much of his psychic insights came to his intellectual consciousness through his dreams. But on the particular night of April 13, with the Moon, the dream-planet, crossing the natal Saturn and Neptune, in astrological theory it was almost impossible for him *not* to have the dream that tried to alert him of his impending assassination.

Between his horoscope and his psychic dreaming, there is no way that it can be said that his psychic factors *did not do their best* to alert him to the potential danger of assassination in a public place on the very date it *did* occur. Now, I ask you: what more could any psychic intelligence-gathering service do? The horoscope gave the overall game plan, and the dreams filled in the particulars. Mr. Lincoln would have been well advised to stay in his office working on his many papers while these dismal psychic aspects passed and defused themselves.

This is, *if* psychic matters had been understood in his time. But they were not. They were scoffed at then as they are today. And how could the nation's leader run scared before a dream? Not easily. As it turns out, Mr. Lincoln's assassination was seen by other psychics well in advance of the event itself — as was John F. Kennedy's assassination, too.

If one refuses to acknowledge the purposes of the psychic alerting systems we all possess, then the worst probably *will* happen. But my point is that if we acknowledge the psychic alerting systems, then we can use them constructively. Mr. Lincoln's alerts were excruciatingly precise.

Lincoln's horoscope shows even more. His natal chart shows that the Sun, Mercury, Pluto, Jupiter, and Venus are in his first house, which, among other things, is the house of leadership. The man was a born leader — and a powerful one at that. He could see into the profoundest depths of issues, and he was to have good fortune in so doing. *But*, during March and April of 1865, the planet Neptune passed slowly over these otherwise excellent astrological aspects.

Among other things, Neptune is the planet of plots and betrayal. The astrological implication, clearly and beyond doubt, is that during this period a plot was hatched, possibly by certain members of his own Cabinet or in the government itself, to remove Lincoln from the scene. Any halfway competent astrologer could have advised Lincoln of this probability. Foreknowledge is the most powerful armament possible.

Yet, nothing of the kind was done, nor was it even possible to do so, considering the anti-psychic climate in which he lived and worked. So, the worst happened. When the great betrayer, Neptune, was conjunct Lincoln's natal Venus, the assassination took place. In astrology, as well as in mythology, Venus represents the arts, especially the dramatic arts. Lincoln was assassinated in Ford's Theater, while watching a play.

Now, did *any* astrologer publish a prediction that Lincoln would be assassinated? Astrological history shows that Luke Dennis Broughton, M.D. (1828-1898), was the second great astrologer in the United States after that earlier great astrologer, Benjamin Franklin. But Broughton certainly did pioneer American astrology which, between Franklin's time and his, had not flourished.

Broughton published a *Monthly Planet Reader and Astrological Journal*. The October-November-December 1864 issue led off with an article about Lincoln in which Broughton correctly predicted that the President would be re-elected. Broughton went on to write: "I might here state that after the [re-election] is over, Mr. Lincoln will have a number of evil aspects afflicting his Nativity...they will be in operation in Nov. and Dec. of this year. During these months, let him be especially on his guard against attempts to take his life; by such as firearms, and infernal machines."

In the spring (1865) issue of his *Journal*, Broughton updated his Lincoln predictions, although the tastes of the times prevented him from openly publishing a death prediction of America's living President by name. But his allusion is clear enough, to wit: "Some noted general or person in high office dies or is removed about the 17th or 18th day [of April]."[2] As it turned out, Lincoln was assassinated on the 14th.

Now, let's not talk of all this as astrology or even solely as a mix of psychic factors, *per se*, but rather altogether as a *psychic intelligence information package*. I defy any intelligence operative to have accumulated a tighter package by so-called "normal" means. And I will state openly that if one works to gain a picture of invisibles by gathering all possible psychic elements together in at least a tentative package, certain beneficial insights may become available. I will further state that it is rather stupid not to do just so.

Earlier I also reviewed the case of Captain Adrian Christian, who dreamt forty-seven years before the events occurred that he should save a sinking vessel. Had he cowered before the skepticism of his crew, and, indeed, of his culture, and *not* changed the course of his ship (i.e., changed one of the factors involved), then over two hundred people, including his own brother, would have perished. I am sure the whole of those saved were grateful he overcame skeptical resistance, which is always and only an intellectual stance, and allowed his psychic alignment to guide his activities.

When we actually experience some aspect of our psychic aptitudes and are thus able to perceive how they relate to actual realities, they tend to take on a more real meaning. If we look at them as intelligence-gathering, survival-cluing aptitudes, then our intellectual awareness of their value of them must change for the better. For me, at least, there is no way around it. My own psychic alignment saved my life in the crisis-event in which, as a child, our house exploded and burnt down. This alignment again saved my life in New York. Psychic inputs have saved the lives of countless people since times immemorial, and since times immemorial those who have ignored them have met dismal fates.

Are there not lessons to be learned from all this? Throughout history, the truly wise have not ignored these lessons and, in fact, *cannot* ignore them. The reason: the obtaining of wisdom always requires getting down out of the softness of the intellectual armchair and making the effort to observe how things really are working and how human nature manifests itself. If one does this, it is impossible to avoid noticing the existence of our psychic sensing

---

2 Holden, James H. and Hughes, Robert A., Astrological Pioneers of America, The American Federation of Astrologers, Tempe, Arizona, 1988, p. 20-12.

systems. It is also impossible to avoid noticing the existence of invisible energies, forces, and factors.

Thus, in spite of the rather large efforts, especially prevalent in our modern period, to put down and suppress interest in psychic stuff, it continues to reemerge again and again — as, of course, it must. As it happens, at the present the overall interest in psychic stuff, for example, in astrology, is now larger than it has been through the sum of the centuries since the Renaissance. Astrology has the defect of being an extraordinarily complex affair whose principles and workings take several years to master and whose mastery depends largely also on acquiring a background understanding regarding fundamental and basic invisible stuff. In accounting for the reemergence of these psychic interests it is not so much that our modernistic intellectual guidelines have "failed" (which they have), but that when people abandon them and seek to reinspect the "raw" stuff of life in order to find new directions they reencounter psychic stuff as part and parcel of that "raw" human experience.

That there should be a period of confusion regarding this is inevitable. Our intellects are not prepared for what is to be rediscovered, and background acquaintance with psychic stuff must be reestablished — or, as some people are saying, "reenchanted." The so-called "New Age" represents, I think, this period of confusion. But if it is a period of confusion, the confusion is the least aspect of it for, in its greater implications, it is also the period in which resynthesizing has begun.

BELIEF IS NOT ENOUGH

Now, many people "believe" in psychic stuff. But is not belief itself is always an intellectual construction which may or may not be founded upon astute proficiencies of observation? Many people who believe in psychic stuff are not at all capable of perceiving its workings and thus, even though they do believe, are not capable of learning how to work with it.

For example, I've met most of the parapsychologists alive and working since, say 1967. Obviously, they all believe in the existence of psychic stuff, and deeply so, or they would not be flagellating themselves with the contempt of anti-psychic scientism. But, not a few of these flagellated souls have told me in private that they have never experienced a psychic event themselves, nor, in some cases, even seen one occur with other people. I could say all sorts of things here, but they are somewhat outside the scope of this book. It *is* possible to observe that one can believe in psychic stuff and *still* not become psychically aligned. And one cannot become psychically aligned unless one also increases one's overall psychic literacy.

The sole exception here involves instances we might call *transient psychic alignment*. These take place in moments of extreme duress, anxiety, confusion, or some other temporary altered state, during which one's direct sensory system overwhelms the conscious intellect and "takes over" temporarily (examples of which we shall see in the next chapter). But then these instances are not really an alignment at all, in that the psychic sensing systems "take over" and temporarily usurp the choice-making intellect — after which the psychic illiterate status quo is resumed.

* * *

Summing up this chapter then, we can observe that people usually do not make an effort to acquire a proficiency they see no use for. The fact that psychic alignment can and does save lives is a valid, good, and wise reason for increasing one's psychic literacy in that it results in a volitional increase of psychic alignment.

Now, you may think that all this is so obvious that it is a usual way to view psychic stuff. Not so — not so at all. In the rather gargantuan amount of psychic literature I've read and researched, nowhere is anything like this even stated, and certainly not unequivocally so.

Look at it this way. People have to perceive what benefits there are in any given thing in order for them to take an interest in it and work at developing it, not to mention fund it. For example, people fund the cancer research industry, even with nickels and dimes, because they perceive that they have a very good chance themselves of getting cancer and dying of it. Thus, cancer research is generally perceived as useful, and so people take great personal and impersonal interest in researching its "causes" and funding it with nickels and dimes.

Well, people may be dying of cancer. But if the psychic patterns I've witnesses over the years are any indicator, in all probability more people die for lack of psychic alignment than because of cancer.

OUR PSYCHIC ATTRIBUTES AND THE BASIC PURPOSES THEY SERVE

o   We can observe that the lack of psychic alignment probably does contribute in major ways to a failure to survive, or to survive intact, in moments of extreme danger. Increase in psychic literacy leads to enhanced psychic alignment, enabling our joint direct sensing and intellectual systems to respond in constructive ways and respond faster if need be.

o   We should observe that low psychic literacy equates to low psychic sensitivity. If such a condition prevails, our intellects cannot make informed choices regarding situations that are carrying heavy psychic factors within them. In such a condition, we will be unable to help ourselves or others when the need arises.

SUGGESTED PRACTICAL EXERCISES THAT WILL HELP IN EXPANDING PSYCHIC LITERACY

o Find someone who has lived through some really serious accident. If the situation is suitable, and it would not be an obvious burden on the person, ask if he or she experienced any kind of psychic intuition or forewarning before the accident occurred. I've found people generally like to talk about this, so as to try to understand it better.

o If you experience some kind of psychic intuition or forewarning yourself, and if there is time enough for you to do so, ask your direct-sensing systems to send along *more* information — and see what happens.

o Make a deliberate effort to become aware of the fact that your direct-sensing systems are probably sending up psychic information all the time, and in several forms.

o Shortly you will be able to notice that unless your intellect "locks on" to psychic impressions, they generally re-submerge and disappear from view. Catch them in writing while you can. Start keeping your psychic impressions in a psychic notebook. Many successful business people do. Every once in a while, read through it.

* * *

Now, I want to dig even deeper into our psychic intelligence systems' networks and seek to show they operate communally as well as individually — to illustrate that the psychic networking transcends individuals. To do this, I want to narrate the psychic aspects of two of the greatest calamities of our times.

VII

Communal Psychic Capabilities and Psychic Networks

As pointed out earlier, we in our cultural West have focused our intellectual ideas of ourselves primarily in the light of the philosophy of individualism, so much so that we tend to view our individual Selves as the major and most important thing in the universe. This is probably not wrong in itself. But it tends to occlude from view the fact that each one of our Selves is amongst the smaller aspects existing in the universe and that there are energies and forces (factors) operating that are much larger than we are.

The more correct actuality is that we live and exist among these larger energies and forces, that we are entwined among them, and that they do impact on us, our activities, and our consciousness. We feel we can control what happens to us by virtue of our individual willpower, but, in reality, many things happen to us that we don't understand, and we haven't the least idea of how they could happen. Even the individual most entrenched in his or her ideas of individuality has to admit that luck and fortune are with them some of the time, and misfortune at other times. The fact is that we are individuals only to a certain degree, but beyond that we are only a part, a small part of the universe, and subject to its fluctuating conditions.

I'm relatively certain that anyone who cannot envision the fact that greater factors do impinge on them is someone who probably will not achieve much psychic alignment or develop their psychic capabilities. Feeling that their individual willpower is enough to direct their lives, such people seldom see any need for acknowledging their own psychic alerting systems or the survival-type information those systems are constantly trying to provide.

I'm also completely certain that those who do become psychic are those who, for one reason or another, begin to realize that there *are* invisible factors outside themselves that impact on them — as well as others — and even upon the progress of what we call human history. But they seldom abandon their sense of individuality completely; they just begin to add new realms of psychic comprehension to their awareness and their literacy.

So far, I've given several examples of invisible factors impinging on individuals at their individual levels, showing that their psychic-sensing systems tried, sometimes unsuccessfully, to alert them to the factors that, indeed, did have consequences in their lives. When I was first trying to comprehend all this (1973-74), it became possible to assume that if *larger* factors did exist, then they probably affected more than just one person.

Further, it seemed not improbable that the direct-sensing systems of individuals could "pick up" on factors that were in the process of impinging on or bringing about events, communal events, that were to affect not precisely themselves, but others — especially if those others were loved ones. I decided to survey the psychic literature to see if events of this kind had ever been noted. I didn't have far to look.

PSYCHIC NETWORKING OF THE ANCIENTS

In ancient times, trying to spy on the workings of invisible energies and forces and trying to peer into the future were held to be extremely important undertakings. The Persians, Indians, Greeks, Egyptians, the Celts and Scandinavians, the Tartars, Chinese and Japanese, the Native Americans, the Romans and Jews all developed ways and means of so doing.

The practitioners of the psychic arts and crafts — oracles, seers, prophets, omen-readers, shamans, and astrologers — all were held in high esteem. In spite of the bad press later ideologies gave them in retrospect, at the time these professionals were given a considerable amount of respect since they were considered in the light of the one thing that can almost guarantee it. They were considered *necessary*.

We'll go deeper into this aspect of ancient history later. But right now, I want to point out something most historians do not comment upon — how these professionals were *utilized*. In our day and time, if we consult a psychic practitioner at all, we do so much under the idea that we need consult only *one* of them. In fact, successful seers develop large followings who hang on every word uttered, while at the same time looking down on others or casting various forms of obloquy in their direction. After all, we live in the age of *competition*, and gravitate to its stars.

The cultures of the past were composed of competitive societies and races, of course, and they certainly had psychic superstars. But their sense of competitiveness did not generally extend into psychic matters. Hardly anyone would have thought of consulting just one seer.

They wanted to consult the best, but in their minds the best was always a composite of the many. Thus, when city-states, kings, nobility, warriors, priests, and ordinary people wanted to consult psychic sources on issues of great moment, they trudged far and wide, often at great hardship, to consult several of them.

The various offerings of the seers were compared and discussed, and a synthesis was arrived at. Upon this synthesis decisions were based, and actions initiated. In large part, the ancients distrusted decisions based only on intellectual reckoning. This method of multi-consultations endured for well over six thousand years. As I'll point out again later in more extended form, hardly could this psychic consulting business exist for even the smallest part of that extraordinarily long time if it had proven itself to be erroneous and thus useless. The ancients had no more time for useless stuff than we do today.

Today, we would call this multi-consulting method a form of psychic networking. The implication is that the ancients realized they were not consulting the individuals through whom certain kinds of information emanated. They were consulting a network of invisible energies and forces. To obtain optimum results, this network had to be pierced at many points, and hence many different psychic practitioners had to undertake this multiple piercing. By using this method, the petitioners hoped not only to bring into focus a larger picture of the many psychic factors that might be involved, but they hoped also to transcend the human frailties that given seers might be subject to.

When I finally realized the nature of this method (after many years of researching ancient psychic stuff), its elegance seemed almost beyond belief. The only remnants of this we have today is in getting what we call a "second opinion," which we do with doctors and financial analysts. Surely, I thought, the basis of this method *must* have developed out of real human experience. And I wondered if this community of psychic piercing was locatable today in our present culture. I did not have to look far; I had only to remember my childhood.

COMMUNAL PSYCHIC CAPABILITIES

I was born in Telluride, Colorado, a small mining town in the High Rockies, an area sometimes referred to as the "Alps" of America. Telluride, set in a narrow valley, was near timberline, and surrounded on all sides with towering peaks, majestic cliffs thousands of feet high, and deep, perilous canyons. The beauty of this environment was almost painful.

And this beauty was dangerous, claiming many lives. The unwary fell to their deaths. Sudden cloudbursts created avalanches and walls of water. In storms, the frequency of lightning was astonishing as it shredded trees, rocks, cliffs, buildings, and people alike. Winter snows piled high on the peaks and cliffs portended avalanches. Needless to say, we were all very sensitive to the vicissitudes and visitations of nature. One had to keep one's wits together and one's extended direct-sensing capabilities active at all times. Simply put, there was no other way.

Many were the times when I witnessed the following. A certain day would dawn. Various telephones would start ringing and people would say something like "there's an avalanche gonna come down today." Certain people would stand on the streets surveying the cliffs around. Groups would form — and eventually they would all point in the same direction, even though there was absolutely no indication that an avalanche would take place where they were pointing. "'Bout three-thirty this afternoon," someone would say. "That's up by the mine," someone else would say. "Better call up there and have them close down a while."

The call *would* be made. The mine *would* close down. The avalanche would occur at 3:45, taking out a building or two, a tailings pond, and, as usual, some electric power lines. Then everything would be as normal. People cleaned up the damage. People waited for the next avalanche.

Our school was a large brick building, standing quite near the mouth of a deep, narrow canyon, in whose depths was a beautiful waterfall a thousand feet high. One day several students didn't come in. When the teacher called to find out where they were, she was told by several mothers that there was going to be a cloudburst that day and that all the kids should be sent home. She went to the principal. Shortly, the bell rang, and everyone *was* sent home — to our great joy.

It was a brilliant, sunny summer day. Hardly a cloud in sight. About noon it was noticed that a huge dark cloud had formed in the peaks above the canyon behind our school. Not a drop of rain fell anywhere in town, but shortly a wall of water, rocks, and mud some twenty feet high roared out of the canyon. It swamped the basement of the school and tore off parts of several houses along the stream's usual route.

Now, no one I knew in Telluride believed in psychic stuff, and certainly it was never much of an intellectual topic of conversation. But the people believed in what they felt or sensed — their "itches" as it was sometimes called. Most of the times their "itches" were amazingly precise. But the major thing about these feelings was that they were communal. If *one* person opined the impending occurrence of an avalanche, no one took much notice. But when the "feeling" phenomenon overtook several, things took on different proportions.

People would stand on street corners and compare their "itches." A synthesis would be worked out, and they would all point in the same direction — or all the kids would be kept at home "'cause the cloudburst's gonna be in the canyon back of the school." Amongst the town's natives there was little argument. For the most part, it was all a silent pageant, taken for granted, and no one called it psychic. But in Telluride at that time, "itches" was synonymous with "psychic." Tourists found it all ridiculous and went hiking anyway, getting themselves in the path of an avalanche or a lightning bolt. Telluride had only a very tiny mortuary, but it had a large room kept stocked with caskets (as we called them) — mostly to ship dead tourists away in.

Remembering all this from my childhood, many years later it seemed to me to represent the basic human experience that the ancients must have evolved into their more complex and more strenuous method of consulting multitudinous seers and psychics. Seen this way, the reason seems plain enough: psychic impressions communally shared can correct each other and arrive at accuracies and syntheses that may not be exactly producible by *one* given psychic practitioner.

If such be true at all, then there must be other examples in which a communal psychic "itch" was perceived and shared by many. I've found there are actually very many — generally recorded not in psychical research archives, but in sociological and anthropological studies. Such researchers, if and when they actually go among so-called primitive or naïve people, are "amazed" to discover a high level of shared intuitive activity among them. In a complete absence of any physical indicators, such communal psychic intuitiveness alerts them to coming conditions: approaching dangers, extraordinary weather changes, and whether or not game or other food stuffs will be plentiful. These group forewarnings also include "knowing" that a given person will soon die and how, and, sometimes, several *years* before the actual event, the date when a new leader will be born.

I should point out that, with only a few exceptions, in general psychical researchers have taken hardly any interest in studying this kind of psychic phenomena, which, on the other hand, disciplines that are generally anti-psychic in attitude (such as anthropology and archaeology) are forced to observe in the process of establishing factual information.

But we can also spot this kind of phenomenon at work in our modern culture, too. I now propose to narrate two of these examples. Unfortunately, both events culminated in the great disasters that were predicted — due completely, in my mind, to the widespread effects of psychic illiteracy, since both could have been avoided had even the merest drop of psychic sensitivity been present. What we will be looking for in recounting these events is the communal nature of the "itches" and how, on the psychic-illiteracy side, they were ignored and went unacknowledged.

ABERFAN, 1966

Aberfan is a grim, coal mining village in Wales, about twenty miles north of Cardiff, and having little claim to fame save for the disaster that overtook it on October 21, 1966, at 9:15 a.m. — a disaster that had been foreshadowed by no less than seventy-six verifiable "itches."

The village sits at the bottom of a narrow valley, the coal mines in the mountains above it. Since the local mining engineers had to have some place to put the coal being produced, they fanned enormous amounts of it out along the mountain sides in what are called "coal-tips." Above Aberfan, one such coal-tip grew to massive size until several residents began to express concern that it might one day collapse and slide down into the village. But the coal-tip had been there for a long time, and, in the peculiar way people hot after money rationalize things, the mine owners paid no attention to the possibility. It had never slid down before, and so it was unlikely to do so in future.

About October 6th, a young girl I'll call Emma, aged ten, said to her mother: "Mummy, I'm not afraid to die." Mother: "Why do you talk of dying, and you so young? Do you want a lollipop?" Emma: "No. But I shall be with Peter and June," two of her schoolmates.

On October 20th: Emma: "Mummy, let me tell you about my dream last night." Mother: "Darling, I've no time now. Tell me again later." Emma: "No, Mummy. You *must* listen. I dreamt I went to school and there was no school there. Something black had come down all over it!"

Later it was learned that Emma was not the only child to have premonitions of dying *in school* when something black slid onto it. In fact, as early as *ten months* before the disaster, dreams, visions, and psychic messages concerning it began popping up all over Wales and England. Three weeks before the disaster, one Mrs. V.C. of Ryde had a "technicolor vision" of a coming tragedy, in which a little girl dressed in a Welsh costume called out the name of "Aberredfan." Eighteen hours ahead of the disaster, one Mr. J.T. of Stacksteads, Lance, had a dream in which he saw a desolate row of destroyed houses and heard the name "Aberfan." Six hours before the tragedy, one Mr. E.H. of Newcastle-on-Tyne experienced a vivid "fantasy" in which the name "Aberfan" was linked to some terrible event.

The reason these psychic precognitions are available to us is that on the day after the disaster, J.C. Barker, M.D., a psychiatrist at Shelton Hospital, Shrewsbury, visited Aberfan, noted the prevalence of premonitions, and launched an appeal through the *Evening Standard* of London requesting persons claiming any foreknowledge of the Aberfan disaster to communicate with him, describing their experiences. He received seventy-six letters from a number of towns, villages, and cities.[1]

In following up on these letters, Barker was able to ascertain that many of the "claims" were indeed "acceptable" because the persons involved either had told others of intuitions *before* the disaster, or they had written them down. Only a few were "unverifiable."

---

[1] Barker, J.C., "Premonitions of the Aberfan Disaster," Journal of the Society for Psychical Research, Vol. 44, No. 734, December 1967.

However, had there existed a "central premonitions registry" to which people could send along their intuitions or telephone them in with the urgency some of the intuitions reflected, there can be little doubt that the name Aberfan would have been noted. The incoming psychic impressions might have been combined with a quick perusal of the existence of the dangerous situation there. Its inhabitants might have been alerted — i.e., a sort of "call up the mine and get them out of there" thing, exactly as I witnessed several times in Telluride during my childhood.

But no such system existed. As it was, on the fateful morning, the village's children all went to school as usual at 9.00 a.m. Fifteen minutes later, the coal-tip gave way in a massive landslide of muck, mud, coal and water. It completely engulfed the school and other parts of the village as well. One hundred and forty-four persons were killed, one hundred and twenty-eight of them children. Emma was buried in the mass grave next to her school chums Peter and June.

And why? Certainly, the mining engineers involved must be held accountable. But in establishing accountability, I think we must begin also to have a look at our basic and abysmal psychic illiteracy. Surely, seventy-six *advance* warnings, achieved psychically, from dozens of people in places not all that distant from Aberfan (and with the name "Aberfan" cropping up thrice) must, in real human experience, amount to something.

Obviously, if a central premonitions registry had existed, none of those now long dead in Aberfan would be joined in a mass grave. This mass grave stands, to my way of thinking, not only as the remembrance of the grievous disaster, but as a monument to our general and often tragic psychic illiteracy. (The word I really want to use is "stupidity," but I'll try to contain myself!)

As astonishing as the Aberfan Event is, there is yet another Event that is more so.

Few now remember or have ever heard of Aberfan, although at the time it made headlines world-wide, and some of the media even deigned to notice the heavy psychic factors involved. But almost everyone has heard of the sinking of the White Star Line's huge luxury liner, the mighty *Titanic*.

But what almost everyone has *not* heard of is this Event's psychic components.

THE *TITANIC*

The bare bones of the *Titanic's* story are well known and are this: On the night of April 14-15, 1912, on her maiden voyage across the Atlantic to New York, the luxury liner side-swiped an iceberg at about 11:40 p.m. and sank at approximately 1:15 a.m. Of the 2,227 people on board (passengers and crew), 1,502 perished — simply and *only*, it is thought, because the *Titanic* did not carry nearly enough lifeboats. However, these unfortunate passengers also perished because our culture has no interest in such a thing as psychically received information or a psychic central premonitions registry.

If we flesh out the tale of the *Titanic's* tragic sinking with human motives, purposes, and goals, and with aesthetics and emotions, we arrive at a far different story than just the bare-bones facts — which is this.

The *Titanic* was the second of three nearly identical ocean-going vessels constructed by the White Star Line. The *Titanic* especially had been designed to be a veritable floating palace containing every luxury passengers might desire. The *Titanic* was viewed as a monument to human ingenuity and success. Not only was it the epitome of luxury, of man's ingenuity, it also was the largest *movable* construction man had ever built.

As such, it was *the* symbol of technological things to come, a symbol of speed combined with advancing technology and luxury, a symbol of man's ever-enlarging genius and enterprise that were to give an entirely different shape to the future. Not only was it unique along all these lines, but it had been designed to be virtually unsinkable, and so confident were its owners in its unsinkability that they felt lifeboats would never be needed — so they dispensed with many of them in order to enlarge the first-class decks.

The *Titanic* thus symbolized modern confidence, pride, status, prestige, power, and the highest satisfactions that any visions of human success and progress could bring.

The very plans of the *Titanic* made history, as did the laying of its keel, and its christening. From its inception, the *Titanic* was accompanied by enormous press coverage. To be on board during its maiden voyage gave a social cachet of no little consequence, and thus the great of the times hastened to make their reservations far in advance. On board, among other notables, were the noted author, W.T. Stead; the philanthropist Isador Strauss and his wife;

the scion of New York John Jacob Astor and his young bride; the industrialist Benjamin Guggenheim and Major Archie Butt (the Alexander Haig of his day), advisor to President Taft.

On board also were and the famous artist, Frank Millet; the noted editor, Jacques Futrelle; and the noted theatrical producer, Henry E. Harris. All these luminaries brought with them small combined armies of no less than thirty-one professional servants to further aid in the luxurious rigors of the Atlantic crossing. The most famous financier of all times, J.P. Morgan, who was scheduled to be on board, cancelled at the last minute. The reason given was illness. But we must remember he retained the services of the famous astrologer Evangeline Adams who was noted for telling people when they should and should not travel. In any event, Morgan's decision not to travel on the *Titanic* was probably the most fortuitous one of his life. In a shock that has not ceased reverberating to this day, all these above-mentioned male luminaries went with the other 1,494 souls of the great, lesser great, and ordinary mortals on board into the icy waters along with the *Titanic's* doomed hulk.

The autopsy, in *material terms*, of why and how the *Titanic* sank was front page news for ten years afterwards, and, in fact, is still argued today, especially recently when the ship's remains were discovered on the ocean floor. Dozens of books and five movies have been produced. There is a *Titanic* Historical Society, and the sinking is observed by annual ceremonies. The fascination with the *Titanic's* sinking is nearly unparalleled in history, and certainly, in modern times, no other event so far can take precedence. The very mentioning of the sinking of the *Titanic* to people who have never heard of it and know nothing of the details inexplicably brings up in them a moment's pause — as if something in their mental clickings misses a beat, as if the event is actually impressed in our collective consciousnesses.

In keeping with the premise that such events are always foreshadowed by psychic alerts, certainly these alerts must have been available well in advance of the actual sinking itself. And, indeed, they were — in spades, as they say. Yet, typical of our present anti-psychic stance which stridently avoids such information you will find none of the *Titanic's* psychic alerts in any history book.

Yet, a psychic autopsy of the tragedy has been done. It goes something like this: The first apparent act of the *Titanic's* psychic sequence began fourteen years before the ship was even a dream in the minds of the owners of the White Star Line. In 1898, a relatively unknown seaman, one Morgan Robertson, wrote and published a fictional story entitled *The Wreck of the Titan*. In his story Robertson pictured the *Titan* as a huge, luxurious fast liner that was designed to be unsinkable. The Company that had built her was out to make a speed record in crossing the Atlantic.

The *Titan* began her maiden voyage in early April and aboard were the beautiful people of two worlds, Europe and America. As the *Titan* sped along the northern travel routes of the Atlantic, she struck an iceberg due to the unconscionable speed she had been travelling in the dangerous iceberg-infested waters. Her "unsinkable" design did not save her, and hundreds of people needlessly perished — because in order to hold more first-class passenger cabins the Company had done away with lifeboats enough to hold all in case of disaster at sea. And, in fact, many people refused to board what lifeboats there were because they believed in the "myth" of the vessel's unsinkability. The loss of life was appalling.

Fourteen years after Robertson had published his story about the disaster of the *Titan*, it proved to be an almost exact pre-play of the actual *Titanic* tragedy. If we line up the details of the fictional and actual event that resemble each other, we find as follows:

	Titan	*Titanic*
Number of propellers	3	3
Displacement tonnage of the liner	75,000	66,000
Length of liner (in feet)	800	882.5
Speed at impact with iceberg	25 knots	23 knots
Number of persons aboard	3,000	2,227
Number of lifeboats	24	20

In 1912, as the *Titanic* neared completion and people were competing with each other to reserve their space on the maiden voyage, the impending destruction of the ship began to "leak" into knowledge through psychic means — through dreams, visions, and premonitions. Psychologist and parapsychological researcher, Ian Stevenson, has collected nineteen examples of these psychic linkages which he believes stand up under scientific scrutiny,[2] but there were

---

[2] Stevenson, Ian, "A Review and Analysis of Paranormal Experiences Connected with the Sinking of the Titanic," in Tantum, William H., Ed., The

many more, many of them published in news media shortly after the sinking.

But there also were "implicit" premonitions. For example, the number of cancellations of reservations for this particular voyage was unprecedented in spite of the great social prestige to be derived from travelling on the maiden voyage. The cancellations mystified the owners of the White Star Line, but what matter, since there was a *line* of notables eager to benefit from someone else's cancellation. At least three seamen inexplicably jumped the ship when it docked at Southampton before setting out into the Atlantic proper. One of these later interviewed said: "I just knew the son-of-a-bitch was going down." Some passengers who had reserved space received cables from relatives or friends asking them not to go on the voyage, but to change to another ship.

Dr. Stevenson lists nineteen "acceptable" premonitions. Of these I'll review but three which illustrate their different types. An English businessman, Mr. J. Connon Middleton, having booked passage on the *Titanic* on March 23, 1912, then dreamed about a week later: "that I saw her [the *Titanic*] floating on the sea, keel upwards and her passengers and crew swimming around her." On the following night he had the same dream. He ultimately cancelled his trip for "other business reasons."

On April 10, 1912, Mr. and Mrs. Jack Marshall and their family were on the roof of their home overlooking the Solent opposite the Isle of Wight, watching the *Titanic* go by on its maiden voyage. After all, at the time, this was *the* event of the century. Suddenly, Mrs. Marshall clutched her husband's arm and said: "That ship is going to sink before she reaches America." As her husband and others tried to soothe her she became frantic. "Don't stand there staring at me! Do something! You fools, I can see hundreds of people struggling in the icy water. Are you all so blind that you are going to let them drown?" As Mrs. Marshall's daughter later reported: "During the next five days everyone was very careful not to mention the *Titanic*, but mother was very nervous, and father looked harassed. It must have been almost a relief for her when everyone knew that the *Titanic* had struck an iceberg; not nearly so lonely as waiting until it happened."

Doomed Unsinkable Ship, 7 C's Press, Inc., Riverside, Conn., 1974, p. 83-170. Also, Journal of the American Society for Psychical Research, Vol 54, October, 1960, pp. 153-171.

The distinguished journalist and editor, W.T. Stead, lost his life aboard the *Titanic*. Stead had a deep interest in occult and psychic stuff and for some years had been obtaining communications through automatic writing from a spirit named "Julia." In the 1880s, Stead published a warning he had received from Julia — that a great ocean liner would sink, and in 1909, Stead gave a lecture to the Cosmos Club in New York in which he pictured himself as shipwrecked and calling for help.

In 1911 Stead consulted with the famous astrologer-psychic, Count Louis Hamon (Cheiro) (whom we will encounter again in the pages ahead). Cheiro told Stead that danger to his life "would be from water, and from nothing else." On June 21, 1911, Cheiro advised Stead through a letter that "travel would be dangerous for him in the month of April, 1912."

Yet, despite Stead's own belief in the occult and almost in spite of Cheiro's warnings, Stead boarded the "unsinkable" *Titanic* in "the month of April, 1912." We can only assume that Cheiro's warnings were ringing in Stead's ears as he plunged to the bottom along with the doomed vessel.

We might at this point well conclude our recounting of psychic stuff connected with the *Titanic's* sinking. After all, we've picked up the main idea that many people pierced into the network or mix of psychic factors surrounding the Event. But we really should try to get some idea of what these factors were — by resorting to astrology, for example, and having a look at the *Titanic's* several horoscopes.

The most fundamental idea behind astrology (as behind all the psychic arts and crafts) is that invisible energies and forces *do* exist. These exist in a wide spectrum of many differing but *identifiable* "qualities," and these qualities contribute to, or sometimes "ordain," how things turn out. Although their spectrum is wide, they can be divided into two general categories: those that are constructive and those that are destructive. Or, put another way, those that contribute to a constructive destiny or a destructive fate.

Although modern astrologers have never been able to explain why it should be so, over six thousand years ago they began to notice that each degree of the 360-degree zodiac, the planets themselves as well as their relationships to each other, and the fixed stars, were factors somehow representative of invisible energies and forces with regard to what we now call "how things turn out." In other words, by erecting a horoscope (a chart of the planets, etc., at "birth") astrologers could "see" what mix of invisible energies and forces was to be active with regard to how things probably were going to turn out for a particular person or undertaking. (A horoscope can be erected for just about anything, including racehorses and stock market ventures.)

The several horoscopes we can study regarding the *Titanic's* astrological factors reveal some chilling aspects. For example, the decision to build the *Titanic* took place in March of 1907, and the financing of it was successfully achieved at that time. For what it is worth, in March of 1907, Saturn, the baleful planet of death, was lurking on the 23rd degree of Pisces. Pisces is the astrological sign of the zodiac that governs, among other things, the oceans and seas.

In astrological lore, the 23rd degree of Pisces has to do with the idea that anything embarked upon for material gain will spell ruin. Saturn, at this point, is sure to confirm impending ruin. All three of White Star's sister ships (the *Olympic*, *Titanic* and *Britannic*) were thus commenced under this unfortunate aspect, and all three met with physical and financial disaster (although the *Olympic* was the luckiest of the three).

However, after the decision to build the Unfortunate Three was concluded, the commencement of building each ship began at different times, and thus has slightly different astrological factors from that point on. The keel for the *Titanic* was laid down on 31 March 1909, when the baleful planet Saturn was now conjunct the Sun (indicating that the ship's glory would be overtaken by death) and this conjunction was square Neptune, lord of the oceans and ruler of Pisces (indicating that disaster would come at sea). I feel obliged to point out that this is *not* hindsight talking. Any competent astrologer would have concluded that the *Titanic* was in for rough times.

As if this were not enough, when the *Titanic* was launched (which is to say, first met water) on 31 May 1911, the destructive planet Mars was occupied with passing over the 23rd degree of Pisces, the negative aspect of ruin under which the ship got started in the first place.

The night the *Titanic* sank (14 April 1912), the trek of Saturn had brought it to the 19th degree of Taurus, which, in astrological lore, is associated with travel to the new world and passivity, hopelessness, and weakness. In astrological terms, the *Titanic* project was hopeless from the start, and, clearly, when it did sink, it did so from weaknesses emanating from the idea it was unsinkable in the first place. Many of those who drowned did so because they believed in the myth of the ship's unsinkability and passively refused to get into the lifeboats at all.

Thus, in astrological terms, it can be seen that the three vessels all were "ruled" by the baleful planet Saturn. The *Olympic* was the "luckiest" of the three unfortunates. During her ocean-going career, the *Olympic* suffered no less than six major collisions with other boats (necessitating costly repairs) but remained in existence until 1937, when she was dismantled for scrap. *Titanic's* other sister ship, *Britannic* (originally to be called the *Gigantic* prior to the *Titanic's* sinking) was converted to a hospital ship during World War I (the professions of medicine and hospital nursing also being associated with Saturn's death-life activity). She was sunk in the Kea Channel in the Aegean in 1916 by a mine or a torpedo. All three vessels brought enormous financial ruin to the White Star Line.

Now, don't bother to ask me *how* or *why* all this should be as it is. I don't know. But the astrological *correspondences* to how things turn out (i.e., how the invisibles will manifest) are obvious enough. Clearly, the directors of White Star Line might have benefitted differently by consulting a few astrologers.

But: there is *one more* awesome psychic factor which no one, as far as I can tell, has managed to point out. This one strikes deep, really deep, into the human psyche, and certainly should be included in the *Titanic's* psychic autopsy.

To my knowledge it has never been pointed out that the very name "Titanic" is the name and symbol of certain destructive forces which the ancients would have quickly recognized as feared "forces." The ancients apparently were familiar, in their terms at least, with the existence of numerous psychically destructive forces which could and did manifest in physical terms.

Of these there were twelve major ones collectively called the *Titans*. Our word "titanic" descends from this early source. Our present meaning for the word is, "of great magnitude, force, or power," but the dictionary also mentions, "relating to, or resembling the Titans."

So, you might ask, here is a word — what's the difference?

It is relatively easy to show that, in what we call a "subliminal way," symbols and images *attract* the energies and forces they represent.

For example, a raised fist in a poster symbolizes rebellion, but it also "attracts" rebellion, in that it inspires it in many of the people who see the poster. Psychologists have long agreed that symbols and images are "psycho-active," which is to say they not only signify what they represent, but also "inspire" activity.

To the ancients, the Titans signified the wild and untamable forces of primeval nature. As the expert on symbols, J.E. Cirlot, points out (in his *Dictionary of Symbols*), in creating a *psychic* model of the universe the ancients correctly assumed there were intermediate stages between the state of chaos and the creation of cosmic order. You can experience this in your daily life. When you go about trying to bring order into some kind of chaos, at first you encounter some rather rough forces that need to be tamed and brought under control before you can achieve order. The only way to really achieve order is to eliminate — in yourself, in your relationships with others, and in the environment — the image-forces that evoke chaos. This can be rather hard to do if you don't realize this is what needs to be done first. Just ask yourself: can chaos be evoked? The answer absolutely must be yes, for we can easily see chaos being evoked around us all the time.

To these forces that evoke chaos, the ancients, in their psychic wisdom, gave the term "Titan" because chaos-evoking forces can grow into *lethal* and *awesome* proportions in no time at all. The ancients were able to identify twelve varieties of chaos-making forces. The twelve Titans were pictured as supermen, yet having all the well-known human failings: greed, envy, jealousy, warlikeness, unbridled desire and ambition, stupidity, and so forth. These psychic attributes not only contributed to the ultimate and predictable downfall of the titanic "supermen" themselves, but in the process released their titanic destructive powers among humanity in general. We are familiar enough with this kind of situation, since we have seen it dramatized in novels, soap operas, movies, and in real life as well.

But the ancients went one step further. They assumed, and correctly so, in my opinion, that although the titanic forces existed within human psychology, they also existed as *factors* in the world's "cosmic aethers," as well. All one needed to do to attract these aethereal, titanic forces was to generate images that *would* attract them. If one can learn to recognize titanic images and that these will attract destruction, one can become a kind of prophet overnight — because destruction and doom is inevitable when these forces are activated.

Now, bearing all this in mind, at least hypothetically, would you name your most fabulous, ocean-going liner (and hefty investment) the *Titanic*? Admittedly, it is hard to make these connections in our psychically illiterate times. But if all things *are* interconnected and linked at some basic level of universal causation (as we now know is clearly the case), then the very images with which we deal are links into the whole, too, and the forces they activate feed back into us and our environment. We can speculate that linkage of this kind may represent a "universal law."

The sinking of the *Titanic* has gone into history as one of the single most calamitous events in modern times. The psychic autopsy of the Event shows that it was *completely* surrounded by invisible destructive factors from its inception onward. Not only were its astrological aspects extremely unfortunate, but the *Titanic's* story is one of ambition, greed, jealousy, and stupidity, all of which *attract* disaster — *titanic* disaster.

COMMUNAL PSYCHIC CAPABILITIES AND PSYCHIC NETWORKS

o We can observe that psychic-type information about future Events is "sharable," which is to say that it can "leak" into human consciousness in bits and pieces via numerous people. This appears especially to be the case where important, large-scale future events are concerned. Thus, it is possible to say that psychic "networks" of information probably do exist.

o We might observe, hypothetically, that these communal "sightings" could be used to good advantage if some kind of central premonitions registry were in common use and in which the piecemeal information could be consolidated into coherent, larger pictures.

o We have to wonder how so many people could possibly "tune in" to this kind of information if the Event did not already exist in some form. The implication is that Events of this kind somehow are in "existence" in some other-dimensional form and, via the people involved, are "feeding back" information into the present from that other dimension.

o We should observe that although this is a complex and mystifying situation, we should not allow its complexities to interfere with observing what's what in practical terms. We should anticipate that with appropriate study the complexities involved will be rendered intellectually explicable in the future.

SUGGESTED PRACTICAL EXERCISES THAT WILL HELP IN EXPANDING PSYCHIC LITERACY

o Try to be attentive to psychic "inputs" originating in your direct-sensing apparatus. If and when you experience some kind of psychic alert, take some time to ask others if they have experienced any similar feelings or impressions. Please do not ask them if they have "received" them, since this term sort of implies that they received them from some place outside themselves. While such may be possible, I've found this concept cuts across and sometimes defeats experiencing one's own direct-sensing system, and it implies that one should await some kind of external message. Remember that frequently communal alerts begin sometime well before the Events themselves may take place. If people you know are aware that you are interested in communal alerts, they will be in touch with you if and when they experience something. Please keep notes. Your intellect will not remember unless you can refresh it with notes.

VIII

A Look at Psychic Excellence

At this point in accumulating background information about psychic stuff, we should now tackle a situation that plagues our modern patterns of judgment regarding it. This situation has never been isolated and discussed before this present book; in my mind, it is one of extreme importance in that it represents the make-or-break point regarding whether we *should* take a constructive interest in psychic stuff or whether we *will not*.

Skeptics and critics of psychic stuff are very quick to point out that there are many self-proclaimed psychic practitioners who, for example, make predictions which do not turn out to be correct at all.

That this is so is unarguably the case — and the fact that it is so gives skeptics and critics the ammunition they need to condemn the whole of the psychic arts and crafts. The skeptics are delighted to focus our attention on this demerit and elaborate on it in order to confuse the actual issues involved — a factor which contributes in no little way to perpetuating our overall psychic illiteracy.

There is at least one salient argument against this skeptical viewpoint, and it is one that can be drawn from actual human experience: the disastrous state of the world which Reason has built. Ever since the Enlightenment broke its first rays (c. 1600), science-oriented intellectuals increasingly felt that human reason, the chief preserve of the intellect, was a better tool for negotiating human progress in the vastness of the cosmos than any other at humanity's command.

At that point in time, exploring the frontiers of reason was, indeed, something of a necessity (as it will always be). But, as interest in reason grew, interest in psychic stuff dwindled — and psychic matters suffered the one thing that was almost certain to cause it to fall into temporary oblivion. They became rationally unfashionable!

The result was that decision-making and predicting became the preserve of reason and the intellect. But, as human experience now knows, decisions and predictions emanating from reason and intellect alone really have not established a very good track record with regard to their own correctness or accuracy. In fact, the errors of reason and intellectual rationalization have been enormous and, in some cases, fatal, and humanity as a whole has paid a huge and bitter price for some of them.

In fact, we live today in a society that is almost completely founded upon allegiances to reason and rationalisms. It is this same society that is teetering on the brinks of several apocalyptic disasters the exact nature of which reason and modern rationalisms cannot even grasp.

At any rate, there is an aspect of wisdom which realizes that if we remain trenchantly focused only on what is wrong with something (other than to observe the existence of the wrongnesses), and never make an effort to isolate the positive, constructive aspects it may contain, then we will never lead ourselves to developing or taking advantage of the latter.

Although today we might indeed have low orders of psychic activity which are inaccurate much of the time, this can be laid at the doorstep of our low-order psychic illiteracy in general. This abysmal situation does not, nor can it, cancel out the fact that high-order psychic practitioners have existed and do exist. And because of their existence we can draw only one conclusion: that high-order psychic potentials and psychic excellence throughout society *are* possible.

Thus, I'd like to use this chapter to refresh our background memories about instances which reveal the existence and excellence of psychic potentials. We do not need to focus too long on the observed demerits of contemporary psychic practitioners. The positive destiny of our future psychic potentials does not at all rest upon their activities, but rather in finding and enhancing those potentials in ourselves.

THREE KNOWN TYPES OF PSYCHIC ACTIVITY

It should be noted that there are three general categories of psychic performance.

The *spontaneous category* includes those psychic events which happen unexpectedly and inexplicably to all sorts of people very much to their surprise, several of which we have already looked at.

The *inadvertent category* includes psychic-type phenomena that occur unexpectedly but with an apparent association to something else, such as hypnosis, anesthesia, near-death experiences, etc. (We will describe in detail two examples of these in the next chapter.)

The third category is represented by *people who deliberately try to achieve psychic proficiencies*. This third category is especially interesting because what we want to do is try to bring psychic performance more under our volitional awareness. If you study people who *try consciously* to be psychic and rate their performance on a scale of one to ten, most people achieve only zero — zilch. The minor statistic these psychically dysfunctional people represent, (which is all too easily observed), gives the anti-psychic factions great joy, and they parade this factor around for all to see, while at the same time burying in deepest obscurity as soon as possible any examples of perfect or near-perfect psychic performance. We need to resurrect some of these examples to make us enthusiastic — to say, to ourselves at least, that it can be done, has been done, and will be done again, now and in the future.

GREAT EVENTS ARE PRECEDED BY PSYCHIC ALERTS

For reasons that are very difficult to explain, great events almost always are foreshadowed by prophetic sightings that get lodged in history before the events themselves occur. If these events were foreshadowed just in their general outlines, we could be done with the psychic hypothesis and attribute them to healthy intellects who could correctly read the trends and winds of change. But these great prophecies are so precise in *details* that the idea of attributing them to anything other than psychic sightings actually brings more confusion into accounting for them than the psychic hypothesis does.

When a seer makes a prophecy filled with remarkable details which on the surface are totally unlikely, and when this prophecy with its unlikely details gets into the local press and becomes recorded gossip before the events occur, and when the unlikely events *do* occur in all their details, I think we are safe in assuming the prophecy is an example of perfect psychic performance.

One of the greatest events the world has ever known was the French Revolution which began in 1789. The two decades just preceding that date are extremely rich in psychic prophecies having to do with details that came about as a result of the Revolution. Thus, I've spent several years studying that period. I have been able to satisfy myself that the Revolution was not a popular rebellion but was brought about by secret societies bent on dissolving the historical monarchic system. It is not my purpose here to argue the justice or injustice of these societies' goals but to point out that these societies were not actually very secret, since a lot of people belonged to them, and the gossip had it that the winds of revolution were in the air. So, psychics who merely prophesied revolution just before the time when the Revolution did manifest can be eliminated from our analysis.

But we are still left with the matter of Nostradamus who lived between 1503 and 1566, well over two centuries *before* the Revolution and the formation of the societies which sponsored it. Nostradamus easily is the most famous prophet to live since the times of the very early Christian prophets; his prophetic quatrains (published in a book entitled *The Centuries*) are much adored by advocates of prophecy on the one hand, and they give consistent heartburn to anti-psychic skeptics on the other.

With regard to Nostradamus's prophecies concerning the French Revolution, the facts are simple enough. Referring to the Revolution, calling it "The Advent of the Common People," Nostradamus made some of his finest, most unambiguous prophecies. More, in the quatrains themselves, we can easily perceive his sense of horror and disbelief as he apparently tried to make sense of what one author calls "the first sights and sounds of modern times."[1]

For example, along with the entire course of the bloody Revolution, Nostradamus noted: "The white bourbon is driven out. Made a prisoner, led to the tumbril (dung cart), his feet together like a rogue...his death conspired will come into full effect, the charge given and the journey to death." This prophecy was made two hundred and twenty-seven years before Louis XVI, the "white bourbon," was taken tied and bound in a two-wheeled dung cart to the guillotine.

Nostradamus also, and in astonishing *detail*, predicted the beheading of Queen Marie Antoinette, and, by name, the death of their young son, Louis: "His arm in a sling and his leg bandaged, young Louis will leave the palace at the word of the watchman, his

---

[1] Hogue, John, Nostradamus & The Millennium, Doubleday, New York, 1987. Hogue competently and elegantly itemizes Nostradamus's correct prophecies.

death will be delayed...then he will bleed [to death] in the Temple at Easter." Which is exactly what happened.

From Nostradamus's time onward, as the march of history proceeded toward the bloody French Revolution (during which some 41,000 people were guillotined), countless major and minor future sightings of it began leaking, via psychic perceptions, into public consciousness. It is probably one of the most foretold Events of all times.

But as the time did draw nearer, and the winds and words of revolution were everywhere, the only future-seeings of it that can interest us are those which contain *details* that the rumors of revolution itself cannot account for. For example, shortly before the first sounds of the Revolution were heard, there existed a great and popular French preacher, one Father Beauregard, who delivered intense, charismatic sermons in the vast Cathedral of Notre Dame in Paris. One Sunday, well amid one of these dramatic sermons, the great preacher paused and staggered in the pulpit. Interrupting his sermon, he said: "Yes, Lord, I *see it*! Thy temple here will be plundered and devastated, Thy festivals will be abolished, Thy name blasphemed."

Getting a fuller hold on his vision, Father Beauregard continued in anger: "But what do I hear, great God? Instead of hymns in Thy praise, I hear this sacred roof resounding to profane licentious songs. And *you*, infamous goddess of Paganism, abandoned Venus, you have the audacity to enter here, to usurp the place of the living God, [and to] seat thyself on the throne of the Holiest of the Holy! Yea, and to receive blasphemous idolatry of thy worshipers? Yea, and too, Oh Lord, the infamy! Thy people will urinate and defecate on Your altar." With which, the famous preacher collapsed in tears, wailing: "Yea, and it shall come to pass herein..."

Needless to say, his audience, packed into the lofty, vast Notre Dame, hardly knew what to think or do except excuse themselves quietly. Yet, only a very few years later, the sacred cathedral was sacked, its altar and walls smeared with human urine, feces, and graffiti — which was later scrubbed up when the Christian edifice was converted into a "Temple of Reason" in which Venus was worshiped and adulated. Details! Yea, details!

And what of this one? In Paris a few years before the onset of the Revolution, the celebrated Count Alessandro di Cagliostro (whose title was probably self-conferred) was holding forth and had attracted a great following because of his psychic predictions, metaphysical insights, and his seemingly inexhaustible supply of money which allowed him to dramatize himself with considerable opulence.

Cagliostro was a Masonic type and had instituted a Masonic Order of his own design, which had attracted as members many from the upper aristocratic crust of the time. At one of these gatherings, at the home of Antoine Court de Gébelin, Cagliostro demonstrated to the assembly the possibility of divining a person's fate through a form of numerology.

Apparently, everyone thought it would be a good idea to have Cagliostro divine the fate of King Louis XVI as well as the fates of some of those at the party. Cagliostro promptly dropped the bombshell that was certain to lock into history his prediction for the King — to wit: "Let Louis XVI, supposed king, cast down from the ruined throne of his ancestors, beware of dying on the scaffold towards the thirty-ninth year of his life...fall, affliction, violent death...delivered to the executioner...before August 23, 1793."

Now, this psychic prediction took place during a time in which anyone openly predicting the death of the king could look forward to a long stay in prison. Needless to say, Cagliostro's prediction more than electrified everyone present. Of Queen Marie Antoinette: ."..unfortunate, unhappy in France, queen without a throne or money, wrinkled and greyed prematurely through grief, kept on a meagre diet, imprisoned, beheaded."

The Princesse de Lamballe, constant companion to the Queen, numbered among those present while these breathtaking prophecies fell from the lips of Cagliostro, was reduced to tears by them. If the Queen was to be imprisoned, then the Princesse could not hope to escape imprisonment, also. When asked about this, Cagliostro replied: "She will be imprisoned and then released. She will not be condemned to death, but she will not escape her fate. Her numbers signify that her fate is first to be beautiful, to be great — then to be unhappy, alone, and massacred in Paris. She will be massacred at the corner of the Rue des Ballets, where she will be decapitated, disemboweled, and her body rendered into pieces by the mad crowd. Afterwards, her head and body parts will be carried on pikes through the streets of Paris."

Cagliostro, apparently in a light trance when he said these gloomy words, then asked: "Is there a street of that name in Paris?" When assured there was, he said: "That will be the murder scene."

When the Revolution began, there was no idea that the King should be killed — only that he and the aristocracy should be stripped of much of their powers and that the French state should be remodeled as a democracy. Events soon got out of hand, and the process of beheading some 41,000 people began, including the King and Queen. Louis XVI was beheaded on January 21, 1793, in the thirty-ninth year of his life. As his head fell into the basket, a group of men and women rushed forward to dip handkerchiefs and clothes into the gore. The King's blood spurted a great distance.

Marie Antoinette was imprisoned and starved, her face wrinkling prematurely, and it is claimed that her hair turned white overnight. She was beheaded a short time after the King.

The Princesse de Lamballe was first imprisoned, then released. On her way from the prison, she was grabbed by a mob at the corner of the Rue des Ballets, beheaded, disemboweled, quartered, and her head was carried through the streets atop a pike — after her murderers had taken it to a very frightened hairdresser who was made to restore its coiffure.

You see. *Details*! There is little doubt Cagliostro was a charismatic, if shady, character, and much about him is open to question. But this particular set of prophecies is not since it was completely visible and much talked about before these strange events occurred. It is very difficult to explain the death of the Princesse de Lamballe, with its truly strange details, by anything other than the psychic hypothesis — that the mysterious Cagliostro did, indeed, see the future.

The network of future seeings that accompanied the French Revolution is very extensive. Another set of prophecies given about the same time as that of Cagliostro was one made by the poet, author, and clairvoyant Jacques Cazotte at a dinner party given by the Duchesse de Gramont in Paris in 1788. It was written down verbatim by Jean de La Harpe, a fanatical atheist and skeptic, so that, as he said, "he could later use the record to show the absurdity of taking prophecy seriously." Thus, it is from the pen of an anti-psychic observer that Cazotte's prophecies were recorded, every detail of which was fulfilled within five years of their utterance.

The prophecies began this way. One of Louis XVI's ministers, Malesherbes, was present at this dinner party and rose from the table to make a toast: "Here's to the day when reason will be triumphant in the affairs of men — a day which I shall never live to see."

While everyone was laughing about this speculation, Cazotte rose to reply: "Sir, you are wrong. You will live to see that day. It will come within six years." He went on to say that he was something of a prophet, and that the Revolution everyone had been talking about was not far ahead. Someone objected, saying that one hardly needed to be a prophet to see the Revolution coming. Cazotte agreed but continued: "The lives of everyone in this room will be affected, and to know in what way they will be affected, prophetic insight is necessary — this you will admit."

All the guests then began clamoring to know their fates. Cazotte, turning first to the Marquis de Condorcet, told him: "You will die on the stone floor of a prison cell after having taken poison to cheat the executioner."

Of Sébastien-Roch Nicolas Chamfort, one of Louis XVI's favorites, Cazotte predicted: "You will cut your veins twenty-two times with a razor, but still you will not die — until some months later."

To Dr. Félix Vicq-d'Azyr, Cazotte said: "You will not open your veins yourself. At your own request, someone will open them for you — six times in one day, and you will expire during the same night."

The famous astronomer Jean Sylvain Bailly was also at this dinner party. For him, Cazotte foretold: "In spite of your good deeds and great learning, there lies ahead only death by execution at the hands of the mob."

Cazotte went on to predict terrible deaths for all the male guests, including Malesherbes, who would die on the scaffold. The ladies present apparently felt omitted and begged Cazotte to tell them, too, of their fates. The Duchesse de Gramont opined that it was unlikely that women would be treated to deaths similar to the men. "Alas," Cazotte said, "You will be treated, all of you, exactly like the men, and you, yourself, and many other ladies present will be taken to the scaffold in the executioner's cart, hands tied behind. Even greater ladies than you will be victims. Of all the victims, male or female, only one will be allowed a confessor before his beheading, and that one is the present King of France."

We can hardly imagine what effect these predictions had on the Duchesse de Gramont's dinner party, but apparently the whole of this set of prophecies was treated with the giggle factor. One of the loudest gigglers was, of course, Jean de La Harpe, who asked about his own destiny. Smiling, Cazotte replied: "Of all here, you will escape the mob and death at this time. A more fitting destiny is in store for you. You will become a Christian." Since La Harpe's trenchant atheism was well known, this pronouncement seemed most unlikely and probably the party broke up in a good mood.

Within six years, *every detail* of this set of prophecies came true, including the fact that Jean de La Harpe entered a monastery and became an ardent Catholic.

The network of future-seeings linked the whole of the French Revolution and its aftermath and its psychic lines of linkage range so far afield that prophecies about it appear in such an unlikely place as the Caribbean island of Martinique. On this somewhat remote island was born in 1763 a seemingly insignificant girl, one Marie-Josèphe-Rose Tascher de la Pagerie, known as a "plump" ugly duckling in her childhood. With her birth began what is perhaps the most extraordinary destiny in history.

When Marie-Josèphe was fifteen, she went with a distant and very beautiful cousin, one Aimée du Buc de Rivéry, to consult a fortune-teller who is recorded in history variously as Eliama or Euphemie David, apparently the daughter of a Carib Indian woman and an Irish sailor. For Aimee, Euphemie David predicted: "You will soon go to France to perfect your education. When you are returning, your ship will be taken by Barbary pirates and you will be sold into slavery. Because you are beautiful, you will be bought for a King of dark skin, and you shall never depart from inside his palace and will live in it like a bird in a golden cage. You will give this king a son, who will come to rule after him. You will be like a queen but will never enjoy public honors. You will command a vast palace. Fear not this prophecy, for you will consider yourself to be the happiest of women. A lingering malady will take you not to a grave, but to a resplendent tomb."

For Marie-Josèphe, the seer knelt before her and called her "Majesty." "Your star promises two marriages in France — which will be in great turmoil. Your first husband will perish tragically. He will be beheaded and leave you two children. You shall be imprisoned and in fear of your own head. But you shall escape the death that befalls many of those around you. Then you will marry secondly a man with olive skin, at first without fortune and unpromising. Yet his glory will fill the world, and you shall first be a queen — and then more than a queen."

Now, what actually happened is this. When Aimée was returning from France after finishing her education in a convent, her ship was captured by Barbary pirates. She was sold into slavery and bought for the amusement of the old Dey of Algiers. This old city ruler, however, saw that she was so beautiful that he offered her unmolested to Sultan Selim III of Constantinople in hopes of gaining favors from him.

There, Aimée was placed in the Sultan's harem where she bore him a son. When the Sultan's first son by another wife died, Aimée's was declared heir. He eventually became Mahmud II, and Aimée became the Sultana Valide, the "French Sultana," otherwise called the "first lady of the palace."

When French authorities finally did learn of her whereabouts, the French Ambassador volunteered to have her freed. However, Aimée, who was by now in love with her husband and son and considered herself the happiest of women, declined the offer. She ruled her "golden cage" for many years, eventually dying of a lingering illness in her age, and was entombed in a mausoleum befitting the wife and mother of kings.

As to Marie-Josèphe, she went to France to marry one Vicomte Alexandre de Beauharnais, with whom she had two children. Both she and her husband were imprisoned during the Revolution. Her husband was soon beheaded. During her incarceration awaiting her own beheading, she clung to her hope in Euphemie's prophecy that she would not die, telling many of this prophecy during the waiting process. With her nerves wrecked, one night she was told to chop off her hair because she was scheduled for the guillotine the next morning. But during that night, the bloody "rulers" of the Revolution were themselves overthrown and killed, and Marie-Josèphe was freed.

Freed, however, she was broke. She became a "fabulous courtesan" to the new regime's masters and eventually also a dealer in black market contracts for military supplies. In this status, she was espied by the young Napoléon who was several years his junior. He fell madly in love with her, and eventually convinced her to marry him. He changed her name to Josephine, a name which is among the immortal names in history, usually preceded by the descriptive term "the Fabulous." As Napoléon's star ascended over Europe, he first made her queen (of Italy) and then more than a queen — Empress of France.

The prophecies accompanying Napoléon's rise and fall are staggering when collected together — but too long to include in this present book, since we want to move up into more modern times.

I've discussed these future-seeings with many people. Although most are impressed with them, and not a few have asked what the larger meaning is, some have said something to the effect of: "So what? The Revolution came and went. The prophecies changed nothing. Everyone got killed, anyway. What good was it to know in advance?"

To answer this, you have to look at the whole history of the Revolution. Just before the Revolution got going, and in its early stages before the revolutionary authorities closed France's frontiers, many people packed up their valuables and left France. Not a few of them did so because, as they said, the prophecies were so consistent that they did not doubt them. Those who left were *not* among the 41,000 whose heads *did* get chopped off.

SEPHARIAL AND CHEIRO

In the latter decades of the nineteenth century, we encounter two future-seeing personalities each of whose works are awesome. Taken together, they, as it is said, "surpasseth understanding."

In 1864 there was born at Harndsworth, Birmingham, England, one Walter Richard Old, who adopted the name Walter Gorn Old and wrote astrological and numerological books under the pseudonym "Sepharial."

It is known that at an early age he studied the Kabala and astrology, then moved on to a variety of subjects including orientalism, ancient languages, and something called "medical dispensing," none of which led to a successful career. In 1889 he joined the Theosophical Society, but he left it after the death of its most charismatic founder, Madame Blavatsky. Apparently, he was known to have the special psychic talent of out-of-body travelling. It is reported that Madame Blavatsky called him an "astral tramp" because of his penchant for wandering about in questionable places in his OOBE state. He was friendly with the famous astrologer Alan Leo (1860-1917).

Eventually, Old found a successful career in that he developed a system of astrological prediction for the stock market and basic commodities futures, from which he made a more than comfortable income. His most profitable income, however, was from an astrological horse-racing system — the dream of many. Before he died in 1929, he had published several books delineating the mechanics of his future-seeing systems which have understandably been of intense interest to many (including myself) but which have yet to produce another Walter Gorn Old.

If we think about it a little, I think we have to take our hats off to a prophet who, unlike many other so-called "predictors," put his *own* money where his prophetic mouth was, especially in the high-risk fields of commodities speculation and horse-racing. But, in addition to his commodity and horse-racing speculations, we find in the "astral tramp" a prophet of stellar magnitude.

We are indebted to Old because he undertook to make his predictions known — in print, in the clearest of details — well before the events he predicted came to pass. For example, Old predicted a coming "great war of nations" in his 1896 manual of astrology. In 1913 he updated his original prediction for this war when he turned in to the publisher W. Foulsham in London a text entitled thusly: *An Astrological Survey of the Great War, Being an Examination of the Indications Attending the Outbreak and the Presumptive Effects of the Conflict.* The Great War (World War I) did not begin until August 1914, and even then, few understood that the outbreak would lead to the enormous European and American conflagration that it did. Further, Old published a series of newsstand pamphlets entitled *The Green Book for Prophecies* that came out intermittently for several years, and in which he updated his predictions.

Even for those convinced about prophecy, a serious, in-depth reading of the astral tramp's collected prophecies will quite shatter your synapses, especially if you look at the dates they were published relative to the events they predicted. You will need to go to bed for a week while your head tries to recover. Let me just pick up some of the high points.

Old lived and worked in a time when power was still held in the hands of monarchs, and so, of course, the fates and destinies of monarchies were targets for every aspiring prophet. Clearly, Old did not like the Germans and Austrians, and so these came under his special scrutiny. In his 1913 prophecy for the year 1914, Old indicated there would be signs of sharp agitation. There would be financial strain and a tendency toward panic on the markets. Disbursements on further munitions of war would give rise to alarm in commercial centers. He referred to his earlier predictions about a coming great catastrophe and castigated England: "In the face of this coming great catastrophe, the politicians of England have assured everyone that never has there been a more suitable opportunity of reducing expenditures on the army and navy." Thus, when the Great War *did* break out, England was totally unprepared for it. Old was later to comment: "So much for *political prescience!*"

In his 1913 prediction for European affairs, Old pointed out that developments in political affairs would not be reassuring and would, about July 25, 1914, lead to a crisis of an awesome nature. There would be war talk throughout Europe and the "Balkan concert will now be disturbed and affairs tend to a crisis in Austria beginning on June 28."

Now, how it turned out. During June 1914, Archduke Franz Ferdinand of Austria, heir to the throne, decided to pay a ceremonial visit to Sarajevo, the capital of Bosnia, where he was to watch Austrian army maneuvers. To extend his visit into a political gesture of friendship, he brought his wife, Sophie. As they drove through the streets of Sarajevo on June 28, both were assassinated by a Serbian nationalist. This shocking event led to the Austrian government's demand on July 24 that Serbia be suspended as a state. Serbia refused. On July 28, war was declared between Serbia and Austria, and the "Balkan concert" was disrupted. Like falling dominos, soon all the other European states were involved in this miserable little impasse. Germany declared war against Russia on August 1. France entered the conflict on August 3, as did England.

In his 1913 prophecy, Old indicated that the aging Emperor France Joseph of Austria, having sat on his throne longer than Queen Victoria had sat on hers, did not "have long to go." He pointed out the series of tragedies that had stricken down Franz Joseph's relatives and that he now sat "in sinister solitude waiting for the blow that would end his eventful career — and shortly after his death would occur the end of the Hapsburg empire." Now, at the time, hardly anyone could conceive of the *end* of the Hapsburg dynasty which had by then been *the* ruling European dynasty for almost nine-hundred years.

Emperor Franz Joseph expired from pneumonia on November 21, 1916, and his heir, Emperor Charles I, was forced to abdicate on November 11, 1918. When Charles signed the articles of abdication, the Hapsburg dynasty came to its end — leaving the somewhat *nouveau* Prussian dynasty, the Hohenzollerns, triumphant.

Their triumph, however, was, according to Old, to be short lived. In his prophecies for 1914, Old turned his attention to the

"Prussian Beast," Kaiser Wilhelm II. Prussia (Germany) would "gather dead sea fruit of inordinate ambitions." "Nemesis awaits upon the earthly representative of the Arch-Enemy, beginning about April 1918." The Hohenzollerns would "bite the dust" and their Empire would "go into eclipse...The despot will be blinded and the cult of 'Blood and Iron' [as the Prussians referred to themselves] is doomed for extinction, so far, at least, as it finds representation in the person of the Arch-Enemy Kaiser Wilhelm II." The "Beast will be given safe conduct into obscurity which, to one who has attempted such heights, must indeed be a hell of debasement and perdition."

Now, what happened: During April 1918, German morale began to collapse. As the Allied forces pressed on, an armistice was signed on November 11, 1918. Wilhelm II ceased to be Kaiser when he signed *his* abdication on November 28, 1918, after having fled to Holland, where he was allowed to live in exile until his death on June 4, 1941, an obscurity that certainly must have been hell for one who had "reached so high."

However, Old was not yet done with these Germans. The defeated Kaiser Wilhelm II possessed a son and heir apparent, Crown Prince Wilhelm, and in 1914, Old focused his prophetic spyglass on this heir. He began by saying: "The horoscope of the Crown Prince of Germany is one that the astrologer instantly recognizes not as a royal, but a decadent horoscope." Clearly, this Prince would lose his inheritance. He would be imprisoned in exile, but around 1922, "he would be heard from again, and in due course be made a forlorn hope by a certain coterie of his people in an attempt to regain the Empire." He would set himself up in the image of the "First Beast" and enter, uneventfully, into league with the chancellor. But by about 1931, he would be entirely rooted out. Yet there was soon to come *another*, a "Third Beast" already "smoldering with the ambition of *la grande revanche*." This Third Beast would set loose "a second great devastation for which the Great War would seem like only a dress rehearsal."

Now, what happened: Crown Prince Wilhelm followed his father into exile on November 12, 1918. He was held, to all practical purposes, a prisoner by the Dutch on the desolate island of Wieringen in the Zuyder Sea. In 1922, he published his memoirs, with the goal of obtaining allies to help him off the island and back to Germany. On November 10, 1923, he was allowed to leave his exile, after which he periodically surfaced in vain attempts to reconstitute his former authority in Germany. In 1931, the chancellor of Germany considered using the crown prince as a front, but this proved unnecessary by affairs in Germany as Adolf Hitler (the "Third Beast") in 1933 began his awesome rise to power and prepared for *la grande revanche* that would make the First World War seem a dress rehearsal for the Second World War.

In his 1914 prophecies, Old turned his attention to Russia by indicating that it was unlikely that the Tsar, Nicholas II, would survive the war, but that at the time he reached forty-nine years of age (1917) there would "be a great revolution" that would "see the end of the dynastic succession in Russia." Further, Russia would not "emerge from the Great War with any measure of success."

What happened: The Russian Revolution occurred in November 1917, and the chilling story of Nicholas II and the royal family is familiar history. They were all murdered in 1918, and the "end of the dynastic succession in Russia" was achieved.

In fairness, it should be pointed out that Old was not completely correct in all his predictions. But he made no major blunders, and his errors when they do show up are minor. Anyone at the time who might have wanted an overview of the complete game plan of the First World War and hints of things thence to come after it, could easily have purchased Old's books or picked up his pamphlets on newsstands in London.

However, Old prophesied things that were, at the time, totally unbelievable, and, like all prophets who predict the unbelievable, his prophecies ran headlong into what I will call "ritualized thinking" in a later chapter, when we begin to dig into the "mechanics" of the psychic factor.

Walter Gorn Old (Sepharial), having been born in 1864, passed into the great psychic beyond in 1929. Contemporaneous to Old lived Count Louis Hamon (Cheiro), who was born in Ireland in 1866 and was found dead on a Hollywood street in 1936. It is practically impossible to tell who the greater psychic was, but it is clear that these two were some of the greatest future-seers of the last two-hundred year period, and few since have approached their excellence either in volume of prophecies given or numbers of prophecies accurately fulfilled. Of the two, Old was something of a grey eminence near the top of future-seeing pyramid, while Hamon was a very visible, ebullient, energetic, and charismatic celebrity-seer who travelled with the jet-setters of the period.

Like Old, Hamon's psychic education began as a child. As he says in *Fate in the Making*, one of his autobiographical tracts: "From my mother's side, Greek and French stock, I inherited romance, mysticism, and philosophy. The subsequent fusion in the fires of life of these combinations naturally produced a being predestined for a career that would not run on conventional lines. My mother from her earliest days was deeply interested in reading works on Astrology, Numerology, and the Study of the Hand. Consequently, almost as soon as I could read, she allowed me to revel in the little library of such books that she had collected. I was only a little past eleven years of age when I caused a sensation in my family by writing a treatise full of illustrations on the Lines of the Hand, a subject, I must admit, not at all pleasing to my father's way of thinking. Shortly after, perhaps to combat my occult tendencies, my father decided to have his only son trained for some religious calling...To my young mind [the Hand] was a mystery like religion itself; it contained the language of the Soul in its prison-house, and the lines of the hand seemed many a time to me a more tangible chart of life than the articles of [religious] dogma I was forced to commit to memory."[2]

It is worth noting here that Hamon, like Walter Gorn Old, began studying psychic tools (such as palmistry, numerology, and astrology) when he was a *child*. Like Old, Hamon left a rather large literary contribution of psychic techniques and, of course, of prophecies published well before they were fulfilled (see bibliography).

In keeping with the interests of the time in which the future of the royal houses of Europe interested everyone, and probably also because members of the royal houses frequently consulted psychic and astrologers, Hamon devoted considerable effort to foretelling the fates and destinies of these houses, especially concerning those of the British Empire and the ruling House of Windsor. It should be said in fairness that many of his larger, more general prophecies are not exactly clear. But when it came to individuals, Hamon's accuracy was fabulous.

In 1925 Hamon turned in to his publisher the manuscript of book entitled *Cheiro's World Predictions: The Fate of Europe, The Future of the U.S.A., the Coming War of Nations, the Restoration*

---

2 See Cheiro. Fate in the Making. Harper & Brothers Publishers, New York, 1931, pp. 2-4.

of the Jews, which was published in 1927, by Herbert Jenkins, Ltd., London. In this book, among other things, he pretty much nailed down the advent and reasons for World War II and the eventual advent of the State of Israel. Naturally, Hamon turned his penetrating psychic eye on Britain's ruling dynasty, the House of Windsor, and made the following prediction for the heir-apparent to the throne, Edward Albert Christian George Andrew Patrick David, Prince of Wales, and his younger brother, the Duke of York.

Hamon's prophecies for the Royal Family are given through complex astrological comparisons that delineate individuals in the entire House of Windsor since its founding, comparisons that are too complicated to summarize in this present book but can be found beginning on page 78 of *Cheiro's World Predictions*.

In 1925 the King of England was George V, formerly the Duke of York, the *second son* of Edward VII whom he succeeded since his elder brother, the Duke of Clarence, had died in 1892. Hamon pointed out that the period between 1928 and 1930, would be unfavorable for George V, and he indicated that His Majesty would be exposed to danger of illness, especially those caused by "air," and that the "portents are strange and ominous and full of meaning for the entire Empire." What actually came to pass was that George V was stricken with severe inflammation of the lungs and pneumonia which commenced in 1928 and lasted to the summer of 1930 when he died, and at which time his first son, Edward, Prince of Wales, became King Edward VIII.

But, in 1925, Hamon pointed out that although Edward would inherit the throne, he would abandon it before his coronation in favor of his younger brother, the Duke of York, for what could only at the time be considered shocking reasons. Now, when you read through the complex prophecy that follows, bear in mind that few have been the kings who willingly abdicated their thrones — and that in Edward's case in particular there seemed little likelihood of his so doing since he was an energetic and popular prince who had acquired the love of the Empire and was looking forward to the time he became King, when he could lead England into the modern age.

The prophecy goes thusly: Hamon pointed out that the horoscope of Edward's younger brother, the Duke of York, had much in common with the second son of Edward VII whom he succeeded as George V. "All through the years 1927 to 1930 the portents are not favorable for the prosperity of England or for the Royal Family, with the exception of the Duke of York. In his case, it is remarkable that the regal sign of Jupiter increases in power as the years advance, which, as I have explained, was also the case of his Royal Father [George V] *before* there was any likelihood of his coming to the Throne. Not only does King George, but Queen Mary also, come under a combination of adverse influences. Nor does the present Prince of Wales [Edward] escape these falling shadows. His astrological chart shows perplexing and baffling influences that most unquestionably point to changes likely to take place greatly affecting the Throne of England.

"The birth date of the Prince places him in a category of individuals who are strangely baffling in temperament. In the case of those who live ordinary lives, these peculiarities escape much comment or have little effect; but where it is a Prince of the Blood, called by birth to fill a high position, it is a very different matter.

"The Prince was born under peculiar astrological combinations which make his character a difficult one to understand. His planetary signs give intense restlessness, a lack of continuity of thought, a difficulty of concentration, and an absorbing love for change of scene and travel, and a lack of what may be called 'a sense of danger.' Physically there will be found a nervousness expressed by restless movements and lack of repose, as in a person 'forever on the move.' Such individuals are apparently wildly changeable and are often accused of being insincere. But as a matter of fact they simply are dominated by different moods — hence their apparent chameleon character."

Hamon then goes on to compare Edward to his ancestor George, Prince of Wales, afterwards Regent, and reigning as George IV (1820-1830). "That George the Fourth, when Prince, married Mrs. Fitzherbert, is supported by historical documents; the match was dissolved by an Act of Parliament which limited Royal Princes to ladies born within the 'circle of Royal Blood,' and his subsequent marriage to Caroline of Brunswick was a disaster...George the Fourth regarded women as mere playthings of an idle hour, but shuddered away from serious intimacy.

"The present Prince of Wales has piqued curiosity many times by rumours of marriages that have faded away into the air. ...The Prince of Wales, who may be fond of a light flirtation with the fair sex, is determined not to settle down until he feels a *grande passion*, but it is well within the range of possibility, owing to the peculiar planetary influences to which he is subject, that he will in the end fall a victim to a devastating love affair.

"If he does so, I predict that the Prince will give up everything, *even the chance of being crowned* [emphasis added], rather than lose the object of his affection."

Now, what actually happened: First of all, in a few pages Hamon hit upon Edward's peculiar psychology, whereas it has taken his biographers some four decades somewhat unsuccessfully to sort it out. In fact, Edward's intricate psychology did not really come into focus until Frances Donaldson published her in-depth biography of Edward in 1974. Certainly, none of Edward's ruinous attributes were visible in 1925, during which time he was acting as an epitome of an heir-apparent and when Cheiro's predictions for him were in the printing process.

In alluding to George IV's fascination with common women rather than ladies of the Royal Blood, Hamon used that King's illegitimate marriage to Mrs. Fitzherbert to indicate that Edward also would fall fatally for and probably insist on marrying not only a non-royal woman, but one who had been married before. In 1925 this was completely unimaginable.

What began to be known about Edward from about 1925 on was that this inordinately charismatic Prince was indeed fascinated with common women. He soon was dipping his wick into a long list of ordinary ladies. But this was seen as Edward's natural prerogative, and it continued to be assumed he would eventually select a lady from one of Europe's royal blood lines to be England's Queen.

However, in the autumn of 1930, Edward, Prince of Wales, was introduced to one of America's gayest divorcees, now married a second time, one Wallis Warfield Simpson. In this woman, Edward encountered the *grande passion* Hamon predicted he was looking for, and this meeting resulted in what is unquestionably the most notorious love affair of the twentieth century. It seems that only a short time had gone by before Edward was trying to envision a means where he might marry Wallis Simpson and install her on the throne as Queen of England when he became King.

That this adventure had absolutely no chance — *none* — of succeeding deterred Edward not at all from assuming that once he was King he could pull it off.

The idea that the English would accept a common American as Queen, much less a once-divorced one, who would need to obtain a *second* divorce to marry Edward at all, was as far-fetched as any idea might be. Edward's addled mind, so clearly described by our astrological clairvoyant, Louis Hamon, now began to surface and reveal itself for what it was — much to the consternation of the English.

The "affair of the century" progressed and solidified until 1936 when George V died, and Edward became King of England as Edward VIII. In the interval between the time he inherited the throne and his coronation, Edward decided the time was ripe to marry Wallis and proceeded to try to *force* Parliament to give its approval. When it became clear to him that he was not to succeed, he opted for a morganatic marriage in which Wallis would not be Queen and their children not be in line for succession to the throne.

But even this plow was not to succeed — even when Edward used his trump card and threatened to abdicate if he could not have the woman of his choice. The English had had enough of the machinations of this woman, whom they clearly could see would be the real ruler of England behind Edward, since Edward's mind apparently was putty in her hands. Having threatened to abdicate, Edward was now compelled to do so, and, in December 1936 stepped down from the throne in favor of his younger brother, the Duke of York, exactly as Louis Hamon had predicted. Edward VIII, now Duke of Windsor, married Wallis Simpson a short time later.

Thus, Louis Hamon's, "I predict that the Prince will give up everything, even the chance of being crowned, rather than lose the object of his affection," became the most astounding prediction of the twentieth century. This prediction can be found at the bottom of page 87 in *Cheiro's World Prediction*, published in 1927, *nine years* before Edward lost his marbles and gave up the throne of England — something the English eventually were grateful for, since Edward was soon revealed to be a Nazi sympathizer.

As an interesting side note, when the "Wallis Simpson crisis" in England was coming to a head, many lotteries were established, and bets were taken on whether or not Edward would abdicate. Most speculators bet he would not. Those who had read Hamon's prediction and bet that he would cleaned up.

EVANGELINE ADAMS

There have, of course, been many good and even great astrologers who have employed the craft to pierce into the activities and workings of invisible factors, and so it is not exactly fair to single out only two of them for treatment in this book. Astrology is a psychic craft because it is used specifically to delve into factors which otherwise will remain invisible or hidden and otherwise have no tangible form save for their results in the concrete universe.

What it takes to make a great astrologer is something astrologers themselves have never fairly faced. Beyond intellectually absorbing the techniques and details of the craft and achieving the proficiency of accuracy therein, it is clear that other human and spiritual capabilities also need to be present in the astrological craftsperson. For example, something amounting to a profound knowledge of fundamental human nature needs to be present, a kind of knowledge that is, in our present times, at its lowest ebb in human history. If this profound knowledge is absent in a given astrologer, they will not inspire confidence in their clients, and their utterances will be shallow.

We can get a better idea of all of this if we understand why people consult astrologers and psychics in the first place. They do so majorly for two reasons, both of which are always of utmost importance to them. First, to discover information that will help them understand and manage a usually serious problem or situation better, and for which (usually) no other form of help is available. Second, to discover what the future holds, a realm in which the psychic arts and crafts are the only ones that are meaningful.

The astrologer, then, must seek to deliver information that is uniquely meaningful, and not just "information" *per se*, and the information that is uniquely meaningful can only be that which is also uniquely accurate. If such information arrived at by psychic/astrological means proves to be so, it is irrational to deny the validity of the processes that produced it.

Just after the turn of the Century, an astrologer by the name of Evangeline Adams (1869-1932) was holding forth in New York City. She had already impressed the world and her clients with an endless list of correct utterances when, in 1914, she was hauled into court in a legal action brought against her as a fortune-teller. Rather than have her lawyer get the case thrown out of court, she pressed to have it brought to trial in order, as she said in her autobiography, to have "the question settled for all time."[3]

In court Adams proved the efficacy of astrology, and the judge ruled in her favor, commenting "that she claims no faculty of

---

3 Adams, Evangeline, The Bowl of Heaven, Dodd, Mead & Company, New York, 1926.

foretelling by supernatural or magical means that which is future, or of discovering that which is hidden and obscure; but she does claim that nature is to be interpreted by the influences that surround it. When the defendant prepared her horoscope of the complainant and calculated the relative positions of the planets at the time of her birth, basing this horoscope on the well-known and fixed science of Astrology, she violated no law." Adams justified having the suit brought to trial by saying she was for equality before the law — even for fortune-tellers.

In her autobiography she noted: "My thirty years' experience is my guarantee to myself that accuracy upon which reliability of my deductions wholly depend. The doctor's mistake is buried, the lawyer's mistake is hanged, but the Astrologian must not make a mistake" — and be able to stay in business, I might add. That she did stay in business and become the premiere astrological luminary in the United States can only be attributed to the value of the services she provided. By her own reckoning her archives recorded that well over four thousand people had consulted her as of 1926 — and among these the names of the great and near great read like a special who's who not unlike the list of luminaries who consulted the astrologer which had infiltrated the United Nations Secretariat when I worked there, as we have already seen.

People consult psychic sources to find explanations for things reason cannot, is not, or is inadequate in explaining — which is to say, a *lot* of things. And which is to say that astrologers also need to know a lot of things besides the intricacies of their craft. In this regard, Evangeline Adams's autobiography, *The Bowl of Heaven*, is very informative, for in it she reveals much of her philosophy, her overviews of natural harmonies and disharmonies and of the perennial human situation, and spiritual insights that are astonishing for their penetrating simplicity.

JEANE DIXON

Since the time of Old, Hamon, and Adams, no future-seer of their caliber has appeared, although it certainly must be noted that during the 1950s and 1960s Mrs. Jeane Dixon, the once great American seer, seemed a good candidate to step into their shoes. Her future-seeing abilities emerged when she was quite young, and she arose to become something of a phenomenon among the Washington political set. Many of her prophecies reached print in advance of their fulfillment through the efforts of Ruth Montgomery who, at the time, was a syndicated political columnist. However, it seems her better psychic functioning got squashed or at least confused within the vapors of psychic glamor and lower-order tabloid "psychic" pap — and, so to speak, she "lost it."

But this "fall" should not, I think, destroy her whole history, as many would like it to do. Mrs. Dixon predicted the deaths of Carole Lombard and Dag Hammarskjold in plane crashes, the assassination of Mahatma Gandhi, Marilyn Monroe's "suicide," the adoption of Communism by China, the partition of India, and the Soviet Union's launch into space of their Sputnik.

Ruth Montgomery, as she says, refused to accept Dixon's prediction that the Secretary of State, John Foster Dulles, would die in the spring of 1959 and refused also to print her 1952 prophecy that serious race rioting would "bloody our American streets in 1963 and 1964." Montgomery also refused to believe her greatest prophecy — that President Kennedy would be assassinated in Dallas on the date the tragedy did occur. This prophecy first saw the light of day in 1952, eleven years before the actual event occurred on November 22, 1963, and Dixon was even able eventually to determine the *name of the assassin*.

This prophecy was well known since it had appeared in *Parade* (March 11, 1956), and, as the fatal day eventually drew nearer, Dixon tried to use her circle of contacts to warn the President not to go to Dallas. When Kay Halle, the influential Washington hostess heard of the prophecy, she told it to Mrs. Alice Roosevelt Longworth, the daughter of President Theodore Roosevelt. As Kay Halle later reported, "What could we do? We Americans simply haven't the capacity to embrace something like this. I knew that the Kennedy's would consider it some kind of mumbo-jumbo. The President would have laughed at the mere suggestion."

Of course, no American President can run scared before a mere psychic — or an astrologer, for that matter. But if Kennedy had had a couple of good astrologers on retainer, he might not have laughed at the "mere suggestion" of Jeane Dixon's prophecy for him. For, at the time of his assassination, the abysmal planet Pluto was getting ready to move in direct opposition to his natal Venus — which means, among other things, the end of a beautiful life as lived so far.

This sorry aspect need not necessarily portend physical death. But, at the time of the assassination, the betrayer planet, Neptune, was moving into conjunction with Kennedy's natal Moon, the natal Moon residing in his "house of friends."

This Moon/Neptune aspect is very similar to the Moon/Neptune aspect which ended in Abraham Lincoln's assassination, as we have already seen. Clearly, Kennedy was in a period when he couldn't think correctly about his friends (in fact, probably could not think at all; for example, he refused to ride behind bullet-proof glass) and, in astrologese, at any rate, the fact he may have been betrayed by his "friends" is not out of the question. But, on the day of his assassination, the terrible blood-lust planet Mars was moving into direct opposition to his natal Sun — indicating a time of great danger through violence. Like with Lincoln, the sum of all this equals a distinct possibility of assassination which, forecasted by Jeane Dixon (she was not the only seer to so forecast) *throughout* the ten years preceding it, duly took place while Washingtonians laughed at all this "mumbo-jumbo."

After Dixon's career ran into its strange eclipse, it is impossible to say no other good future-seers appeared on the scene, but it is possible to say that psychic history entered a period in which stellar, inspired, accurate, and charismatic future-seeing personalities have not emerged. On a quieter key, though, apparently a few have, among which is the New York psychic-astrologer, Charles House.

Born in Memphis, Tennessee, House began studying astrology in 1970 when he was thirty. In New York, by 1972, he was, as the *Press-Scimitar* said, making "bold predictions" which by 1973, also found their way into media coverage by, among others, such diverse newspapers as the *Staten Island Advance*. It is little wonder, for in March 1972, House predicted that a scandal of major proportions would rock the Richard M. Nixon administration and result in Nixon's resignation as President. After the Watergate scandal had erupted, House updated his predictions for Nixon by indicating he would "begin reevaluating his political career during June 1974" and would resign during the summer. Nixon resigned on August 9, 1974, the first American President ever to do so.

House correctly predicted the unlikely landslide election of Ronald Reagan because, among other positive astrological aspects, "the fortunate planet, Jupiter, will be transiting his mid-heaven at the time of the election." On March 20, 1988, House presented a public session, attended by this author, at the South Street Theatre in New York specifically to give his predictions for the upcoming November presidential election. He unequivocally stated that

Michael Dukakis didn't stand a chance, not only "because his chart shows he is victim of his own inherent communication problem which will confuse the issues he says he stands for," but "because George Bush, like Reagan, will have the fortunate planet, Jupiter, transiting *his* mid-heaven at the time of the election indicating that he, too, will win by an overly large majority."

This prediction went against what most other astrologers were saying, at least those that got themselves on TV and into the media. In a later interview with House after the election in which Bush had won by a landslide, I asked him why most other astrologers had predicted in favor of Dukakis. House said that most astrologers are liberals, like he himself is, but that unless run-of-the-mill astrologers can rise above their ritualized political thinking, their political preferences will cloud their interpretations of political horoscopes. House further indicated that it was a good thing Dukakis did not get elected because he has the baleful, authoritarian, uncompassionate planet, Saturn, on the mid-heaven of his natal horoscope whose aspects, when added to his "afflicted" communication problems, would not be suitable for the Commander-in-Chief of a democratic nation.

* * *

So, there we have it — some examples of psychic excellence, characterized by *details* which no amount of intellectual rationalizing or rational expertise alone can account for. I think these not only could, but should, inspire us to move off the dime and get to work reconnecting ourselves to our own psychic potentials and to the psychic arts and crafts.

Palmistry, numerology, and astrology are arts and crafts that serve to help isolate or "condense" accuracies in future-seeing. There is little evidence that these crafts, in themselves, can be responsible for making the judgments necessary for accurately forecasting the astonishing *details* of future events. The clairvoyant aspects of the psychic factor are strategic, and these clairvoyant aspects must be integrated with the mechanics of the crafts. Without these clairvoyant aspects, the crafts themselves can well represent labyrinths of "occult" possibilities amongst which the non-clairvoyant practitioner must make rather mechanical guesses.

Even so, as is often mentioned, the best psychic practitioners often can make mistakes. Well, so can anyone who drives a car, but this hardly keeps cars from being driven. Anyone who tries to think can make mistakes, too. But this hardly keeps everyone from trying to think. What we are after in the context of this book is whether or not psychic stuff and its allied crafts can serve us.

This question is already answered in part, and not only in this book. *OMNI* magazine, in its January 1989 issue (page 76) speculated whether or not an astrologer could intuit as much about someone as psychologists could, and they reported that psychologists Anton DeMan of Bishop's University in Quebec and Huub Angenent of Rijksuniversiteit te Groningen in Holland decided to find out. They gave the dates and times of birth of thirty subjects to an astrologer and then asked psychologists who knew the subjects well to agree or disagree with the interpretations of the astrologer. The psychologists agreed with the astrologer's character analysis seventy-three percent of the time.

It really must be pointed out that psychologists in general are far less successful, even after having spent several years with patients, and the patients sometimes have spent considerable amounts of money.

At any rate, if any of you are considering a stab at obtaining the presidency, perhaps a few good astrologers can help you sort out the possibilities and say whether or not the fortunate planet, Jupiter, will favor you.

A LOOK AT PSYCHIC EXCELLENCE

o We can observe that individuals with highly-developed psychic proficiencies *have* lived at various times, and that their excellent proficiencies were developed out of the raw psychic potentials generally existing in our biopsychic human nature.

o We can observe that many earlier, great psychics and practitioners of the psychic arts and crafts probably had interests in psychic stuff during childhood and began their studies of it quite early.

o We should observe that although this early interest ultimately manifested itself in adult psychic competency, the fact that it was early undertaken probably made it easier for the young forming intellects to integrate the specific kinds of general background information and psychic crafts necessary for adult psychic proficiency to function, sometimes at white heat.

o We should also observe that in our present culture the sector of our population insulated the most from information about psychic stuff is children. They are not exposed to it in any constructive, organized manner and, indeed, are taught it is irrational, or even worse. Only certain adults begin to recognize the value of psychic sources and then have to work somewhat assiduously to correct the imbalance in their intellectual overviews to accommodate psychic literacy.

SUGGESTED PRACTICAL EXERCISES THAT WILL HELP IN EXPANDING PSYCHIC LITERACY

- It is somewhat difficult to develop any practical steps regarding the contents of this particular chapter. One thing that can be done, however, is somewhat enjoyable if you have developed some seriousness in enlarging the scope of your psychic literacy.

- This is to read any of the available books detailing past, successful psychic predictions. Several of these will be found listed in the bibliography.

***

Up to this point I've dealt principally with our direct-sensing systems and their processing of invisible types of information. Before we move into Part Two, I'd like to round out the scope of our background information by discussing, via two examples, another type of power apparently inherent in our psychic potentials.

This power is so astonishing as to unnerve intellects which are already positively predisposed toward psychic stuff — the power to alter biological processes themselves and, even, to reconstitute genetic patterns.

IX

Miraculous Healing

Up to now we have discussed psychic potentials in the light of their information-gathering powers. But other kinds of psychic potentials exist which are considerably different in character and so extraordinary that the term "miraculous" has always been used to describe their effects. When I first planned this book, I had decided to focus only on those psychic potentials which had to do with information gathering, since those potentials are so widely experienced and specifically developed in selected individuals and in the psychic arts and crafts. But a great deal of progress is being made, as we shall see, in the new and rapidly widening fields of psychic energies and their implications to physical conditions of the human body. These new fields clearly portend that it is only a matter of time before, for example, miraculous healing will be better understood.

So before we begin a larger review of the special factors that are giving birth to the psychic renaissance, some discussion of bioenergetic implications seems fully in order. I'll also give two extraordinary examples of miraculous healing which, if they do nothing to explain how they occurred, at least illustrate something of what we might expect to understand better as discoveries continue. These healing powers have not been much acknowledged during the modernist scientific epoch, although there is a long history of them which can hardly be denied by fact gatherers. They represent the potentials of our human biopsychic organisms to transcend biological laws as we *presently* understand them, and thence to do things we do not understand at all.

OUR BRAINS

We have been taught (during the last two hundred years) to assume that all our biological and mental processes emanate from our physical brains, and that the brain is the central control center of all our life processes and activities.

Is this assumption correct? If it is, then we have a problem of some magnitude. So far in this book it has been established that the future can be perceived and, in some cases, acted upon. But if we stick to the physical-brain assumption, then the implication is that our physical brains somehow, of and in themselves, can perceive the invisible future.

Personally, I have no trouble with this assumption *per se* because it is quite possible that matter *is* in touch with invisible stuff. But it is possible to observe, as we have done in the preceding chapters, that *something* about us is psychic, and that the vast majority of brain researchers are having a terrible time in attributing anything of the kind to the brain as they currently conceive it to be. After all, so far as it can be seen, the brain is composed of physical matter — chemicals, tissue, atoms, electricity, fluids, etc., and "processes" (such as electrical and hormonal) that somehow, on their own, manage to result in what we call, somewhat redundantly, our life processes.

If the above materialist assumption is to hold true, then somehow the physical materials of our brains can perceive the immaterial and invisible future.

But: It is also generally believed that matter in and of itself can perceive nothing at all, much less the invisible future. All this leads into complexities that strongly challenge and fatigue the current state of our intellects — anyone's intellect, including those of brain researchers. However, rather than trying to address that incredibly deep issue, all we want to do for the purposes of this book is observe that *something* about us *is* psychic. We want to increase our psychic literacy and, as a result, somehow learn to work with our psychic elements, even *before* brain researchers arrive at a full and total understanding of how the brain works.

In pursuing psychic literacy, we are obliged to observe that, apparently, there exist psychic-type powers that can change physiological and biological processes, more or less instantaneously, without bothering with the slower, long-term changes familiar to physiologists. Anything physiological *must* somehow involve brain mechanisms. But if material-biological changes occur relatively instantaneously, and those changes are outside the laws of biology as we understand them, then the is brain "causing" the change, or is the brain "responding" to the change? If is it the latter, then the presence of factors *external to the brain* must be admitted.

Thank goodness we don't have to resolve this issue in this book, either. I'm not up to it, anyway. But we *can* observe instances in which extra-brain "agencies" seem implicit.

Since these agents are invisible, they fall into the psychic arenas we have been discussing. And we need a glimpse of them to round out our accumulating reservoir of psychic background information and give us further reason for taking a long-term interest in psychic matters.

As you read through what follows, you might like to bear in mind that two of the world's leading brain experts, after years of studying the issues involved, were much of the opinion that at least one thing is not located in the brain — the mind.

Wilder Penfield, the famous neurosurgeon and brain researcher, opined, after exhaustive research, that the mind was not lodged in the brain. The mind had no specific, centered location within the body. The mind appeared to be everywhere — in the muscles, tissues, cells, bones, organs.

Sir John Eccles, perhaps the most distinguished and foremost expert on the brain and nervous system, felt that Self and brain are not synonymous, but that their association is only temporary and only the result of a coincidental encounter — which is another way of saying that the control center is not in or of the brain — which in turn is one way of saying that we must possess a psychic control center which, in the terms of *its* functioning, is superior to our brains.

And now, here come the two stories that will knock your socks off. Hey, you skeptics. Don't even *think* about debunking these two cases. Their documentation is so voluminous it would choke a *Tyrannosaurus rex*, and it is so unimpeachable that only absolute and obvious idiots could seek to say the phenomena involved were faked or can be explained in some other "normal" way. *Anything* that explains these two cases is *not* going to be normal any way you look at it.

THE JOHN TRAYNOR EVENT

In 1882, in Ireland, there was born one John Traynor. From all accounts, he grew up to be an average Irishman (if the Irish can be accused of any such thing as average-ness) of lower, middle-class status. He had already lived his mundane life as a worker-laborer by the time the Great War (World War I) broke out. He was mobilized into the Royal Naval Reserve. A short time later at the battle of Antwerp he was shot in the head.

He lay in a coma for over five weeks. But when the surgeons finally found time in their over-crowded hospital, and since Traynor was still alive, they operated on his skull and pulled pieces of bone out of his badly damaged brain. Thereafter, he regained consciousness, recovered completely, and was posted to Egypt. There he was shot again. When he recovered from this wound, he volunteered for the landings at Gallipoli, which turned out to be one of the most dreadful and useless confrontations in modern military history.

At Gallipoli, in April 1915, during a bayonet charge, Traynor was again shot in the head, and two bullets hit his chest. One passed through, but the other lodged under his right collarbone, completely severing the brachial plexus. With these important nerves to his shoulder and upper arm severed, his right arm was now to be totally paralyzed forever. Four successive operations to sew the nerves back together failed. The surgeons finally recommended that his arm be amputated since it would be totally useless. John Traynor, bless his Irish heart, refused.

Shortly after he began to have epileptic seizures. Both legs were partially paralyzed, and he could no longer walk. The epilepsy grew worse, and he became doubly incontinent. He was confined to bed or a wheelchair. In April 1920 his skull was trepanned (removal of part of the skull), and a silver plate was inserted into the hole to protect his brain. In other words, John Traynor was in a physical condition of the worst kind. Back in Ireland, he became a total burden to his poor wife who eventually could not manage, and arrangements were made in July 1923 to house him in the Mossley Hill Home for Incurables where his pension from the Ministry of Pensions would support him for what was assumed to be the rest of his short life.

Before he could be so permanently disposed of, however, John Traynor had heard about pilgrimages to Lourdes, where the Virgin had appeared to the young girl, Bernadette Soubirous, and which had thereafter become the most famous healing shrine in the world. Traynor spent his last gold sovereign as a down payment, even though the priests in charge of the pilgrimage told him he would probably die on the way, and this would be a serious inconvenience to them.

Undaunted by the priests' reluctance, Traynor persuaded his wife to pawn anything they had left and raised the balance of the cost of the pilgrimage fee of twelve pounds. Once embarked on the journey, his condition worsened, and he had several epileptic seizures. Later, the priests in charge admitted that had the seizures occurred when the train was near a hospital, they would have dumped Traynor into one, where, of course, he would eventually have died.

Arriving at Lourdes, he was placed in the Asile Hospital where he promptly suffered a devastating *grand mal* seizure and began bleeding from his mouth, nose, and anus. This caused him to be examined by three doctors. They found: "Epilepsy: The fits during the journey have been recorded. Paralysis: involving the median, musculo-spinal, and ulnar nerves with typical *main en griffe* deformity and wasting of all the muscles of the right upper limb, wasting of the right pectoral and auxiliary muscles. Skull and brain: a trephine hole 2 cm diameter in the right parietal area, pulsation of the brain palpable and the area is covered by a metal plate. There is loss of sensation and voluntary movement in the lower limbs. There is constant incontinence of urine and feces." Signed: Drs. Azurdia, Finn and, Marley.

Translated, this diagnosis means that Traynor was a complete wreck, as close to a defecating, urinating vegetable anyone might become. He could not walk, and his nerve and muscular structures were clearly beyond any hope of repair.

On July 26, 1923, Traynor was wheeled to the baths in the Grotto of Lourdes. The brancardiers (volunteer stretcher-bearers) who help the invalids in and out of the baths, held him down when he began to thrash around in the water. He had tried to get to his feet, but the brancardiers mistook this as the beginning of an epileptic fit and held him down.

After the bath, he was taken to the procession of the Blessed Sacrament, and the Archbishop of Rheims passed in front of him carrying the monstrance. At this point, for the first time since his arm nerves had been completely severed at Gallipoli eight years before, Traynor realized he could move his right arm.

He did so, in fact so vigorously that he snapped the bindings that kept his formerly useless arm from flopping around. The brancardiers thought he was becoming hysterical. They injected a sedative into him. Back at the hospital, Traynor found he could walk a few steps. whereupon he was administered another injection which knocked him out for the night.

The next morning, before the watchful brancardiers knew what was happening, he arose and ran out of the hospital in his gown to the Grotto where he knelt praying for twenty minutes. This was a distance of several hundred yards over a gravel path. He then walked slowly back to his ward, where he washed and dressed himself to the complete astonishment of everyone involved.

Crowds began gathering at the hospital once word of his recovery began to circulate. The doctors — many of them now — examined him again. His right arm was usable, his legs performed a normal gait. The epileptic fits had ceased, and the opening in his skull was considerably smaller. It was only when he was interviewed on the train back through France by the Archbishop of Liverpool that he and everyone else began more fully to realize the awesome extent of his recovery.

News of the recovery had proceeded ahead of him to Liverpool, and enormous crowds had gathered at the station, so large that the train bearing him had to halt outside the station. Traynor dismounted and only reached his poor home with the help of policemen. The crowds were calmed by the Archbishop, and the whole affair went into printed history when the Liverpool *Post* described its "extraordinary scenes."

John Traynor's cure at Lourdes is perhaps one of its most famous — due to the fact of Traynor's long-existing Army medical records and the fact that his abysmal condition had been confirmed upon his arrival at Lourdes. Before the "bath," his arm's nerves were still in their severed condition; after the bath they had grown back together again. In a few weeks, the hole in his skull closed completely with new bone and was identifiable only by a small depression. Four years later, the Medical Bureau at Lourdes (which carefully and *slowly* judges upon the miraculous aspects of cures) declared that Traynor's total cure could not have resulted from natural processes. A copy of the Bureau's report was forwarded to the Archbishop of Liverpool, who seems to have lost it, and the cure was never officially proclaimed as...yes, a *miracle*.

And what of John Traynor? When he advised the Ministry of Pensions he was not any longer entitled to receive his pension, he was informed there was no machinery to discontinue a pension to one who had been granted it on the grounds that his wounds were incurable. Thereafter, he used his pension money to go to Lourdes every year, where he volunteered as a brancardier. In Liverpool, he went into the moving and hauling business, and he was often seen heaving two-hundred-pound sacks of coal. He lived to be sixty years of age, and when he did die, it was not from his earlier wounds or from epilepsy, which had never returned. He died in 1943 of a strangulated hernia, presumably acquired from heaving sacks of coal.[1]

Now, let's do all ourselves a favor here and not confuse the basic issues of the Traynor Event with theological issues involving the Virgin Mary or Catholicism. The basic issue is this: John Traynor was born, as far as anyone can tell, a completely normal male. He suffered catastrophic physical and neurological damage during the War which left him a grim, permanent invalid of the worst kind, and all the doctors and priests who saw him held no hope. On July 26, 1923, *in the space of a few minutes*, he was restored to *complete health*.

It hardly does any good to say this was "impossible," for extensive records exist showing that the Traynor Event did occur. We may think, if we wish, the impossible occurred because the Blessed Virgin intervened. Personally, I have no problem at all with this. If the Virgin *can* intervene, by all means, let the Venerable Holy Mother do so. But let us take some interest in what had to happen in Traynor's body for the Event to take place.

The Traynor Event clearly shows that what we call the human brain-body-mind combination is capable of *complete regeneration* under certain circumstances. This is the basic issue.

And, inescapably, it is a psychic issue. Are we to assume that Traynor's brain, as his central control center, did all this? If we so assume, then we are obliged to admit that our concepts regarding the role of the brain remain somewhat at odds with all this, and that the theories we are presently using to found our present assumptions are probably *very* "incomplete," as they say. But even if we accept the brain-central-control hypothesis, then, in Traynor's case, we are confronted with the probability that the brain, as a biological *mechanism*, can, at times, function in a way that is greater than the sum of its parts. Since this is somewhat like asking a standard automobile to rebuild its damaged fender on its own, you can see the scope of the issues involved.

---

[1] John Traynor's tale is narrated, among other sources, in Lourdes, a Modern Pilgrimage, by Patrick Marnham, Image Books, Garden City, New York, 1982.

It is really more sensible and *much easier* to entertain a psychic hypothesis, to wit, that we possess a psychic center which is greater than the sum of the parts of our mechanistic brains and bodies — a psychic center that can *completely* restore brain-mind-body conditions to complete health in a *few moments of time.*

HOW TO DEBUNK CURES AT LOURDES

Because instantaneous cures at Lourdes "fly in the face of all we know scientifically," as it is said, they have long been subjected to microscopic investigation by various anti-psychic cliques. It is one thing to explain away transient psychic events like those which have been reviewed in the first eight chapters of this book. But it is something else again to explain away a person who has been "miraculously" cured, since that person remains healthy and is thereafter a walking embarrassment to "all we know scientifically." Therefore, it is not an easy task to explain these cures away. But many try to do so — and, as I see it, it is part of our psychic literacy project to see something of how they go about it.

Anti-psychic rationalizing has found one "dependable" way to explain what happens in these cases: show the original diagnosis to be wrong, that the afflicted were not suffering from what doctors said they were.

Ever since the Grotto at Lourdes opened for business, as it were, in 1858, several thousand cures have been claimed. About three million pilgrims visit the shrine annually, including approximately twenty thousand who are sickly. The shrine contains a large room which is filled with cast off crutches and wheelchairs. However, the Catholic hierarchy doesn't accept all the cures as miraculous. For example, of the ninety-eight claimed cures between 1925 through 1950, the hierarchy accepted only about ten percent of them as miraculous.

In 1957, one D.J. West, M.B., CH.B., C.P.M., published in a book entitled *Eleven Lourdes Miracles*, a "medical review" of the eleven miraculous cures between 1937 and 1950. Via the book's 124 pages, West exposes his readers to exhaustive clinical details of the maladies of those cured and focuses on the competency of their doctors' diagnoses. He then finds himself able to conclude that in all cases the diagnoses were bungled or wrong — which means, essentially, that the doctors involved were incompetent.

Now, West's *own* book reveals, by count, that altogether several dozens of doctors had worked on these cases, and many more medical technicians. But the sum of West's conclusions is that in no instance was a correct diagnosis ever achieved. Having reached this plateau of observation, West then goes on to speculate that in some instances the patients "may have been" suffering more from miscalculated medical remedies more than any given illness, and that if these remedies were abandoned, the patients might have experienced "a natural" alleviation of their grueling symptoms. And he assumes that such explanation accounts for some of the cures at Lourdes, since by going there they did, indeed, abandon their dependence on the former remedies.

In such a way, then, the doctors' diagnoses are set aside: Hodgkin's disease, liver abscesses and fistulas, Addison's disease, tuberculosis peritonitis, adhesions from gastrectomy, rheumatic spondylitis with compression of nerve roots, nephritis, vaginal cancer, tubercular abscess of the neck, gastric ulcer, pulmonary tuberculosis, Encephalitis lethargica, persistent intestinal hemorrhages, and so forth.

Since these diagnoses were not, upon his inspection, supportable by the records available, the afflicted were not suffering from them — and thus the cures of them could not be upheld as cures. He then glides to his conclusion: that since it was not truly known what the afflicted were suffering from, the miraculous nature of their claimed cures was in complete doubt.

In so gliding, however, West manages to skip past the one observable fact that *is* completely pertinent. The afflicted *were* suffering from *something*, and their suffering was ghastly. And, in each of the eleven cases, the "something" had caused protracted sufferings, lasting, in two cases, nearly ten years. In fact, the sum of all the years of suffering of the eleven cases amounted to seventy-five years between them — an average of 6.8 years of suffering each. None of the cases responded to medical treatments, however imaginative they might be. And, in some instances, although the doctors continued to try to treat the afflicted, it was generally admitted professionally that the diseases had reached a point of no return.

However, each of the afflicted dragged their suffering bodies and minds to Lourdes. There, as far as I can count in West's own pages, in *a sum of thirty minutes between them all*, all were cured — permanently. West's little book completely avoids any discussion of this fact, leaving the final impression that the cures "might" have taken place naturally, even if the afflicted had not dragged themselves into the waters at Lourdes. Since this "explanation" is easily recognized within the prevailing patterns of Western reasoning, it makes the sense that, admittedly, is otherwise lacking. Hence it is accepted, and the cures at Lourdes are, so to speak, "de-miracle-ized."

It is worth noting, for the record, that J.D. West was an affiliate of The Psychical Research Society in London and published his little book under the auspices of The Parapsychology Foundation in New York, both establishments failing to notice the obvious — that traumatic afflictions existing over long periods of time were vanquished in thirty minutes at Lourdes. I have tried without success to fathom how an *assumption* that doctors *may* have erred in diagnoses has much to contribute to how things actually turned out at Lourdes.

Now, it might appear that I'm trying to pump up Lourdes. Frankly, I am, but not altogether. I am much of the opinion that when medical remedies are of no avail, one has a human right to go for the Lourdes-type of approach, or any other method or place that might accomplish what the medical remedies are failing in doing. But there is more to all this than just Lourdes, for the history of "miraculous" cures by invisible means is very long and predates the emergence of the Holy Mother and the Holy Family by many centuries.

The earliest known tradition of healing is that of shamanism, of which there have been various models. But, in general, the job of the shaman is to enter psychically into the invisible energies and forces "causing" affliction, to intervene and deal with them on their own terms, correcting the invisible factors, the sum of which is manifesting as illness. In fact, modern psychological techniques roughly (very roughly) approximate shamanic processes in that they attempt to enter into and correct invisible stuff "causing" various conditions. If, then, invisible stuff can be entered into by our inexpert psychological methodologies, the existence of the possibility to do so must be admitted, after which the questions revolve around the exact nature of the invisibles. Shamanism, of course, deals with invisible "universes" still quite alien to our prevailing thinking, but once the existence of invisibles is admitted, then the situation becomes one of exploration, some of which we'll take up in Part Two.

At any rate, cures at Lourdes are attributed by Catholics to the "intervention" of the Holy Mother, and it cannot be the purpose of this present book to enter into the theological issues involved. Therefore, in keeping with further expanding our psychic literacy, it would be of interest to learn of a "miraculous" cure which does not associate itself with the intervention of the Virgin. Some time ago, I began a search for a suitable example of this kind — suitable from the viewpoint that medical records concerning it were professionally available and beyond challenge. I found one — in spades, as they say.

THE "FISH-SKIN" EVENT

On May 25, 1950, a sixteen-year-old boy named John was admitted to the Queen Victoria Hospital in East Grinstead, England, where he was to undergo plastic surgery by the renowned surgeon, Sir Archibald McIndoe, and his team. The anesthetist for the operation was Dr. Albert A. Mason, who, by chance, was not part of Sir Archibald's usual team, and, by chance, was also a skilled hypnotist.

Mason assisted many doctors in their operating arenas by administering anesthetics to their patients during the course of the surgery. Normally, one would think that the anesthetist would know precisely what was wrong with the patient in advance of the operation. But in hospitals things frequently do not go along in proper order. Mason did not know what was wrong with young John who, when delivered for surgery, appeared to be covered with wild profusions of warts. Mason assumed that since Sir Archibald was famous for plastic surgery, he was going to use skin grafts to get rid of, as he later wrote, the large warty excrescences that covered the patient's legs and arms and most of his body.

John's hands were horrible, enclosed with a rigid horny casing that had cracked and become chronically infected. He had been born with this "disease" and, naturally, was treated at school like an outcast because of his obviously ugly appearance and the appalling smell issuing from the many infections.

Dr. McIndoe was going to attempt skin grafts on the palms of John's hands. They scraped the hard coating from the boy's palms and replaced it with some patches of unblemished skin from his chest. A month later it was seen that the operations had not succeeded. The newly-grafted skin had thickened and turned black. A second attempt proved no more successful.

At this point, Dr. Mason, who continued to think the boy was suffering from extensive warts, suggested to Dr. McIndoe that perhaps hypnosis could help. Mason, himself, by using hypnosis had successfully removed warts from other patients. At this point Mason believed warts were the issue. If hypnosis could remove one wart, perhaps it could also remove the thousands covering John's body.

Dr. McIndoe, already annoyed that the skin grafts were not successful, was not responsive to this idea. Somehow, Mason did not yet understand that it was not warts that were the issue, and McIndoe did not understand that Mason did not understand the true nature of "fish-skin" disease. The two had not exchanged their respective diagnoses. In their conversations, Dr. Mason had never mentioned "warts," and Sir Archibald had never mentioned the true diagnosis of John's condition. This failure in communication set the stage for one of the most astonishing miracles ever.

Apparently still thinking that Mason *did* understand John was suffering from a genetic defect of his body's skin, Sir Archibald sourly suggested that Mason himself undertake this impossible approach of a cure through hypnosis.

Mason duly hypnotized John, and while John was in the hypnotic trance told him that the "warts" on his left arm were "going to fall off" and not come back. About five days later, the horny skin softened and began to fall off revealing what now appeared to be normal skin. In another five days, John's left arm was completely clear from wrist to shoulder.

Rather pleased with his success, Mason took John to Dr. McIndoe, bragging that hypnosis did well with warts. McIndoe was shocked — "Jesus Christ," said he, "do you know what you've done?" He brusquely informed Mason that they were not dealing with warts but with a rare congenital condition known as ichthyosiform erythroderma of Brocq and suggested that the hypnotist go to the medical library and look it up.

It was now Mason's turn to be shocked. Ichthyosiform erythroderma is a congenital condition, meaning it is also structural and organic, in which the skin has no oil-forming glands that would enable its outer layers to flake off and renew themselves. The skin would just go on building up until a hard, black armor-plating would accumulate. Mason found that one of England's leading hypnotists, Dr. Stephen Black, had already concluded that this appalling and disfiguring condition had been considered incurable since 1904 and would remain with the patient throughout what was to be an obviously short life.

Dr. Mason, somewhat unnerved, since he had caused not a normal hypnotic cure but a miracle, now became somewhat famous for having done so. McIndoe presented the strange cure at a meeting of the Royal Society of Medicine, at which several doctors who attended claimed themselves to be "profoundly impressed" (an understatement if I've ever heard one). One doctor, "surprised" that a structural, organic congenital condition should respond to any kind of treatment at all, much less that of hypnosis, felt that a total revision of the current concepts of the relation between mind and body was called for. A dermatologist was astounded and noted that the cure was unprecedented and inexplicable. The case thereafter gained in celebrity as more and more specialists became apprised of what had happened.

Thereafter, the story becomes considerably more complicated. Encouraged by the initial success with John, Mason continued hypnotic treatments involving other parts of John's body. The legs, which had been completely covered by the black armor, improved by some 50 percent along with 95 percent of the arms and a complete clearing of the palms — although the fingers were "not greatly improved."

A year later, John's mental state, as might have been expected, "had changed dramatically." He had developed into a "normal happy boy" and gotten a job as an electrician's assistant. The cure was not total, but it seemed to be permanent as far as it went since the cured areas stayed cured.

When Mason asked John if he would care to try to clear up what remained of the black patches, the boy "agreed to try." But Mason found, to his bewilderment, that he could no longer hypnotize him. In fact, John seemed somewhat frightened by the idea of being hypnotized. Mason decided to leave the situation as it was.

He went on to undertake hypnotic cures with eight other cases of congenital ichthyosis, reporting in the *British Medical Journal* in 1961 that every one of them had been a complete failure. However, an Oxford general practitioner, Dr. C.A.S. Wink, published an account of his own successful hypnotic treatment of two similar cases — two sisters aged seven and five. Like Mason, he had worked on one part of the body a time, but although a great deal of the skin had cleared up, he also had failed to bring about a total clearing of the entire body.

The questions began to pile up as mysteries. As the psychic investigator, Guy Lyon Playfair, points out,[2] why should a hypnotist succeed with one patient and not with eight others, and why should he be unable to hypnotize his star patient at a later time? Why should Wink succeed with *two* patients? Why should various parts of the body respond and not others? And, finally, why should the body respond at all when the condition is congenitally structural in that the affected skin suffers from an *absence* of certain dermal tissues? When one considers this last question, only the wildest conjecture is possible — as long as the situation is limited only to physiological phenomena and the image-beliefs that govern the "normal" medical view of them.

Mason's own original conclusion was that a "psychological" factor lay behind the cause of ichthyosis or else it was possible to influence a congenital organic condition by psychological means or, of course, a combination of both. In either event, though, just what psychological factors may be involved clearly lay beyond any known explanation or, in fact, any accepted logic and reasoning. The explanation, whatever it is, clearly is a psychic one.

Thirty years later, when Mason was living in California and had become a psychoanalyst, having given up hypnotism altogether, he wondered if, perhaps, John's skin had somehow contained "tiny remnants" of glands that had "come to life" under the stimulus of hypnotic suggestion. But, he added, the stimulus for such a profound change must, itself, be "equally profound." And, I might add, equally psychic in origin.

Now, if we consider the Fish-Skin Event very carefully, we can perhaps spot something that has escaped the notice of others. Previously, I mentioned the idea of entering into and correcting invisible energies and forces which, as psychic *factors*, "cause" given situations. Clearly, if one is to foresee the future, one must, at some level of perception, enter into the invisible energies and forces "causing" that future. It is but a short step from entering those kinds of invisible energies and forces to entering those that are "causing" physical conditions. In fact, something like this has always been the hypothesis underlying shamanic healing and other forms of miraculous cures.

---

2 Playfair, Guy Lyon, If This Be Magic, Jonathan Cape, London, 1985.

With regard to the Fish-Skin Event, the hypnotist, Mason, at first thought John's condition was a matter of warts. In his experience, he knew warts could be gotten rid of by hypnotic suggestion. John, only sixteen, doubtless did not completely understand the genetic nature of his skin's defect, and probably thought that Mason was just another doctor going to cure his warts. So, the two got together and, in the hypnotic state, entered into the invisibles. Thus, apparently, all the *necessary* psychic factors were in place, and the "cure" came off.

The most interesting point is what was *not* involved. Neither Mason nor John thought that removing warts was impossible. However, *after* Mason and John became aware that curing a genetic effect was "impossible," John could no longer be induced into a hypnotic trance, and Mason found out that he could not cure others he tried to work with, i.e., they now could not "enter" the invisibles, since an intellectual belief had now blocked the "entrance."

Thus, we approach the touchy area of *belief* and *disbelief* (both of which, I'll not hesitate to point out, are intellectual factors only). All the people cured at Lourdes believed they would be cured there, or at least that a cure was not impossible. In Mason's case, he *knew* he had cured warts by hypnosis before and that he probably could so again. Young John did not know that he "could not" be cured. The actual physical conditions in these cures apparently are irrelevant to the invisible psychic process that must be involved. But belief and/or disbelief appears to be relevant. When Mason's and John's intellects began incorporating "impossible" belief-elements, the particular mix of all the psychic factors involved was altered. And further cures could not proceed.

A SPECTRUM OF PSYCHIC POTENTIALS

Now, getting back to our brain-not-brain problem, are we to assume that John's brain had much, or, indeed, anything to do with altering genetic materials? It is true that no one really understands the actual mechanisms that lead to any kind of healing. And it is not impossible that these mechanisms one day will be found somewhere in the brain. But genetic change? Does the brain contain "codes" that can change genetic materials of the body within which and of which it is an integral part? You can cling to the brain hypothesis if you want, but, personally, I think this is pushing it a little. It is far easier to agree with the eminent researchers Penfield and Eccles and hypothesize that there exists a greater "organ" possessing enormous powers — which, although completely invisible to our present materialistic knowledge, certainly must exist. And it was this "organ" that John Traynor and Mason somehow activated — although, of course, quite inadvertently.

This "organ" certainly falls into the "psychic" category, since it has demonstrated (in these two cases, as well as in thousands of others) that not only can it, for example, perceive the future (transcend space/time), but it can remodel the physical materials of our bodies (transcend physical limitations).

John Traynor did a fortuitous thing by removing his poor body from the environment littered with negative images about any possible cure for him and went to Lourdes, a place where cures were *possible*. At Lourdes, he found the proper and correct psychic stimuli and linked up with them. Both Mason and the "fish-skin" boy thought that the removal of "warts" was *possible*.

Is it as simple as that? Do our intellectual images of reality "control" that reality and its possibilities? Apparently, the answer is in the affirmative. Apparently, our *real* control center (wherever it may be) can do miraculous things — provided all the psychic factors necessary are correctly lined up. Apparently, this control center is not essentially in and of the brain, but that the brain is part of it.

The Traynor Event and the Fish-Skin Event, as well documented as they are, show us that the human mind-body, if either catastrophically damaged or genetically imperfect, is, under certain circumstances, capable of regeneration via the invisible powers of our central psychic potentials.

MIRACULOUS HEALING

o We can observe that under certain conditions (which our sciences are not at all prepared to identify) remarkable psychic-type cures have been known to take place.

o We can hypothesize that in such cases certain invisible factors must be present for the cure to turn out or manifest.

o We should observe that if the "mechanics" of such cures could be discovered they would be of enormous value.

o We should observe that we have no chance of discovering such "mechanics" if our overall psychic illiteracy persists.

SUGGESTED PRACTICAL EXERCISES THAT WILL HELP IN EXPANDING PSYCHIC LITERACY

I think you might agree that suggesting practical exercises for the type of thing discussed in this chapter is somewhat daunting. But...

o   If at all possible, find someone who has experienced a "miraculous" cure of any kind. I've found many people who have not experienced dramatic things such as are described in this chapter but who have experienced smaller cures regarding such things as pimples. Many feel they have "caused" a wart to fall off. If you can locate such a person, get into discussion. Normally, such things are not discussed, because in our psychic illiteracy we believe such discussions reflect a trend in us towards irrationality. Belief in "irrationality" gums up the workings of your intellect regarding psychic stuff.

o   If you like to meditate, take up the subject of "psychic stuff being irrational" and reflect upon its sources. Try to recover those instances in which such ideas entered your intellectual mind streams. When your intellect can perceive the nature of these sources, it will erase the mind-patterns stimulated by them.

* * *

What we have been looking at so far is a *spectrum* of psychic factors — a spectrum which, indeed, is probably very wide. I do not know what all the A-to-Z elements of this spectrum are. But, at one end are those psychic factors that foresee the future and alert us as to times and events that will be either fortunate or unfortunate, and at the other end are those psychic factors that can alter damaged and genetically imperfect bodies. All this is to say that our psychic factors are all fountains of life, and some of them even may imply *eternal* life — for if genetic "fish-skin" disease can be altered by means that are essentially psychic, so perhaps can our genetic aging and death codes.

In addition to providing a minimum pool of background information necessary for dealing with the developments that will now be described in the rest of this book, I've made an attempt to illustrate why we should take interest in elevating our psychic literacy overall. But the information and issues involved are still so complex as to be unmanageable. We will not get very far with enhancing our psychic literacy unless we can instigate what amounts to a new intellectual synthesis regarding psychic stuff.

The study of psychic phenomena needs, or we need, a synthesis that cuts through confusions and illuminates basic ideas our intellects can recognize as constituting the essence of human experience — and in recognizing these ideas *begin to work with them*. At this point then, and with all this background information in mind, we are somewhat prepared to construct the rudiments of a new psychic synthesis and see how these past psychic phenomena actually correlate with new discoveries taking place. Shortly we'll be able to conclude that a psychic renaissance is coming, and, perhaps, that it has already commenced.

PART TWO

Psychic Literacy

A New Psychic Synthesis

THE FAILURE OF THE MODERN PSYCHIC SYNTHESIS

Quite early in my laboratory career in parapsychology (beginning in 1969), I began to wonder about something that had struck a few other psychic researchers but had really received no attention. This was: why, throughout the history of organized psychic research, had psychic phenomena *not* made frequent and robust appearances in laboratory settings, when, on the other hand, they did so in the normal course of life?

One of the more embarrassing factors in laboratory research was, as it was often remarked, that psychic phenomena remained "elusive" in *all* the various parapsychological laboratory research setups. While it was true that researchers could, and often did, accumulate statistical evidence for the existence of ESP, etc., still, robust appearances were so rare as to be almost nonexistent. And, when they did appear, it was not very long before they vanished altogether.

An explanation for this got going — robust psychic manifestations did not "like" laboratory settings. This meant there was something wrong with the various laboratory set-ups, and researchers were always on the lookout for ways and means to make their laboratories "more conducive" to the appearance of robust psychic stuff.

Since I had openly talked a great deal about this matter, it eventually came about that I was charged with trying to solve the mystery in some way.

Now, parapsychological laboratories are rather cheerless places. They tend to be filled with challenging equipment (often just stacked around and with no apparent purpose), worn couches, examples of bad art (if any), and many are even windowless. Everyone except the most devoted are glad to get out of them as quickly as possible. Psychologically speaking, they tend also to be filled with grim, but devoted, researchers whose accumulated disappointment in not making big breakthroughs is quite tangible — even if they do manage to smile at subjects.

Furthermore, there is a distinctive caste system that divides researchers and their subjects. Most of the latter soon get the impression they are just seen as rats being put through some psychic paces designed and devised by the researchers. In large part, this is the truth. As soon as a given subject fails in producing what the researchers expect of them, even the enforced smiles vanish.

Many (but not all) researchers have little or no interest in what their subjects have to say about psychic things, or in how the subjects feel they can produce psychic phenomena. When I asked the noted parapsychologist Dr. Gertrude Schmeidler about this, she responded that subjects used to be asked to comment on how they felt they were able to produce certain psychic phenomena. But since they all said something different, no one could make any sense of the accumulating commentaries and stopped trying to do so.

We are talking about fifty years of combined parapsychological research here, during which period no significant breakthrough had ever been made and in which large-scale psychic demonstrations remained "elusive." To my way of thinking, then, it was not the purpose of psychic stuff to appear in laboratories. I based this conclusion much on the idea that if ESP testing did *stimulate* purposeful functioning, then psychic proficiencies probably *would* manifest. But not only did psychic proficiencies fail to appear in laboratories, they tended to get even more dysfunctional over time — being driven into oblivion, or into what parapsychologists euphemistically came to call "psi missing."

One of my own "claims to fame" consisted of the fact that I survived the cloying routines and environments in the parapsychological laboratory and, over time, my own psychic proficiencies tended to get better — a factor that did not go unnoticed.

Thus, in grasping for a place to start in trying to bring illumination into this matter, I started with myself. Why should I survive the rigors of the parapsychological system when other subjects could not and did not? My own estimate of my psychic proficiencies was that they were rather average and not spectacular in the first place, since the archives easily showed that others had had spectacular proficiencies far outstripping my own.

But, once dragged into a laboratory, their proficiencies soon failed nonetheless — a factor that had something to do with parapsychologists developing a lack of interest in, and aversions to, testing "gifted" subjects and acknowledged psychic superstars. Indeed, in retrospect, had I at the outset been an acknowledged superstar, there is little doubt that the parapsychological scene would have had little more than passing, and quite detached, interest in me. Fortunately, when I began laboratory experimentation I was a psychic nobody, an ordinary mortal with no pronounced psychic proficiencies.

But these observations merely compounded the inexplicabilities at issue.

When you are not getting anywhere with something, you should recheck your basic premises. Which is to say, recheck the synthesis of the fundamental ideas underlying your efforts — a "synthesis" being the composition or combination of parts or elements which form a whole. Indeed, it is easy enough to see that if, in a synthesis, even one idea is wrong, then the whole will be lopsided or counterproductive in some way. In a sense, then, because the average parapsychological laboratory was counterproductive to producing psychic phenomena (something parapsychologists themselves admitted), one of the basic premises underlying the whole of the parapsychological endeavor *must* have been wrong.

Considering their problem here, one might have thought that parapsychologists would have grasped this themselves. But no. As a whole, people don't like the idea that their fundamental premises, their basic assumptions, might be in error. And parapsychologists are not excluded from this reluctance.

At any rate, what, then, was the difference between my basic assumptions and those upon which parapsychology was founded? The basic assumption in psychic research has always been that psychic aptitudes were *powers of the mind* — which is to say, mental activities. Although it took me two years to discover it, I actually disagreed with that basic premise. To me, psychic aptitudes were powers *not* of the mind, but powers in themselves, *and* powers that at times actually transcended "mind," or cut across it, or, even, were capable of operating when what we call "mind" was asleep or unconscious — or, even, when clinically dead.

Indeed, since my childhood I had not for one moment believed psychic capabilities were functions or products of the mind. I was more likely to attribute them to the soul or spirit which, in my estimation of things, are both greater than mind or intellect — and can, therefore, occasionally supersede mind-intellect-brain when, in their wisdom, it is necessary to do so. Indeed, I felt quite confident in this discovered assumption in that a great deal is now known about the mind-brain thing, and psychic capabilities have not really shown up in all that is now known about it.

This is, of course, a matter of personal philosophy. But it enabled me continuously to function in dreary laboratory settings. I was *never* testing my mind. I was testing some other agency in which psychic capabilities were natural endowments.

Now, all parapsychological laboratories are set up to test powers of the mind and nothing else. In fact, the normal instruction to subjects is to focus "in your mind" upon psychic capabilities, and to use "mental processes" to produce psychic results. If, then, psychic potentials are not part and parcel of "The Mind," it is unlikely they will manifest within the guidelines of this basic, and quite erroneous, uninspected assumption.

WHAT ARE PSYCHIC POTENTIALS REALLY PART OF?

But if psychic capabilities are *not* fundamental activities of the mind. what, then, are they fundamental to?

As has been shown, they are — as a priority — fundamental to the survival of the organism. We might assume that mind-intellect also has this survival as basic to *its* functioning. But, by observation, the mind often gets itself in a situation which not only disregards survival, but often becomes a *factor* which deliberately hastens non-survival or destruction. Simply put, mind-intellect breaks down upon occasion, aborts its own survival "instincts," and ends up between a rock and a hard place.

All these things considered then, the psychic synthesis that has governed overviews in parapsychological research between c. 1920 and the present were *fated* to fail. Psychic capabilities "belong" to something other than the mind — at least in the way the mind is currently being understood.

A new psychic synthesis thus must be mounted upon discoveries having to do with locating the actual agents that psychic potentials "belong" to. If these might be discovered, then we will be looking not only at a new psychic synthesis but a psychic renaissance.

The second half of this book will now serve to expand our understanding of the actual nature of these psychic potentials and where we can expect to find them in reality and in our experience.

By the end of this book, you will hopefully have a general idea of what this new psychic science is destined to look like.

A NEW PSYCHIC SYNTHESIS

- We can observe that the psychic synthesis paradigm prominent between 1920 and 1985 has failed. This paradigm, including its expectations, fully anticipated locating psychic potentials in the mind as mental activities that could consciously be controlled by the self-same mind.

- We can observe that in pursuing this paradigm, parapsychologists did not look for any other "sources" of psychic capabilities. Indeed, since brain researchers have not found any brain-mind elements that are identifiable as psychic, they felt they were on good grounds for rejecting the psychic hypothesis as a whole.

- We should observe, then, that a new psychic synthesis is called for on the grounds that psychic stuff continues to occur widely, and that parapsychology has failed in demonstrating them to be products of the mind hypothesis.

SUGGESTED PRACTICAL EXERCISES THAT WILL HELP IN EXPANDING PSYCHIC LITERACY

- If the occasion permits, take some time to ask people if they feel psychic capabilities are products of their minds or of something else. Keep a list of their responses. I think you will be surprised by some answers. If they opine psychic capabilities are part of their minds, ask them how they know this to be true. Don't argue the point or try to convince them otherwise. Just nod and keep your own counsel.

XI

The Meaningful Difference Between Psychic Energies and Psychic Forces

As you will have noticed throughout the first part of this book I've depended a great deal on the phrase "invisible energies and forces." The "and" in this phrase is there for a purpose, implying that it is possible (and advisable) to distinguish between an energy and a force.

The Ancients, in their wisdom, had no trouble at all in distinguishing between an energy and a force, either in the material or invisible realms.

Simply put: *energies* nourished life, while *forces* could kill, and often did. They understood, and unquestionably so, that when life-nourishing energies got out of balance they turned into deadly forces. To them, Life was energy (a multitude of energies) of which biological organisms were but its expressions in varying forms. The Ancients also assumed (and correctly so) that everything in the cosmos was Life, even the atoms of matter. It was clear to them, however, that the energies of Life could and did get out of balance rather often.

The knowledge that there were both visible and invisible forms of Life was unquestioned. What *was* argued were the degrees of influence the invisibles had over the visible. But that the invisibles *did* influence everything in major ways was unquestioned.

This knowledge was actually perpetuated in social streams up to and through the European Renaissance, after which these same life streams began increasingly to lose contact with it. For reasons that are hard to imagine, modern science seems to have lost contact with it altogether.

One of the results is that we now use "energy" and "force" as synonyms, and we are almost completely incapable of comprehending that there *are* very great differences between them. Yet the perceivable differences are again beginning to be recovered, and again via ecology by necessity. Ecologists now well understand that the energies that nourish life *must* be maintained in proper balances, and that the introduction of imbalances — i.e., forces — must be very carefully guarded against.

Exactly the same is true regarding the invisible, psychic realms. Imbalances introduced into the invisible energies turn them into forces, often devastating ones.

For the benefit of our intellects, I want to work through the actual definitions of these two terms. But first, let's build some visualizations of them. For example, recall the avalanches described during my childhood, whose advents were perceived as a group function *before* the avalanches took place. Snow, of course, represents an energy. It melts into water. All living things need water. But when snow or water become out of balance, they both turn into destructive forces.

Get the idea of an ocean in its basin. It nourishes the life in it, providing not only the environment for that life but an electro-chemical basis for their nutrients as well. There is a certain amount of wear and tear, of course, but overall, as long as the ocean is in balance everything benefits, and often even the normal wear and tear serves constructive purposes. However, if something like a severe riptide develops in the ocean, it sucks everything into it, and the destruction can be enormous — as many people have found out.

THE PSYCHIC OCEAN

In traditional occult terminology, the psychic realms have often been described as altogether comprising a "Psychic Ocean." The analogy remains a good one. That this "Ocean" is somewhat invisible to our five physical senses and to our intellects does not make it any less the ocean that it is. In this psychic ocean there is normal wear and tear, but it also "develops" forces and force-patterns that, if large enough, "drive" toward destruction everything that gets caught up in them.

In this way, then, we can conceive that the psychic ocean, as the composite of invisible energies in balance, nourishes the psychic components of Life. These same energies out of balance, turning into forces, produce destruction.

We can thus visualize the psychic ocean as the psychic *environment* in which we live, and which nourishes the invisible aspects of our lives. We can further visualize that *each of us constitutes a psychic life-entity both in our own right and as a part of the greater psychic environment.*

Any given psychic-life entity in this environment can, if it gains enough power and becomes out of balance in the greater whole, cause destructive riptides in it.

Further, we can visualize the psychic environment as one that naturally will have, or will develop, psychic "storm" systems in it. That these psychic storms *do* exist has, surprisingly and only very recently, now been demonstrated scientifically — as we shall see ahead.

INTELLECTUAL DEFINITIONS OF "ENERGY" AND "FORCE"

All of the traditional psychic arts and crafts have focused on trying, first, to perceive the invisible environment and, second, forecast fair and foul "weather" in it. This fact implies the absolute necessity of being able to perceive the differences between energies and forces. Otherwise, the invisibles will somewhat resemble an Irish stew in which the ingredients are indistinguishable from one another. If an energy is mistaken for a force, or vice versa, the psychic arts and crafts are rendered useless. Likewise, *all* the spontaneous psychic experiences described earlier herein deal with energies out of balance (forces) and, in some cases, restoration to balance.

In whatever intellectualized dress these disciplines have been forced into by intellectual contrivances, still, at base, they all deal with invisible energies and forces. Further, we are obliged to observe that whatever the intellectualized interpretations may be, it is quite unlikely that the essential nature of the invisibles differs *just because of those interpretations.*

For example, the basic elements of water do not differ just because one language calls them "water," another "aqua," and yet another "Wasser." Neither, then, do the basic elements of the invisibles differ just because the Kahunas refer to them via the language of a certain intellectualized mindset, and the Kabbalists via another, the astrologers another, and modern psychologists yet another. In fact, the basic elements of the invisibles do not differ even though anti-psychic cliques refer to them as "bosh" and "cow pancakes." The invisibles still are the invisibles, and they exist in two states — balance and imbalance.

In other words, the invisibles are *there.* They are basically themselves and possess their *own* integrity. The labels we evolve to refer to them do not at all change their basic nature, constituents, and "structures." Put more intellectually, *our* semantic differences do not at all have any effect on the real nature of the invisibles.

But it must be pointed out that our semantic differences *do* have meaningful impact on our intellectual workings and thus on the overviews we establish because of them. For example, if astrologers intellectually assume they are dealing with the "planets," the Kahunas think they are dealing with "*unihipili*," the Kabbalists with the "Tree of Life," and the anti-psychics think they are dealing with "impossibles," then it is entirely possible that each of these will achieve completely different, and often divergent, intellectual viewpoints about the invisibles.

What can these intellectualized differences matter to the invisibles themselves? Not very much, I dare say. But they matter a great deal to how we construct our intellectual overviews about things psychic. Basically, these intellectualized overviews *divide* the realms of psychic study which, otherwise, should be coherent and integrated.

If we sit back and try to take a long look at the invisibles, it should be possible at least to agree on one thing. Whatever the invisibles are, they are first and foremost *invisible* — until we can modulate our intellects into appropriate conditions to perceive and acknowledge a *self*-experience of them.

Yet there is a problem here. If we intellectually think we must experience "planets," "*unihipili*," the "Tree of Life," or "impossibles," then in all likelihood we will not experience anything at all — for the above are just *names* for the invisibles.

There is yet *another* problem. Even if we do manage to transcend or clear out our intellectual labels, then we still cannot self-experience the invisibles unless we can become "aware" of their impacts upon, or their interactions with, our direct sensing systems.

And we cannot align our direct sensing systems and our intellects unless we can first intellectually conceive of the *basic* ways in which the invisibles impact upon or interact with us.

Now, I tortured my brains with this issue for a long time. I probably would still be torturing it if, in struggling through information being turned out from the cutting edge of quantum physics, my intellectual processes had not locked on to a salient bit of information: As far as quantum physicists can tell, the whole of our universe can be reduced to two basic things: energies and forces.

At first this distinction confused me, for, like almost everyone else, I thought the two terms were synonymous and interchangeable. But since some bells were going off, I finally threw in the towel of my intellectual certainty and opened, yes, a dictionary. Now, I well know that the average reader doesn't like to struggle through definitions, so I'll make this as painless as possible.

Our term "energy" is derived from the Greek *energos* which means "active" or "actively working." This definition is expanded into a very serviceable one: "capable of or having active vitality of expression."

The radical difference between "energy" and "force" becomes visible only when we compare the definition of the latter to the definition of the former. Our present term "force" is derived from the Latin *fortis* which means, essentially, "strong," which further means "to induce, to press or push, to cause energy to be brought to bear, and to *bind* energy for or toward a given purpose."

In other words, an energy is an active potential, capable of its own expression. But when it is *bound up* so as to induce a specific motion or change it becomes a causative factor in its own right. Likewise, when the force is "unbound," the energies it had contained revert to a neutral state of vitality, capacity, or potential.

We can further illuminate our intellects by getting the idea that we are looking at *two* conditions of the same thing. Energy that is "free" and energy that had been "bound up" and given forceful direction. We can enlarge our intellectual image of this by observing that electricity is, apparently, a free form of energy. It becomes a force when captured in dynamos and fed through wires to, for example, *drive* computers and heat curling irons. Also, masses of people "contain" a lot of free energy. They become a force when bound together by, for example, some political, religious, or intellectual ideal.

In the rawest state conceivable, the invisibles are "free forms" of energy. They become *forces* when they become *directed* or *bound up* into given directions or channels. And the power of any given force is probably directly proportional to the energies *bound up* in it.

These two definitions, if understood, can illuminate our intellects considerably. First of all, both states can be experienced at the individual level. We can sense our energies and even estimate their fluctuating "levels." But we know that to utilize them to any given end we have to direct them in given directions. In other words, to bind them up into a force that is profitable and not destructive. If we discover in us forces that are, like riptides, sucking us toward destruction, we will want, somehow, to unbind and free the energies captured in them. Likewise, if we see psychic riptides in others, or in society, we should want to do something about them, or, if that fails, get out of their way until they are spent.

But, if our *personal* energy-force quotients were all there is for us to deal with, there would hardly be any need for the greater psychic arts and crafts. The double fact is that our personal energy-force quotients impact upon and interact with the energy-force quotients of others; and, horrors, there exist energies and forces that are independent of ourselves but which impact upon and interact with us and everyone else.

The overall result is a complex web of energies and forces which are, of course, always invisible — until a given intellect can be brought into a condition proficient enough to perceive them.

As far as I can determine, humankind began recognizing the existence of this invisible energy-force complexity quite near the onset of human experience on Earth. *All* psychic disciplines were evolved with the goal of perceiving, monitoring, keeping track of, getting out of the way of, profiting from, and forecasting what the invisibles were up to and how their effects would manifest in the concrete realms.

When these disciplines, all originally focused on the same invisibles, became so intractably institutionalized (astrology, Kabala, Masonry, etc.), their adherents became intellectually isolated in their own formalized precepts, with the predictable result that over six thousand years of historical communication between the disciplines broke down.

The next thing on which we should quickly focus our attention is the fact that energies and forces can be constructive or destructive, and I propose to examine this in the next chapter. But first:

THE MEANINGFUL DIFFERENCE BETWEEN PSYCHIC ENERGIES AND PSYCHIC FORCES

o   We should be able to conceive of the fact that invisible energies and forces are what they are, and that the way different disciplines label them serves to bring no change in their natural "laws" but do serve to confuse our intellects concerning them.

o   We can observe that there is a radical difference between an energy and a force — whether visible or invisible — and that somewhat appropriate definitions have been provided above.

o   We should observe that if we desire to reach *any* psychic literacy, we must more or less abandon the intellectual, competitive situations between the psychic disciplines and their arts and crafts, so as to reacquaint ourselves with basic human experience. Doing so implies the need for a new psychic synthesis which makes psychic experience accessible and understandable.

SUGGESTED PRACTICAL EXERCISES THAT WILL HELP IN EXPANDING PSYCHIC LITERACY

o It is really quite difficult for us to perceive something we are not already perceiving in ourselves. If we could perceive it, we would already have done so. It is far easier for us to observe others and to identify what *they* are not perceiving and then look into ourselves to see if we are not perceiving the same. Doing so often unclogs our own intellectual arteries. Thus, begin observing others with an eye to observing what they are *not* perceiving. Don't be surprised to discover that many people fail to perceive many things that are even visible to their physical senses. In other words, observe other people's perceptions very carefully. Doing so may awaken sleeping perceptions in yourself.

o The active presence of invisible energies and forces are usually quite visible in others. To begin to enhance your own sleeping proficiencies, watch for telepathic linkages between others, for example. If you chance to observe an apparent instance of intuition in someone else, and can talk to them about it, do so. Ask them to describe their experiences. Our intellects are always more impressed with someone else's experiences than with their own.

XII

The Constructive and Destructive Nature of the Invisibles

By now you may have begun to get a pregnant idea that the total of all the invisibles is much larger than any of us individually, and, in fact, larger than humanity as a whole. If so, you have found your intellectual way to the right psychic ball park.

The sum of all the activities of the invisibles is enormous; we might say cosmic-enormous. Apparently, unless you can "suffer" this realization, your intellectual equipment cannot build a correct picture of what is involved. Your volitional proficiency in dealing with psychic stuff, with psychic energies and forces, is directly dependent on this realization.

For example, the survival of sailors and seafarers is directly dependent on their accepting and understanding the fact that the oceans are greater than they. Since this is so, they must learn to *work with* the oceans, rather than insisting the oceans adapt to *them*. When any given sailor gets the idea that he has conquered the oceans and is therefore superior to them, he will certainly find out differently. Astronauts have found out something similar in that they must accept the knowledge that space is greater than they, and that it is they who must learn to work with it rather than the other way around. The slightest mistake in space leads to instantaneous disaster.

Our present culture is much founded on the idea that the powers of the individual, properly cultivated and believed in, can overcome *anything*.

Well, when it comes to overcoming the vast oceans of the invisibles, good luck and good-bye. History well illustrates the fact that unless individuals learn to work with the invisibles — and not attempt to overcome them — such individuals quickly become history themselves. This realization relates to a second fundamental reality that must be acknowledged.

"Overcoming" the invisibles equates with learning to work with the complex factors that characterize the vast scope of invisible activity. We overcame the oceans by learning to work with them. We are in process of overcoming space by learning how to work with it.

In fact, it is really very difficult to discover *any* area of human endeavor that is excused from this formula. Our modern and postmodern culture is (to its continuing amazement) discovering the prices to be paid as the result of trying to superimpose human designs over the natural orders and laws of things all the while caring nothing for them in the process. It is becoming increasingly clear to some of us that when humanity collectively or individuals on their own seek to try to impose activities on natural conditions which are incompatible or not "agreeable" with nature, something is going to give way — and it is *not* going to be the natural conditions! These can be disregarded only at great cost.

HARMONY AND DISHARMONY

To further enlarge upon this, we now need to resurrect two words that have become extremely unfashionable, especially during the last hundred years — "harmony" and "disharmony." It is somewhat a mystery as to why, exactly, these two words were retired from usage by our modern culture. But something seems to turn on the idea that modern, scientific man blundered forth into the Age of Science and Technology much under the mistaken idea that Scientific Man could not possibly be the cause of disharmonies. If this latter term was no longer needed, then the term "harmony" was not needed either — and thus the two terms were retired from modern dialogues. In a sense, Science (as a faith) put mortal man in the "top man" position. And since everything was being converted into "science" in our modern age, the expectation was that man shortly would align his total utopian existence with materialistic orders. At least, this was *scientism's* vision for the future.

Furthermore, "harmony" actually means "heaven," while "disharmony" is associated with "hell." Thus, the two terms carried inconvenient religious connotations, and withdrawing from the religious "mess" greatly preoccupied the intellects of the early (and later) scientists.

Basically, "harmony" means attuned, having all parts agreeably related. "Disharmony" means lacking or defective in harmony, disagreeably related. The whole of the workings of the universe can be described via these two terms. When all its parts are agreeably related the whole works well. When not, something awful is going to happen.

And the same can be said of the invisibles which, themselves, are not excused from the cosmic whole. When they are agreeably related in a "positive" situation among all their "parts," harmony manifests. When not, a "negative" one results.

With this "universal law" in mind, the ancients, in utilizing their evolved psychic arts and crafts, tried to determine existing and potential harmonic and disharmonic "conditions" of the invisibles — to take advantage of the former and get out of the way of the latter. Apparently, they understood that such "determinings" were possible and feasible and intellectually had no problem in so considering.

My purpose in providing, in Part One, such a lengthy amount of background information ought now to become visible. For we can easily see illustrated in it many psychic-type situations which are either harmonic or disharmonic in character. But we can even go further at this point via more illustrations. Essentially, when sailors sense or intuit great storms coming, their intuitions, arrived at far enough in advance, give them the option of heading for port to get out of the way. And in the centuries before our present technologically-advanced weather warning systems, our nautical predecessors depended a great deal on their own intuitions and other forms of psychically-gathered intelligence.

TAKING ADVANTAGE OF CONSTRUCTIVE AND DESTRUCTIVE FORCES

Yet, even storms at sea can be taken advantage of if they occur within the scope of one's designs, and psychic intelligence gathering opportunities are at hand. It is therefore not surprising that many kings and queens of days gone by kept a reserve of psychic "intelligence agents" near at hand. To wit:

When Queen Elizabeth I (1533-1603) gained the throne of England, she was only twenty-five. She ascended the throne in the face of insuperable odds and maintained it against similar odds until her death forty-five years later. History has judged her a super-dynamic personality, which, it is safe to say, she clearly was. Most of the average biographies written about her tell her tale with great clarity, but all of them either slide quickly past, or omit altogether, the fact that she leaned very heavily on an assortment of court psychics and astrologers and made a point of keeping track of psychic predictions. Attempts have also been made to destroy all evidence regarding not only her interest in psychic stuff, but especially her dependency upon it.

During her reign, one of the most momentous events the European world witnessed developed this way. Phillip II, King of Spain, saw that if he could negotiate a marriage with Elizabeth, he could add England to his possessions. Elizabeth saw this too and declined his proposal. Not to be defeated in acquiring England for himself, on the ostensible grounds that the Protestant Elizabeth had executed the Catholic Mary, Queen of Scots, Phillip decided to launch his armada, the most powerful war fleet ever assembled to that time, to conquer England. The ultimate success of this adventure was a foregone conclusion, one clearly understood by Elizabeth herself.

What, then, was to be done to save England from the grasping claws of the Spanish?

Elizabeth debated whether or not to send England's very slight men-of-war to encounter Phillip's powerful armada on the high seas and had to consider the pessimistic view that her smaller vessels would be blasted to hell and back. Her other option was to allow the Spanish to invade England and fight the battle on land where she had a better chance of winning.

However, in consultations with her court psychics and astrologers, it was determined that the battle should be fought at sea because, as her chief astrologer, one John Dee, predicted, a disaster in the form of a terrific north wind would strike the Spanish fleet while still at sea. The large vessels of the armada would be unmaneuverable, their tall masts breaking in the fierce winds. On the other hand, Elizabeth's smaller men-of-war combatant vessels could easily negotiate the storm, move close to the foundering Spanish vessels, and sink them.

So, with only this psychic intelligence, acquired weeks before the actual conflict, to guide her, Elizabeth sent her men-of-war to conquer the Spanish armada. At the appointed encounter, wild north winds duly appeared and lashed the one hundred and thirty heavy war galleons of the invading Spanish fleet, crashing many of them together, and overturning others, so that the more maneuverable English men-of-war could take an enormous toll. History records that scarcely half the completely defeated Spanish armada returned to Spain. The Queen had taken advantage of a fortuitous disaster, and she could only have done so because the disaster was predicted by a seer.

Elizabeth continued to consult astrologers and psychics to the day she died, a factor which probably helps account for her long and extraordinarily successful reign. It is worth noting that John Dee's successful career came under the careful scrutiny of other European leaders who saw the advisability of detaching him from the service of the Queen — and promptly took propagandistic steps to ruin him, not because he was a psychic "charlatan" as later historians dubbed him (no one at the time would have dared to challenge his proven track record), but because he gave Elizabeth advantages others did not like her to have.

Dee, based on his astrological calculations and his psychic surmises, correctly espied a future moment of disharmonious weather which might be turned to England's advantage. Considering the fact that embarking on this particular mission was a vast, expensive, and time-consuming affair, Elizabeth risked a great deal (certainly her throne and possibly her life) by depending on psychically-acquired intelligence.

Elizabeth was only doing something rulers had done from times immemorial. As I may have mentioned earlier, some time ago I came to the conclusion that the ancients persisted in utilizing psychic intelligence because, and *only* because, it was profitable to do so. Cicero certainly said as much when, in observing the Delphic oracle which was already ancient in *his* own now ancient time: "Never could the oracle of Delphi have been so overwhelmed with so many important offerings from monarchs and nations if all the ages had not proved the truth of its oracles." And even the skeptical author, Eric Russell, is forced to admit in his book *History of Astrology & Prediction*, by saying: "The powerful men who made rich gifts to the [Delphic] temple were not taking part in a religious act of vague and general propitiation but virtually a commercial transaction in which they paid out hard cash for information about a future event. If the ratio of success to failure had been the ordinary one of pure chance, it seems unlikely, to say the least, that caravans laden with gold and silver and precious spices and perfumes would have continued to wind their way over the tortuous roads to the shrine."[1]

---

1 See Russell, Eric. History of Astrology & Prediction, New English Library Ltd., London, 1972.

We can contrast Elizabeth's Armada Event to one in our modern period, the assassination of John F. Kennedy. His assassination was presaged, as are all great events, not only by the once-proficient Jeanne Dixon, but by several other sources. Indeed, his horoscope (the details of which we need not go into here) implied disharmonies of great danger on the day he visited Dallas. Had Kennedy changed even one factor in his visit — by riding behind bullet-proof glass as his security advisers recommended — he could have fortuitously turned the assassination attempt to great popular advantage. But although Elizabeth I was possessed of refined psychic literacy, the unfortunate President was not — and, doubtlessly those involved in the assassination plot were content that he wasn't.

Now, considering the intellectual orientation of our present culture, the reintroduction of the terms "harmony" and "disharmony" probably will not be an easy thing to accomplish. But since the basic purpose of *all* the psychic arts and crafts is not only to perceive the existence of the invisibles, but to distinguish their harmonic and disharmonic *trends* — and thence, together with intellectual activity, to *balance* their outcomes regarding human advantages.

Clearly, harmony equates to constructivity, and disharmony to destructivity. "Constructive" literally means "to build together," while "destructive" means "to build apart." We can perceive, then, that in the psychic sense destructivity involves building apart from the natural elements which otherwise should be observed. Constructivity implies building within and together with natural elements that should not be disregarded.

By now we can begin to espy that the invisibles modulate or phase themselves in and out of harmonic and disharmonic patterns, and thus, in themselves, can temporarily manifest either as constructive or destructive potentials. It is the purpose of the psychic arts and crafts to keep track of these modulations.

But, humans can, by disregarding the invisibles (and other situations, as well), *induce* destructivity and/or induce constructivity. For example, it is rather well accepted that Adolf Hitler and his Nazi court (by war-like, that is, disharmonious, means) induced a great deal of destructivity, both physical and psychical, that is *imprinted* on human consciousness forever more. On the other hand, the Venerable Mahatma Gandhi (by pacific, i.e., harmonious, methods) induced constructivity, both physical and psychical, which also is imprinted deep into human memory.

PSYCHIC CREATIVITY

Before we close this chapter, we have yet one more word-concept to review as it relates to psychic stuff. Human initiative is always linked to what we call "creativity" — whose exact meaning, mechanics and processes remain elusive. So much so that while on the one hand we possess thousands upon thousands of books and information papers trying to isolate its *modus operandi*, on the other hand the situation it represents is so complex that many researchers abandon studying "it" altogether.

Generally speaking, we relate creativity to *positive outcomes*, sometimes centering on new, workable visions and discoveries, and sometimes centering on the resolution of old, intractable situations. Since this is so, we become confused if and when we begin to realize, as we must, that destructive people also employ creative initiatives in pursuit of, yes, destruction.

We are so used to considering creativity only in its positive sense that we do not even possess a word for its negative sense. In other words, there is a hole in our intellectual approach to the matter entirely.

Our term "creative" is taken from the Latin terms *creatus* and *creire* which mean, simply, to produce. It is rather a large jump from that ancient, simple definition to our modern one of "to invest with a new form." The fact of the matter is that people are producing things all the time, which is to say, in the ancient context they are perpetually creative. In other words, creative does not apply to where, why, or how things *originate*, but simply to human *products*.

In the simplest sense possible, people are producing two things — constructivity and destructivity — with the added complexity that it is, usually, very hard to tell which is which, since this can be determined only by how things turn out. That is to say, it is hard to tell without employing psychic proficiencies. Without incorporating psychic intelligence, it is really very difficult to predict how human initiatives are going to turn out.

For example, Hitler gained the power he did because people felt his initiatives would turn out well, and because of this he was able to mobilize the inherent powers of the German masses and use that invested power to his own ends. Only a very few, at the time, could foresee the abysmal outcome of the Nazi regime — and in almost all cases those were psychic types — including, of course, Winston

Churchill. On the other hand, the Venerable Mahatma Gandhi was at first widely considered a scurrilous rabble rouser whose initiatives only seemed full of impending doom. Only a very few could foresee the positive outcome of his initiatives and, again, these were psychic types. In the end, the outcome of the Venerable's initiatives led to the liberation (for better or worse) of the British slave state, India.

It is almost impossible to say that Hitler was not creative and that Gandhi was. The command of creative avenues enjoyed by the former was, in fact, considerable. As the monster's career rose into the cultural stratospheres, he was indeed hailed along the way as a creative genius by Germans, the English, and many Americans alike. On the other hand, Gandhi was castigated as a fool and worse. Well, so much for human foresight uninformed by psychic graces.

Thus, creativity-as-production breaks apart into two lineages, the destructive and the constructive. *Psychic* creativity then implies the production of special psychic products, primarily the proficiencies necessary to see and foresee how human initiatives are going to turn out. That proficiency in this regard also must incorporate proficiency to monitor invisibles in the first place is, by now, a foregone conclusion.

It would seem that there are no human initiatives that are not founded on either constructive or destructive psychic impulses, or perhaps a complicated mix of them. We know by experience that such impulses *attract* other similar impulses. What we really do not understand, generally speaking, is that these impulses are intrinsically invisible and, therefore, psychic in nature. In common parlance, we refer to these impulses as "vibes." Few of us are those who have not experienced vibes. But, I'm getting ahead of myself here.

THE CONSTRUCTIVE AND DESTRUCTIVE NATURE OF THE INVISIBLES

- We can observe that the "universe" of the invisibles is gigantically large, and that we are, as it were, "embedded" in it. Thus, to learn to survive in it, we, like sailors on the oceans, must learn to work with it — with its moods, tempers, trends, activities, and cycles.

- We can observe that when psychic energies and forces are "agreeably" related, a positive harmony can be expected; when their relationships are not "agreeable," negative, disharmonious situations will eventuate.

- We should observe that in the harmonious-disharmonious balance can be found lineages of destructivity and constructivity, and that once the balance leans one way or another, these lineages will attract similar impulses.

- We should correct our idea of creativity, in that creativity refers to what is produced through human initiatives, and human initiatives are capable of inducing both destructivity and constructivity.

SUGGESTED PRACTICAL EXERCISES THAT WILL HELP IN EXPANDING PSYCHIC LITERACY

o   Although most of us try to face each new day as a brave new world, normally we make very little attempt to try to observe the presence of destructive and constructive trends around us. We generally like to be optimistic, and we may feel that deliberately looking for destructive stuff makes pessimists of us. Yet we live amid a constant supply of human initiatives, *all* of which are headed towards destructivity or constructivity. Hardly any human initiative "hangs up" in time and never changes. Therefore, trying to become aware of both negative and positive psychic impressions may represent the onset of actual pro-survival proficiencies. As usual, note them down in your psychic book; otherwise your intellect, which has a lot to do by now, may forget them.

***

Our intellects learn very fast by viewing visual graphs, charts, and pictures. The following two synopsize what has been talked about in this chapter. They need to be superimposed over each other to achieve the larger picture they represent together.

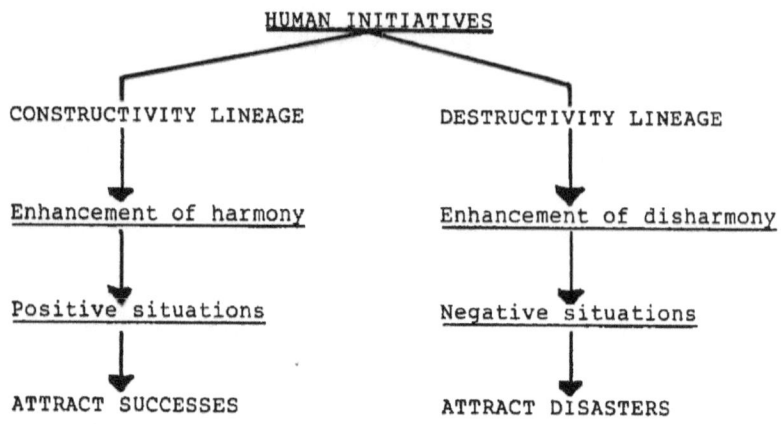

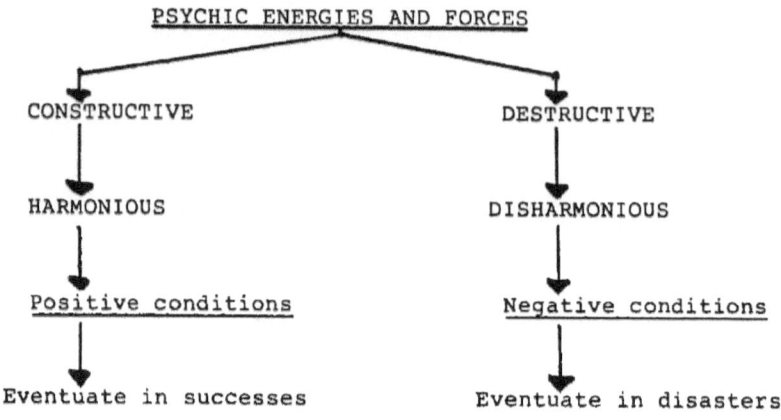

Now, the ancients had two terms that identified what we might in contemporary terms call "success-attraction" and "disaster-attractions." These two ancient terms have fallen much out of use, save in what many would call the lower superstitious echelons of the public. Once in a while, however, a writer will get them up and dust them off. We now need to get our dusters out, too.

XIII

Fate and Destiny

In 1961, when I was, as they say, still trying to get my sea legs *vis-à-vis* living and surviving in New York City, I fell in with a certain rather exciting literary and artistic group of extreme individuals who were all bonded together by two things.

First, they were all trying to succeed in making it into the higher levels of New York's culturati where wealth, influence, and money lay, and where also would be found something most people crave but usually cannot get anywhere — public appreciation and acknowledgement of their valuable "contributions."

The second thing that bound them together was that they had not succeeded but nobly were still *trying*. In fact, some of them had been trying for twenty or thirty years. Two of them had even punched through into the limelight, but, mysteriously and embarrassingly had quickly and inexplicably resubmerged back into New York's rather large population of cultural nobodies.

This group had two echelons. The top echelon contained those who had been trying the longest, and, perhaps, had come closest to claiming shares of the limelight. The "other" echelon (everyone was careful not to call it the "lower" one) consisted of neophytes and aspirants who were still trying to get a grasp on what they might "contribute," on what the Cultural Establishment "wanted from them," and who seemed trapped in the question of "what the hell was going on, anyway?"

"What was going on" remained, I suppose, something of a mystery to the group entire. None of them ever succeeded in claiming or even reclaiming any extensive share of limelight status. But I liked this "group" very much because life within it periodically took on excitement and because the group liked to fight about the meaning of life's deepest and profoundest issues on the way to getting drunk — a condition in which the profoundest issues didn't need to be resolved anyway.

In this group was a youngish woman (a rather tough number) born in Scotland who liked to stir up the group by stating: (1) that she knew that *she* was destined to be nobody, destined to die young; (2) that a lot of people were so destined; (3) and that the group represented a small collection of them. Now, in this group this was like pouring gasoline on embers almost dead, but not quite. Such statements revivified the members' flagging exertions of trying to mount the cultural ladder. For, you see, everyone in the group felt they indeed had a destiny. The fact that these destinies were not really clear to anyone in no way altered the essential fact: everyone knew they had a destiny, and each made haste to leave no doubt of this in others' minds.

The unofficial leader of the group, a man who had once been awarded a Pulitzer Prize but who had gone down the tubes thereafter by overly pursuing drink and sexual gratifications of various kinds, liked to censor the Scottish maid by pointing out that she did not have a sense of Destiny at all, but "liked to justify her own abject sense of failure by masturbating Fate!" You see — excitement!

Then would follow enlivening, beer-drenched "discussions" of what constituted Destiny and what constituted Fate and, especially, who was being "led" by the former and who was in the "grip" of the latter. Nothing was ever resolved, of course, and eventually I drifted away from this lifestyle — somewhat content to abandon Destiny and/or Fate to those who might have them.

Thus, it came as somewhat of a surprise twenty years later when it began to dawn on me that, whatever they were, the concepts of Destiny and Fate had something to do with the "machinations" of the invisibles. After which I began to feel obliged to try to make sense out of them, something which my exciting group had failed to do. After spending not an inconsiderable amount of time ferreting out information about these awesome and sometimes terrible twins, I found as follows.

To begin with, we in our present Western culture don't like the idea that our lives are "directed" by anything other than what we want to be "directed" by. We have been largely programmed to assume we are self-motivated and thus self-directed. But direct observation and direct experience demonstrates that many of us end up in places and suffer psychic-type events considerably different from those designed by our self-motivations. Despite this, much of our Western convictions about our essential individuality do not change.

Yet we can look at other people and, more or less, see the inadequacy of our ideological individuality. We often point out that someone "was *born* a bad seed and was going to turn out rotten no matter what," or someone "was destined to triumph and succeed." In fact, "it's in the stars" is *still* used, even though in modern intellectual circles the concepts of Fate and Destiny are considered as belonging to the Dark Ages of superstition, having no place in the age of Scientific Enlightenment. The fact is, while we avoid discussing the issues involved, since at present they are culturally taboo, we use the appropriate terminologies anyway because somehow and upon occasion they are meaningful to us, even though our intellects have no idea of what they mean.

For example, do you understand intellectually what Destiny and Fate mean, and that there is actually a difference between them? On the surface of our intellects we use the two terms interchangeably, as synonyms. I certainly did so for a long time and was thus much subjected to the confusions arising from this lack of precision. Why do we have the *two* words in the first place? It is because, like "energy" and "force," they actually have two radically different *original* meanings.

Let's decode Fate first. It derives from the Latin *fatum*, meaning very precisely *what has been spoken, decreed, or already directed*. Clearly this refers to *an outcome* — most specifically, one that is fatal. Our term "fatality" is derived from this Latin word.

But look at Destiny. It derives from the Latin *de + stinar* which means *to stand or set aside for a special purpose*. Clearly this refers to an outcome, too, but "purpose" implies something that is *to be attained*.

Admittedly, the line of demarcation is very narrow here; it is fairly easy to see how the two meanings can become confused. But if we consider the two meanings calmly and transcend the confusions, we can see that Fate refers to an ominous negative outcome while Destiny refers to a potentially positive one. No one has ever had the purpose of *attaining* something fatal, even those who commit suicide — ostensibly to get free of an intolerable life. No one seeks fatality, but rather to extricate oneself from it if one can find out how to do so. Fate and pain have much in common. But we hardly ever think of pain in connection with Destiny.

On the other hand, Destiny implies not the *closing down* of a future, but the *opening up* of one. In "setting aside for a special purpose to be attained," a future is implicit.

We can simplify all this considerably if we conceive that Fate is close-ended while Destiny is open-ended. Fate implies ultimate extinction or entrapment in lines of invisible energies and forces that will culminate in, yes, destruction. On the other hand, Destiny implies just the opposite.

We may get the two verbally confused, and our intellects might use the terms without really knowing what they actually mean. But they are seldom confused when it comes to artistically rendering them into visual images. In fact, the Fates are always visually portrayed as the Hounds of Hell or malevolent, dangerous characters, witches, shadowy types in hoods, or sometimes just plain, but ominous, black holes. But look at images of Destiny! Destiny is almost always portrayed as stalwart youth, sometimes bearing a torch or lantern, but always gazing into a luminous, if unspecific, future.

In the context of this book, then, Fate and Destiny can be seen as representing the two most basic archetypes of the two observable fundamental conditions of the invisibles — the destructive and the constructive, the disharmonic and the harmonic. If we cast back to the many examples given in Part One, we can espy Fate and Destiny "at work" in many of them — mostly Fate, thus far. In the next chapter, and throughout what follows, we'll see something of Destiny "at work," too.

Admittedly, distilling exact definitions for Fate and Destiny is made a little more complex due to the fact that various cultures have discovered, and given names to, *varieties* of both. Writers and artists then have personified these varieties, giving them human names, mythological and modern. Dramatists have even created very dramatic plots in which one version of Destiny manages, of all things, to *marry* a version of Fate, whose "children" then are born mixtures of their "parents" and thereafter have great difficulty in dealing with anything except irresolvable machinations.

Anti-supernatural intellectual purists worked to erase the concepts of Fate and Destiny from our intellectual landscape — and on the surface it would seem they have succeeded. But if you study society carefully, you can espy a vivid, vital interest in them under other names. For example, consider soap operas, and especially the big one, *Dallas*, whose dramatic plots are nothing more nor less than ongoing encounters between Fates and Destinies. Then there is, yes, *Batman!* — whose special purpose is to battle Fates of one kind or another. And *Lethal Weapon II*. And remember the *Star Wars* trilogy. Our utter fascination with Fate and Destiny is still very much a vital part of human nature. Anti-psychic enthusiasts well may erase two mere words from usage. They will probably never, however, be able to erase what they refer to.

FATE AND DESTRUCTIVE FORCES

The ultimate result of destructive forces is almost certainly a foregone conclusion: destruction. If someone psychically gets caught up in or "sucked in" to riptides or convolutions of destructive forces, visible or invisible, they can be seen as headed for some kind of doom. That doom is a Fate in the complete meaning of that word.

It is really very difficult to extract oneself from the lines of force-activity that will culminate in doom precisely since we usually cannot see in advance that we are caught up in them in the first place. Usually the truth of the matter begins to dawn on one's intellect only when the Fate hovers into sight and becomes obvious; and then it is sometimes much too late to do anything about it. Often someone's direct-sensing systems will try to impinge alerts on their consciousness, as we have seen. Even so, many people ignore them anyway.

At any rate, if someone embarks, even unknowingly, on a course of action that will eventuate in a doom, apparently all the factors that will manifest that doom begin to line up. The clock starts ticking, as it were. The only feasible way to avert this doom is to foresee where decisions and activities *actually* will lead — and this involves, and clearly so, using not only the limited powers of intellect but direct psychic capabilities and the psychic arts and crafts. Another factor is involved too: actually paying attention to the alerts gained via psychic methods. Many people do not pay attention to psychically-derived information even if they have been made fully aware of it — and we have already seen several examples of this earlier.

DESTINY AND LIFE-GIVING ENERGIES

The ultimate result of life-giving, life-sustaining energies is constructivity, although this might not be as foregone a conclusion as that involving destructivity. Apparently, it is much harder to create constructively than it is to create destructively — even if we know the differences between these two kinds of creating.

One reason is this: we are altogether surrounded by many more destructive forces than we are by creative energies. The ocean of human nature is filled with psychic storm systems large and small and, seemingly, perpetual. A large part of our individual creative enterprises has to do with surviving these storms, surmounting them, getting out of their way, and picking up the pieces after they have passed.

If someone manages all that is implied here, they almost certainly will be considered successful. But look at this: It is exactly among successful people that the highest ratios of psychic literacy and interests in psychic matters are found. Anyone can easily meet their doom without being too psychic; but one cannot meet one's destiny if one does not have active psychic potentials. Just observe people over time. You will see this is the case.

FATE AND DESTINY

o   By looking around at other people, we can observe that Fate and Destiny, alias many other names, are of continuing interest at many levels, for we sense that their activities and machinations are, in fact, "driving" much of what we call "*our* lives."

o   We should observe, though, that our modern intellectual stances have largely decreed the issues of Fate and Destiny to be throwbacks to the "age" of superstition and thus are intellectually taboo. Although our intellectual attitudes thus detach social consciousness from any overt, intellectual considerations of their possible reality, versions of Fate and Destiny themes portrayed in various forms are prevalent due to the fact that they reflect recognizable psychic activities which are part and parcel of human nature.

SUGGESTED PRACTICAL EXERCISES THAT WILL HELP IN EXPANDING PSYCHIC LITERACY

- Reminding ourselves that our intellects learn more from observing others than ourselves, ask a few people if they sense they have a destiny and invite them to talk about it. If you want to see instances in which people quickly detach themselves from their intellectual noise, this topic should do it. Be prepared to sit back and *listen*, for it is quite likely that most people will have a great deal to say once you make them comfortable and they feel okay to say it. Try to find out when the person first experienced a destiny impression and in what form. Be careful in asking them if they feel they are on or off their destiny tracks. This may induce discomfort. *WARNING*: asking people if they have a sense of their *fate* may cause them to get irritable quickly and view you with suspicion or, even, anger.

XIV

Our Hidden Psychic Agendas

The ancients evolved many terms via which they identified and referred to the many different aspects, activities, and machinations of the invisibles. However, our present culture has inadvertently evolved one the ancients never thought of. This term has evolved outside the psychical research and parapsychological frameworks. Although it is not thought of as a psychic-type term, indeed it serves to bridge the visibles and invisibles. In doing so, it takes on great psychic connotations. Anti-psychic types have not yet espied these connotations, so it is okay to use it. Thus, it has a certain cachet and has proliferated almost everywhere.

This term is: "hidden agendas."

Now, one of the great functional purposes of all the psychic arts and crafts is to locate and unravel hidden agendas of all kinds, especially those agendas that are "hidden" in the invisibles. We can, of course, look around at the tangible, concrete aspects of life and acknowledge the existence of visible, locatable agendas. But, as countless sages have observed: "nothing is what it seems." They refer to hidden agendas.

OUR HIDDEN PSYCHIC AGENDAS

In the background information given so far, we have observed many Events of which people were psychically forewarned in certain ways. We have to consider that *if* there could be forewarnings, then the Event was somehow "scheduled." Since scheduling always implies the existence of an "agenda," we are obliged to acknowledge the existence of "agendas" that are hidden from our intellects but, apparently, not from our psychic direct-sensing systems.

The question we then have to consider is this: since our psychic elements *do* try to alert us to things to come, does this mean we are enmeshed in hidden psychic agendas of some kind which include the manifestation of specific events? If we acknowledge the evidence, clearly the answer is yes. I'll quickly admit that the implications of this go very much against our precious ideas of who and what we are, along with our present conceptions of time and space. It resurrects the old arguments of predestination, versus free will, which at various times have split cultures and been philosophically argued into confused impasses by theologians and scientists alike.

Now, the evidence that hidden agendas do exist seems to me to be very convincing; it has a ten-thousand-year history which can be traced back to the oracular shrine at Dodona, established shortly after the Flood. And recent evidence that our psychic elements continue to try to alert us to coming times and events included in future scheduling is equally convincing. Ergo — we *do* have hidden psychic agendas, and their nature must be of immeasurable importance to *each* of us. This is reason enough to take an interest in them.

However, this is a very tough idea to take on board. Everyone would be glad enough to get psychic clues with regard to making big bucks or finding treasures. But few people are interested, for example, in learning at which point in time they or their loved ones are going to die. Yet, we apparently have many possible "death events" scheduled in our hidden agendas, many of which could probably be avoided *if* we pay attention to psychic clues. When we do not, apparently we can sit back and await the worst.

Between 1974 and 1982 I gave dozens of workshops and seminars on psychic matters, and once when I had finished taking and answering questions a woman came up to me. I'll call her Estelle. She burst into tears instantly, obviously stressed out and sad. I knew immediately that she had experienced a psychic clue and had ignored it, much to her regret. I wrapped her in my arms until she could talk.

The gist of her tale is this: her mother got her yearly physical, and the family doctor pointed out that she had a minor condition that could quickly be repaired by minor surgery. The mother would be in and out in a jiffy. Nothing to worry about. Two weeks before the minor surgery, Estelle had a dream in which a figure in light appeared to her and told her to take her mother to another doctor for a second opinion.

Now, as Estelle said, she did not at the time believe in psychic things like dreams, and so she mentioned nothing of hers to her mother. The minor surgery went alright, but the mother went into shock in the recovery room and died almost immediately from "complications" of the operation. When an autopsy was done, it was discovered the doctor had been in error, and the mother had not had the minor condition in the first place — a fact which Estelle believed a second opinion would have discovered. An enormous legal to-do followed, and Estelle was awarded a large settlement.

Even so, Estelle had felt suicidal for a long time and could not erase the feelings of her own guilt, which had enormous repercussions and made of her, among other things, a psychic seminar groupie trying to make sense out of the psychic realms. Estelle said she was crying not simply because she had flubbed her psychic clue, and her mother had died; she had eventually handled that. She was crying because as a result of my lecture she realized for the first time that she had been a model product of the anti-psychic culture in which she lived. Her intellectual stance contained a negative image of psychic matters, and it was *this* that had caused her to ignore the urgent alert given in her dream.

Estelle was quite clever. She wondered if I could confirm *her* idea that her mother's death was somehow "scheduled" and suggested that it must have been already formed (recall our definition of Fate) somehow. She had concluded such, since only this could account for the information presented to her in her dream. I agreed that I thought such was the case.

But Estelle then went on: if she had taken up the psychic clue provided in her dream, she would have taken her mother for a second opinion and discovered the first doctor's error. In doing so, would she have *rescheduled* her mother's hidden psychic agenda? There was only on answer to this, since it was so obvious. Yes.

Estelle then observed: "Well, then, fate (*her* word, not mine) was not completely intractable. If we only knew what to look for, we could 'reschedule' a great deal of what's going to happen to us." I owe something to this woman, for she clarified a few things I, myself, was grappling with at the time.

I'll use a very sad example of all this out of my own life. In August 1988 I visited my parents who live in Texas. When they were taking me to the plane after the visit, my lovely sister who also lives in Texas went along. She had long been married to a successful Texan farmer. They owned great sectors of land, had a beautiful home, with four children and nine grandchildren. Yet my sister, a pillar in her family and community, was just approaching her fiftieth birthday. I sat with her in the back seat of the car, and as we were talking about Texas matters, such as the price of cows and cotton and the changeable weather, I suddenly got the impression she was going to die. I put this thought quickly back in some dark recess of my swampy intellect and was glad enough to call it some kind of random imagination.

As I was tucking this unwelcome "piece of imagination" in some dark mental drawer, my sister mentioned she had been experiencing "migraine headaches." Now, you'd think that with all I am saying I know about psychic stuff I might have put two-and-two together on the spot, and instead of catching my plane might have diverted us all to the nearest hospital to get her a full checkup. In retrospect, this would have been a very hard thing to do. It would have scared my mother and stepfather to no end. My sister probably would not have gone, stubborn thing that she was. My brother-in-law, who thinks psychic stuff is cow pucky...well, how could I justify alarming my family with a mere psychic impression of death for one yet quite young?

All the members of my family are a stubborn lot, and besides, as my sister went on to mention, "migraines" are plentiful in Texas, and she knew a lot of people who had them, and doesn't everyone take aspirins for them? So, we disposed of the "situation." I caught my plane, hugging her closely, the impression of "her dying" having already vanished into the dark recesses out of which it had come.

One morning four months later, a few days before Thanksgiving, completely "unexpectedly," she died instantly of a massive brain aneurysm. I attended her funeral in great grief, kicking my psychic ass all the way — as I will do forever — finding myself much in the same spot as Estelle whose dream figure tried to alert her to taking her mother for a second opinion before the mother died of some doctor's abysmal stupidity. After the funeral, one of my sister's sons and a couple of her friends told me she had had her *own* premonitions of her approaching death-crisis.

At any rate, in my sister's case the *psychic* "autopsy" looks like this. My psychic factors picked up on the fact that my sister was approaching a death-crisis. At that very moment, apparently my sister's own direct-sensing systems had picked up on the fact that mine had picked up on her death-crisis situation, so she began *verbalizing* her symptoms. The next stop *should* have been this: I should have said, "I've just had a psychic impression that involves your possible death, and spontaneously you have just verbalized some alarming symptoms which, taken together with my psychic impression indicate we should go post-haste and see what the real reasons for your headaches are." We should have gone to a hospital for a brain scan and some expert opinion as to the real nature of her "migraines." Medically and psychologically, much can now be done to reduce the risk of strokes, and this is rather well known.

At this point, though, all our intellects would have misfired. To try to drag my sister into a hospital because of *my* psychic impression of her forthcoming death would have resulted in a family disruption of no little magnitude — an Event in itself, if you know Texans. Texans don't keep company with psychic stuff. You get the gist of all this, I'm sure.

Could she have been saved from this particular death-crisis? We'll never know, for sure. But I believe so, for it is the purpose and function of our psychic systems to alert us to forthcoming dangers so that we might take active steps to avoid them by changing their scheduling.

Now, I must be honest. I am very touchy and not a little embarrassed over all this. (I could hardly bring myself to including this degrading event in this book.)

Here I am, an "acclaimed psychic." Yet, I flubbed this one because I paid more attention to non-psychic stuff. And even worse, when I later had a good look at my sister's horoscope, the aspects clearly indicated she was to experience a serious health matter concerning her head on the day she died. Jesus, what more "alerting" can one have? So, if any anti-psychic garbage-mouth wants to come to me and tell me that psychic stuff is superstition, they can do so only at the risk of some physical danger to themselves. In other words, don't bother.

If we want to get into the nuts and bolts of our psychic elements, we have to stiffen our nerves a little and get ready to look at a few things we all normally avoid — such as our own precious images of ourselves, the problems people have in dealing with psychic stuff, and the situations of life and death and what is really going to happen to us between these two awesome portals.

Let's start with what is really going to happen to us. Of this, most of us have no idea at all and just bump along encountering this and that along the way. What is the reason for this typical ignorance? Well, one thing is this: I've made some point in establishing the fact that most people deal exclusively with intellectual patterns they and others have constructed to represent this or that portion of life.

A good many of these intellectual images (stereotypes) are decidedly fictional, and thus this is to say that most of us live a life that is mostly composed of fictional contexts based upon our own constructed intellectual programming.

In large part, we inherit these programs about what we should or should not believe from our family and educational backgrounds, and many of these inherited ideas are surely based in, yes, modern intellectual *superstitions* (of which believing psychic potentials are mentally pathological is one). Over these, we deposit some more ideas of our own making. And then we try to achieve those things that are in keeping with our ideas. Basically, those ideas we entertain the most are those that are compatible with the prevalent notion that our lives are under our direct conscious control — and that by using strong conscious willpower and energetic determination we can do anything we want.

This is, indeed, the Western way of thinking about life, and anyone who dares to suggest differently is considered a wet blanket or worse. Now, it is abundantly clear that some parts of our lives *are* under our direct conscious control. But it is also clear that some parts are not. Given our allegiance to the modern myth that all and everything in our life is under our direct conscious control, we don't like very much to think about those things that are not — for example, our hidden psychic agendas.

What we do instead is project these mysterious factors into fictions (fables, novels, TV, and movies) and watch them wreck and ruin fictional characters. But normally we completely resist acknowledging that these same mysterious factors are working within us, too, and in the ebbs and flows of times and events around us.

Our problem is that we think we are isolated and immune from the interlinked ebbs and flows, when in fact our lives are the stuff of these currents and eddies.

Our failure to see our involvement in this complex psychic labyrinth of hidden energies and forces is a dysfunction, and this dysfunction does what most dysfunctions do — it prevents us from seeing that a dysfunction is even present.

It should be clearly pointed out that this dysfunction does not concern our psychic elements, which try to work in spite of it. It is an *intellectual* dysfunction, pure and simple. In other words, we are idiots about our psychic elements and the hidden agendas they are monitoring. Anyone who has lived through a deeply dismaying death-crisis as I did, or Estelle did, will know exactly what I'm talking about. When we are too intellectually dysfunctional about these hidden matters, we reap the Fates that go along with our intellectual dysfunction.

Now, the strangest thing of all is this: most of us intuitively know that all this is so! Yet, to keep ourselves in alignment with our anti-psychic society, most of us would rather literally die rather than become considered a psychic freak in the eyes of our peers.

But if you want to learn to work with your psychic elements, a first step in doing so is to acknowledge that they are apparently "on the case" on your behalf. *They* are monitoring the invisible factors and agendas that are applicable to you, whereas your waking intellect is probably completely incapable of doing so on its own. So we have to get our act together and get ready to peer into the invisible realms — no matter how uncomfortable things like death-crises are. In these realms there exist what really should be called our hidden psychic agendas. They are "hidden" usually, and only because, we don't want to see them. But strong circumstantial evidence of their existence is all around us.

How many times have you heard someone say that someone was born to be famous, was born a bad seed, was born to be successful and rich, was born to be a leader or born to fail? How many times have you met a person and felt the meeting was scheduled? How many times have lovers met with the immediate knowledge their love was *destined*, and they had only been waiting to reach the times and events in which they would meet? How many people have felt they were born to do something special and eventually achieved it? How many people have dreamed they should be doing something other than what their intellectual pressures have led them into? How many people are grateful to finally find their "true calling" after years of failed efforts in other areas?

All these things we feel are "there" can only be associated with a hidden agenda of some kind — one that is invisible to our intellects. Psychic data is being dumped into our intellects out of a hidden psychic agenda. One can either accept or ignore this data, but ignoring it often brings about a disaster — while accepting it often produces miracles.

Throughout history, many people have seemed to be closer in touch with their hidden psychic agendas than others. For example, Alexander the Great, Napoleon, Churchill, and General George Patton all knew well in advance they had been born for the specific purposes their lives eventually fulfilled. The hidden agenda plans for their lives apparently existed in some...let us say "parallel" consciousness. Actually, a great many people "know" or sense what they were born to be or do, and, apparently, the "hidden" purpose of a life need not be as grand as Napoleon's or Churchill's. It can also be quite mundane — yet equally successful in its own terms.

Considering the rather plentiful evidence that hidden psychic agendas exist, it is really very hard to escape having intellectual knowledge regarding their actual existence. Yet, with but rare exceptions the whole of our Western culture has managed to not only succeed in this escapism, but to view escaping as the appropriate thing to do. The exceptions are, of course, highly achieved psychics and psychic-crafts experts, who can tune into these agendas on behalf of other people and perceive something of the agendas' "plans," often in great detail.

For example, Count Louis Hamon, the world-famous Irish clairvoyant-palmist-astrologer (who, as we have seen, used the professional name of "Cheiro") was consulted by a vast spectrum of notable people, many of whom visited him several times. Among them was the British Field Marshal, Lord Kitchener (1850-1916), one of England's most highly-decorated military heroes and strategists. At the time of one of these consultations (July 21, 1894), Kitchener was then forty-four and wanted to know the year of his death. Cheiro did his thing regarding this and was able to identify the first part of June 1916 (some twenty-two years hence), as the most probable month and year of death-crisis when Kitchener would be sixty-six.

Kitchener then wanted to know the details of the death. Cheiro pointed out that it was to "be by water, most likely caused by storm or disaster at sea." Cheiro recommended that Lord Kitchener *not* travel by sea during June 1916, thus avoiding this death-crisis. Shortly, this prediction became part of the public domain, for Kitchener took astonishing risks with his life in land battles during World War I, which surprised many. He included mention of Cheiro's prediction in letters, and, as he told those concerned for his safety, the risks "do not alarm me because I know I shall die at sea, as Cheiro has said, and not until 1916." So, Kitchener, an Army man and not a Naval officer, felt he was safe on land regardless of the risks involved in the land campaigns in which he took part.

Historians still have a problem as to why Lord Kitchener boarded the naval vessel *Hampshire* on the evening of June 5, 1916, which set out to sea and inexplicably sank during a storm. Lord Kitchener was among those drowned. But, at any rate, here we have the problem of understanding how Cheiro could in 1894 "see" a death-crisis event coming down the lines for Kitchener in 1916 — twenty-two years in advance of its actual happening. If we accept that this *can* be done, then at least three things are necessary.

First, the future event must already exist in some way we do not understand. Second, if it exists, then it is part of some kind of hidden psychic agenda. The third factor requires that some function of human consciousness be able to link into this plan to perceive it. If we try to be psychic, and at the same time believe that a future planned agenda does not already exist in some form, then, of course, we are going to shoot ourselves in our psychic feet. Apparently, Cheiro accepted as a fact that the future already existed in some sort of a plan-form, and with training in the psychic crafts, he was able to link into these plan-forms.

Cheiro was both an astrologer and an inspired palmist. We have no record as to how Cheiro was enabled to specify Kitchener's probable death date, but presumably Kitchener had a life-line that terminated somewhere around his sixty-sixth year. If this was so, then it was but a short step to his horoscope to find a set of astrological death-crisis aspects around that year. If we consult Kitchener's horoscope, we find, in the first house of life, Neptune, ruler of the seas, in Pisces, the sign of water and seas. We have met the disastrous Neptune earlier herein. In this position in Kitchener's chart, it implies, among other things, he was a clever, plotting son-of-a-bitch — which I think few who are familiar with his biographical details will deny. We also find Mars and Venus in Kitchener's sixth house, the house of health.

Turning, then, to June 5, 1916, we find that Mars, among other things the planet of accidents, moves into direct opposition to Kitchener's natal Neptune in Pisces, with Neptune itself beginning its transit of Kitchener's natal Venus (the planet of well-being) in his house of health. We also find that in June 1916, the planet Mercury, ruling thinking and mind, was retrograde in Gemini — and badly aspected to his natal Neptune-Mars arrangement — indicating that during this period Kitchener would not be thinking clearly (which may be why he forgot Cheiro's prediction in the first place).

Now, astrologically speaking, these are rather skimpy enough aspects to predict a *death* from, seeing as how Mars would be opposite Kitchener's natal Neptune once approximately every three years. But they are sufficient enough to predict a death-crisis by water while at sea. So Cheiro must have drawn additional information from Kitchener's handprint (and possibly included direct psychic clues). Putting it all together, he predicted the death under the circumstances it did take place.

Cheiro was reading Kitchener's hidden psychic agenda, which included dangerous ocean-going situations once every three years. He cautioned Kitchener about going on the ocean, and should he avoid doing so he could also avoid the death-crisis situations that he would encounter "probably at sea."

Cheiro was able to give similar, accurate predictions (not all of them fatal) for many other historical figures: Nellie Melba, Prime Minister Gladstone, Pope Leo XIII, the Czar of Russia, King Leopold of Belgium, Sarah Bernhardt, Blanche Roosevelt, Mark Twain, and other luminaries, all of whom were eager to consult him since he could "peer" into hidden psychic agendas which they, themselves, could not.

As mentioned before, we believe our lives and our futures are always under our conscious, waking control, that we have absolute powers of choice and determination, and that we can create our futures based on these powers alone. Even in the best of times, this is clearly not the case. Yet we have a huge, huge investment in this postulate, and it is what we have been taught. But, if our psychic elements *can* inform us of the nature of times and events included in hidden agendas, does not this possibility need to be incorporated into our intellectual minds?

All of the examples given in the first part of this book represent psychic-type events people experienced, hardly any of which were under their conscious, waking control and, indeed, quite alien to their (and our) accepted standards regarding conscious choice and determination. It is clear their lives "turned" one way or another as a result of these invisible psychic agendas. Further, earlier I included the two "medical" tales to illustrate that our psychic powers can go far beyond just giving us clues as to our psychic agendas. Apparently, if revved up enough somehow, our psychic powers can *change* those agendas *completely*.

No poll has ever been taken to discover how many people sense their lives are being lived, for better or worse, according to some invisible psychic agenda. I think a poll of this kind would produce some meaningful statistics — which, in turn, would amply suggest why we should not remain psychic illiterates.

It is true we can create conscious agendas for ourselves and support them with our conscious powers of choice and determination. I am not at all suggesting we should give up our conscious powers of creating active agendas and simply toss ourselves into the psychic labyrinths around us (which is what some people do). But if there are invisible psychic agendas operating in and around us, certainly it is the epitome of stupidity and foolishness to think we can consciously construct a successful life without taking them into account.

All the evidence shows that *clever* people try to rise above their intellectual dysfunction in this regard and try to find out what these invisible psychic agendas contain — and in so doing, apparently, they learn how to work with them. It is also apparent that when they do *not* learn to work with them, certain disasters soon follow.

The various kinds of psychic elements we encountered in the first part of this book tried to give *clues* to the various people who experienced them as to what the invisible psychic agenda had in store. The obvious reason for these clues was to enable the conscious powers of choice and determination to take notice of these invisible agendas and do something about them. The people who failed in being able to take notice of these clues failed simply because of their own high levels of psychic illiteracy. Those smart enough to accept their clues benefitted from them. The common-sense message is clear enough.

SENSING ONE'S DESTINY

In 1978 I met a man who had one of these strange tales to tell concerning his hidden psychic agenda. In 1960 he had just finished his internship in brain surgery and was looking forward to a highly profitable career in this field. He had, as he said, "just gotten himself set up and money had begun to roll in" when he experienced a "ridiculous" dream in which he saw himself as a paleontologist digging up fossils in Africa — a dream which he soon forgot about.

He was well on his way to brain-surgery glory when he "chanced" to visit the American Museum of Natural History in New York, a place he had never been before. There he saw fossils galore, dinosaurs reconstructed, and the history of man being pieced together through the efforts of paleontologists. "I can't begin to tell you what I experienced," he told me. "I saw my purpose, what I was meant to do, what I *really* wanted to do. I wasn't exactly happy in brain surgery, but I had felt it was the thing to do because of its high rewards. I went back to school right away. Everyone thought I was completely nuts, but I was only sorry I had wasted time becoming a brain surgeon. And I remembered that dream!" He is now digging up fossils in Africa and is as happy as a bug in a rug. In life, to be able to be happy certainly accounts for something, doesn't it?

My own life is an obvious lesson in all this — to me, at least. Despite the many psychic-type events I experienced as a child and youngish adult, I was a dysfunctioning psychic illiterate until my fortieth year (I still am in some cases, as we have seen regarding my sister) and had very little real ideas about my own hidden psychic agendas.

When, in 1950, I entered the small Westminster College in Salt Lake City, what I really wanted to study was art. I had been painting since I was six. Painting turned me on (it still does). The smell of paint and canvas was ecstasy (it still is). Everyone had encouraged my artistic bent while I was a child and said, "my, how talented he is." Now, however, everyone said art would not be a profitable profession. My mother at first wanted me to be a priest, or at least a doctor. My girlfriend (we were planning to get married someday) thought I should aim for law, where the big bucks were. My college counsellor, who was also a history professor, thought I should take up history — "there would always be a demand for good history teachers," he said. (How wrong *he* was!)

It was all very confusing. Finally, I arranged an academic schedule that would allow me to carry a double major in art and biology, somewhat thinking I would eventually take up advanced biological research.

Not long after, I was on the front steps of the college's major building looking out over the campus, wondering what I really would become, or, more to the point, what would become of me. I experienced a sort of "change-of-mind-space," or sort of a "benevolent breath" — and *knew* that one day I would do something "big" in parapsychology.

Now, I can assure you that in Salt Lake City in 1950 no one knew or wanted to know diddly squat about psychic stuff, and the psych department had nothing but awful things to say about it. So, I paid no attention to this strange foresight, forgot it, and art and biology it was. After college, I joined the Army and spent three years in the Far East. After that, art won out. I came to New York, the world's art center, "to be a painter" and took a job at the U.N. to support myself until I "succeeded."

In 1969, nineteen years after I had experienced the change-of-mind-space on the front steps at college, I chanced to meet Cleve Backster at a party. This was a man who, at the time, was making a stir. Backster was a polygraph expert who had hooked up his office plants to lie-detectors and found they showed emotional responses when people had thoughts like, for example, putting a lighted match to the plants' leaves. In a sense, this meant that plants had consciousness — an idea considered preposterous by mainstream science. Reports of his work were creating quite a ruckus.

Next, I found myself in Backster's lab thinking thoughts towards plants and watching them respond on the lie-detector. It was fabulous. I was very good at it. When Dr. Karlis Osis at the American Society for Psychical Research heard of this, he invited me to come to the Society to try clairvoyant and "out-of-body" experiments. These turned out to be very successful, which led to parapsychologist Dr. Gertrude Schmeidler at City College, who suggested trying some PK-type experiments in which I would try to influence thermistors (temperature registers) by will alone.

When all these experiments were highly successful, the feathers hit the fan. When the media got hold of all this, their imagination took off. After all, if a person can affect a thermometer in a sealed vacuum in the next room, the implication was — as it was interpreted by many — that one might also trigger an atomic bomb by thought alone. Everything was possible.

In 1973 and 1974 these speculations and imaginations were given space throughout the media, including *Time*, *Newsweek*, *Horizon*, and even the noble mainstream magazine *The Smithsonian*, to name just a few. All featured my name prominently, where before I had been just an insignificant artist dwelling in New York with the rest of the twenty-five thousand aspiring artists dwelling therein. As parapsychologist Dr. Janet Mitchell noted: I had "burst over the parapsychology scene like a roman candle," and this "roman candle" continued for a twenty-year period during which I worked full-time in trying to uncover the secrets and mysteries that surround psychic stuff. The impact of my psychic career has, indeed, been "big." I'm saying this not to brag but to illustrate a point.

This point begins with the fact that for a long time I had no idea as to how all this came about. In 1950, I had no real idea of what psychic stuff was all about, yet during May of that year I "suffered" a premonition that one day I would work in parapsychology. In 1969, I had no wisp of an intention of working in parapsychology and certainly no idea that I could make a living for twenty years at so doing. Yet, a "chance" meeting with Cleve Backster led to other "chance" meetings, which led to other "chance" opportunities, which led into the strange limelight that seems to surround psychic matters. For a long time, I considered the whole affair to be composed of chance — since this is what it seemed to be.

I was not even aware that there was a problem with this interpretation until I read the account of Adrien Christian, whom we have met earlier in this book, who dreamt of saving a ship with his brother on it forty-seven years before the event transpired. Then, slowly, I began to put two and two together. The Chance Theory certainly did not explain *at all* how I could have had my own moment of future insight on the front steps of my alma mater back in 1950 which hinted at a "big" career that did not begin until 1969. Indeed, I had quite forgotten about this future insight, anyway, and in the interim period between 1950 and 1969, getting into parapsychology was the farthest thing from my mind. You see, for one thing, everyone said there was no money in it. (I now know differently.)

Now, I must ask you, dear reader. Has the situation regarding the existence of hidden psychic agendas become contextually clearer for you? Do you see the problem — and the opportunity — here? Thousands of people experience glimpses of some future thing which then takes place, often with many years separating the glimpse from the actual event. Our scientific disciplines have taught us to regard the *whole* of this as superstition, or at most, as coincidence and chance. Garbage! And a stinking pile of it at that.

CONSTRUCTIVE AND DESTRUCTIVE ELEMENTS IN HIDDEN PSYCHIC AGENDAS

Now, to expand our contextual understanding of hidden psychic agendas a little more, we can observe that they contain two major lines in them. The first line concerns those times and events we will encounter that will be beneficial to us. The second concerns those times and events that will be inimical. In keeping with the ancient, historical psychical traditions, I will henceforth refer to the first as the agendas of the *Fortunes* (or Destinies), and the second as the agendas of the *Misfortunes* (or Fates).

My experience with people more or less convinces me that they "know," at some sub-level, that they *do* have hidden psychic agendas. Many have even told me, totally unprompted, that they feel we are being somehow shaped by the future — which does equate to hidden shaping plans. When people try to find out "what the future holds," what they are actually doing is trying to plug into the agendas that are yet invisible to them.

These agendas resemble confusing labyrinths until we realize there are two major kinds of threads running through them: the Fortunate threads and the Misfortunate threads. People are quite willing to find out where their threads of Fortune are leading, but they usually recoil at looking at their threads of Misfortune. Yet it is these Misfortune threads that can bring down *any* house of Fortune — *if* we are not prepared to cope and/or avoid Misfortunate times and events and the adversities they entail.

Another complexity is this — and it is a real lulu: I know of no one whose hidden psychic agenda does not intermesh, interlink, interconnect, or intersect with the agendas of others — in fact, many, many others. When the famous Trappist monk, Thomas Merton, wrote his best-selling book entitled *No Man is an Island*, he touched upon one of the deepest, most powerful mainstream currents in the psychic realms. Simply put, none of us are "islands" completely independent of others — although it is true that certain individuals can and do become more powerful "peninsulas." Still, even these individuals are linked to the activities of many, many others.

The idea of a hidden psychic agenda is complex enough. But when one tries to conceive of *interconnected* hidden agendas, the picture quickly turns into one of very complex labyrinths, indeed — so complex that our first gut response might be that we are not up to the task of wending our way through them.

Yet, as we shall see in more detail ahead, with a little effort on our part we can do a few things to get at least a partial grasp on all these labyrinthine twists and turns.

First, we must note that the labyrinths contain two major threads or trends — those of the Fortunes (construction) and those of the Misfortunes (destruction).

Second, we must realize that our personal hidden psychic agenda intersects or is interconnected with those of many others. We will elaborate upon this point in the next chapter.

OUR HIDDEN PSYCHIC AGENDAS

- We are now in a position to confirm what people have sensed throughout the ages: that our lives are somehow associated with hidden psychic agendas.

- We can observe that if our intellects are psychically literate enough to be sensitized to and accept psychic clues being pumped out by our direct-sensing systems, and if we are sensible enough to *want* to consult some of the psychic arts and crafts, these hidden agendas can be altered by volitional decision-making.

- We should observe that our socially-induced psychic dysfunction often leads to unfortunate results.

SUGGESTED PRACTICAL EXERCISES THAT WILL HELP IN EXPANDING PSYCHIC LITERACY

o In an earlier suggested exercise, it was pointed out that talking with people about psychic clues they failed to respond to (and what happened as a result) would help broaden the intellectual platforms needed to enhance psychic literacy. We are at a point now where you might ask the same people if they sensed the Event involved was contained in some sort of invisible schedule — and if that schedule might have been alterable if they had done something about it.

o Make a list of people that are important to you. Take some time to study the list and try to sense whether your relationships with them have developed out of Fortunate or Misfortunate elements. It is suggested you do not tell them you are doing this. Henceforth, try to be alert to psychic promptings that might have something to do with these relationships. I can almost guarantee some of these promptings will take place.

NOTE: We do not, of course, experience psychic promptings all the time. But you might begin to consider the implications of any that might strike you. Many psychic promptings we do experience might have nothing to do with us personally, as we have seen in the Aberfan Event narrated in earlier. Your decision to act on any of these promptings is, of course, a matter of your own volitional choice.

* * *

I'll close this present chapter now with the comment that the more I've learned about psychic stuff, the more difficult it has become for me to imagine *why* we moderns became an anti-psychic society. The only possible explanation is that *behind* our more local, more immediate personal psychic agendas lurk larger hidden *master agendas* or *super-agendas* that have to do with the nature of the times and events in which we live. And, yes, in my opinion, anti-psychism obviously belongs to certain psychic energies and forces that trend toward destruction. For the "turning off" of our psychic capabilities surely leads in that direction. But, again, I'm getting ahead of myself.

XV

Psychic Linkages

At this point, we need to change our contexts a little and begin to head for some technical stuff.

In 1969, when I began parapsychological research in earnest, I joined several research groups whose goals, generally speaking, were focused on two aspects: getting psychic stuff to appear in laboratory settings and then trying to observe *how* the stuff did its thing *within* terms (this is very important) that our present-day science might accept.

This sounds simple enough, doesn't it? Well, you'd just as well try to get milk out of turnips. First of all, apparently our psychic elements do not give any high priority to appearing in laboratories to be scrutinized within the terms of scientific theories that have them stereotyped as pathological superstitions. And so they seldom do, and then not in any great plenitude.

Second, parapsychologists have psychic stuff stereotyped as "paranormal" powers of mind — and not correctly identified as powers of Life itself. This salient mistake of interpretation took place quite early in psychical research, not long after it was formally founded in 1882 — and the uninspected assumption that our psychic potentials represented paranormal powers of *mind* has never been revised since.

Thus, parapsychological research efforts generally have labored under the following burden: the necessity of discovering *acceptable* scientific explanations that would fit paranormal powers of mind into the limited and limiting theories of scientific materialism which — as a philosophy and for no real scientific reasons at all — has from its start already decided psychic stuff was irrational nonsense. This is something like trying to build the Golden Gate Bridge out of toilet paper. But many people thought it could be done and, with no end of parapsychological contrivances and strange logic, proceeded to try.

This rather unrewarding commitment had not a few strange outcomes, one of which, I think, we should point out to help break apart the stereotypes that emerged from them.

During its first forty years (1882 to approximately 1925) psychical researchers randomly investigated psychic stuff of all kinds. The laboratory concept had not really solidified, and researchers generally were willing to interact with psychic stuff wherever and in whomever they found it. During this period there was a great deal of active psychic stuff going on in society.

Because of the excessive presence in society then of phenomenal psychic stuff and because of the early researchers' willingness to interact at a human level, the early archives of psychic research are filled to the teeth with excellent reports on various kinds of psychic stuff. But, from the start of formal psychical research, the researchers were all aware that they had science to deal with. And so they began to avoid getting involved with the varieties of psychic-type stuff especially hated by anti-psychic scientism.

Among the things that should be avoided, they thought, was the whole of occultism and the traditional psychic tools and professions which, among other things, included astrology, numerology, palmistry, mesmerism (a type of hypnosis), shamanism, and prophecy. All these irritated scientism to no end. And, so, into the "unscientific" bin they went. No "respectable" psychical researcher or parapsychologist has ever studied any of these in any formal sense, and they avoid doing so to this day.

Now, the magnitude of this prejudice is not apparent until you realize that perhaps as much as eighty-five percent of all psychic stuff the world has ever known has emanated from occultism and the traditional psychic arts and crafts, with the remaining fifteen percent emanating from spontaneous occurrences. Thus, right from the beginning, in their attempts to align their goals to ideologies of anti-psychic scientism, psychical researchers lopped off eighty-five percent of their source materials. This is now like trying to build the Golden Gate Bridge out of fifteen rolls of toilet paper. It's just not going to happen. So, eventually psychical research collapsed, much to the I-told-you-so smirks of anti-psychic scientists.

However, in the 1930s, psychical research was resurrected under the umbrella term of "parapsychology," mostly under the energetic auspices of the famous Dr. J.B. Rhine.

Parapsychology's basic premise is to rigorously employ scientific methods in the study of psychic stuff, with the idea that if science's own methods are so used and succeed, science would be *forced* to accept psychic stuff as real. Since the chief method science depends on is continuously repeatable statistical analysis, this, then, was to be the new tool to research psychic stuff. Meanwhile, parapsychology continued the former embargo on occultism and the traditional psychic arts and crafts.

All might have been well and good *if* psychic stuffs would decide to continuously repeat themselves for purposes of statistical analysis — which it is now clearly known they refuse to do. But. Parapsychologists *have* managed to accumulate sufficient, partial statistical data that would readily be acceptable under normal scientific standards — if they came from practically any other field than parapsychology. Science adamantly continues to stereotype parapsychology as philosophically dissonant to its major thesis, that of scientific materialism.

Since parapsychology accepts science as its sovereign power, it has never formed a power base of its own (as has, say, psychology). It remains a pouting satellite begging acknowledgement from its sovereign and trying to appease its scientific demands.

In rejecting eighty-five percent of its source materials, formal psychic research essentially has lost contact with eighty-five percent of the human psychic-stuff principles it claims it is researching. It is really very hard to complete the puzzle with eighty-five percent of the pieces missing. As a result, parapsychology has never been able to create an overall philosophy — a greater picture — of its own that makes any sense at all.

TRACKING DOWN THE ESSENTIAL PURPOSE OF PSYCHIC STUFF

I should point out here that I am speaking from hindsight born of long experience. When I first got into formal parapsychological research in 1969, it never dawned on me that I was stepping into a large situation whose fundamental premises were themselves incorrect. At the time, I agreed with the hypothesis that the scientific method was the only way to go. I agreed with the supposition that occultism (which I had studied deeply beginning about the age of nine) and the traditional psychic tools and professions were not amenable to scientific method. And, at any rate, the early experiments I was a subject in were more than successful — in this case, success meaning repeatability, which led to my so-called "superpsychic" status.

But this superpsychic status, combined with my earlier scientific training, and the fact that I could blend somewhat into the parapsychological-cum-scientific woodwork, brought invitations to pursue research at bigger and better research centers with dollar/man-hours of my own to do something with.

Now, there are five general areas in which researching psychic stuff can be pursued: (1) theory, (2) statistics, (3) trying to isolate the biological-mechanistic sources of psychic stuff, (4) chasing psychic phenomena around, and (5) practical applications. I decided to focus on the last, not only because better research proposals could be written, but because it was an empty field — a field which had not been pursued by any of the earlier psychic researchers.

Simply put, no one had any idea at all what psychic stuff could be *used* for.

The picture was this: all efforts were either directed toward legitimately insinuating psychic stuff into science and/or trying to fulfill science's demand that a biological-mechanistic explanation be found that would "allow" for the existence of psychic stuff. This was where the commitments were — and most still are — in the United States; but not, for example, in the Soviet Union, which apparently had aimed *its* psychic research at practical applications.

Now, when you go for the practical applications of something, to a large extent (but not completely) you can leave scientific polemics and imbroglios behind. Generally speaking, people are usually interested in something if uses for it can be found, whether or not science can account for it.

And so in looking for possible practical applications of psychic stuff, the first question to ask is what purposes and functions it serves in the first place. It is clear that clairvoyance, if it was good enough, could serve espionage functions — which certainly would be a practical application in which numerous people would have a lot of interest. But, if this *was* possible, it would only be bending a psychic function to a human design. This would still leave the large issue unresolved, which is this: psychic processes exist naturally in everyone. What is their overall purpose in doing so?

At the time, I certainly had no answer. But it seemed to me that if we were to be able to access psychic stuff for practical purposes, we would certainly need a much larger overview of them than was available from the stereotyped approaches characteristic of American parapsychology and traditionally popular belief networks.

In the winter of 1974 I was invited to go to Washington as a consultant to give a ten-minute briefing (for potential clients who must remain unidentified) during which I would give my ideas for new directions that might be pursued. I spent three of these strategic minutes outlining what I have just said above, stating that while the search for convincing scientific evidence must, of course, continue, trying to convince anti-psychic networks of a psychic reality represented a dismal catch-22 situation.

During the next five minutes, I outlined what I saw was the larger problem. I pointed out that if we took the largest overview possible, it could be seen that the psychic realms and parapsychological research altogether did not make any common sense, instead representing a diverse collection of conflicting, unassimilated facts, beliefs, legends, myths, and theories. I pointed out that even scientists need to think from a common-sense platform, and that no one really knows what to do about something that does not, no matter how voluminous research archives become, make any sense at all.

I proposed a project that would begin to collect and evaluate all available information about the psychic realms, with the primary goal of trying to fit it all into a sensible larger picture and with the secondary goal of trying to discover possible practical applications. I pointed out that no one in parapsychology had undertaken such a project, but that it definitely was needed. I said two years would be required to do this and gave a large budget for the project, broken down into dollar/man-hours. This left two minutes for questions, and I narrowed my eyes, pursed my lips, readying myself to defend my arguments.

The room was silent. Finally, one question was asked: would two years be enough? I said that three would be better, for it might take the better part of a year to write a final report.

The potential clients said they would get back to me. Three months later, much to my everlasting surprise, the three-year project was approved. A small staff was assembled, and thus began the largest evaluation of psychic and related matters ever undertaken.

At the beginning of this project, I and others involved actually believed that when all the facts were in, they would fall naturally into place, and we could then provide the sense so far missing. But, by the middle of the second year, a dismal realization had set in. All the facts taken together were not going to make sense. You could take history, the occult, the mystical, psychical research reports, psychology, aesthetics, the spiritual, science, consciousness studies, and even religions, and more, more, more — and still the whole of them would not fit together into a unifying picture that portrayed anything sensible about psychic phenomena.

My project was going to fail, and embarrassingly so. What to do now?

We sat around a large table, brainstorming, drinking wine (good wine), and feeling sorry for ourselves among our massive piles of books, xeroxed manuscripts, shelves of journals and unpublished reports, trivia, and so forth — awaiting the emergence of a new idea that would put us in touch with the links missing. We made crude jokes about missing links and drew lines between one kind of psychic phenomenon to another, until we saw links everywhere.

Just look at all this, we said. There *are* links everywhere!

In this rather inadvertent way, through a haze of good wine and toppling piles of books, the concept of *Psychic Linkage* gradually clarified itself.

The thing *all* psychic phenomena have in common, no matter what else they might be, is that they function as links between the human mind-body organism and something else.

Intuition is a link between the person and something he or she needs to know. *Clairvoyance* is a link between distant places and events. *Telepathy* is a link between people and, even, animals. *Precognition* and *prophecy* form links with the future. *Postcognition* is a link with the past. *Psychokinesis* is a link through which some kind of energy flows to create physical effects. *Past-life "memory"* is a link with past lives. *Apparitions* are links with different dimensions. *Spirituality* is link with harmony (heaven). *The Devil* is a link to disharmony. *Dreams* and *visions* and *inspired ideas* are links to the unconscious, which, in turn, is linked to past and future events.

You can go on and on. The whole comes together within the concept of *Psychic Linkage*.

Like the fish swimming in water, the last thing the fish will probably notice is the water. We are swimming in a sea of physical *and psychic* linkages, an environment of connections so omnipresent that *unless* we turn our attention to deliberately trying to perceive the environment in detail we probably will not.

The flaw in psychical research and parapsychology is that psychic phenomena are considered things in themselves, when actually they are the *results* of linkages.

Now, this *is* a completely new idea, although it seems instantly familiar.

The image we have of human beings is that each individual is a separate biological unit, independent of all others. This is, of course, true to a degree. But at a certain point, our separateness gives over to communal linkages that *join* us together with our visible and invisible environments, with others, with past, present, and future events, with other dimensions.

The greatest missing link is that our concept of ourselves is not correct. We are not independent, biological organisms. We are *biopsychic* organisms linked together in many ways, including ways that are psychic.

The concept of *psychic linkage* is a veritable workhorse. With it, sense can be made out of *all* disparate psychic phenomena. The whole of psychic phenomena — from mother-child telepathic bonding to astrology will fall into place. Without it, psychic phenomena will not make sense.

As it happened, about the time our final report on this project was ready, in other fields, especially at the cutting edge of physics and in the ecology movements, the concept of the *interconnectedness* of all things had begun its rise into popular prominence and became a hot buzz word. Interconnectedness means linkage. All things are, in some form, linked to each other and interdependent on each other. When linkages break down, so does interconnectedness.

The place where we today are learning to see that interconnectedness means the most (outside of advancing physics) regards our precious biosphere, Earth's delicate environment. Today, almost everyone understands that our biosphere is made up of interdependent links that must be preserved if our biosphere is to maintain itself in a healthy, positive state. You can adapt this analogy directly as a description of our psychic environment. When our psychic links are in shambles, we are unhappy and suffer. When our psychic links are up and working, we are happy and creative.

If you think this through, it is possible to see that psychic links can be inactive or active. Sometimes they become spontaneously active, as in the examples given earlier. Achieved psychics have activated certain psychic links on a more permanent basis. Intuitives also experience linkages. Information flows along psychic linkages. In our Information Age, we have come to understand that everything, no matter what it is, is first and foremost some kind of "information" package. Since this is the case, we in our Information Age are now in the best possible place to begin to understand psychic stuff and initiate a new intellectual synthesis for it.

All psychic phenomena are information linkage-exchanges of some kind. Telepathy is not a thing-in-itself. It is a particular kind of information exchange. Clairvoyance is not a thing-in-itself. It is a particular kind of information exchange. The prophetic events given earlier herein are not things-in-themselves but information exchanges.

We live in a universe of networks of information exchanges of all kinds. And our psychic interconnectedness is our key to entering those networks. Communication among all beings and Life's collective functioning are the apparent and easily demonstrated *purpose* of all our psychic potentials, including the psychic arts and crafts. If you put psychic linkage together with information theory, it is easy enough to see that a new day of human psychic endeavor has begun. The fundamental key to this new day requires only that we shift our incorrect images of the human from the past ones that portrays us *only* as independent biological organisms to ones that see us as interlinked biopsychic entities.

None of the biological knowledge we have gained needs be set aside or lost. But the biopsychic hypothesis will open doors to new concepts about ourselves. It is really very difficult and counterproductive to try to comprehend our psychic "parts" as things independent of our biology and vice versa. All the available facts of biological and psychical experience taken together easily substantiate the biopsychic hypothesis and show we are biopsychic organisms.

If this is so, then it ought to be relatively easy for us to take volitional steps to sense our psychic linkages with others and with invisible potentials. In fact, most people *do* sense these linkages — and, of course, always have. But our Western sciences have avoided tackling the implications for reasons already stated. But contemporary Soviet scientists have not. They have even evolved a term for these linkages — bio-communication, of which we shall learn more later.

PSYCHIC LINKAGES

o   We can observe, as we already have, that there is a yawning gap between the ideological directions of "scientific" scientism and real human experience. In real human experience, linkages, both biological and psychical, have been sensed from times immemorial.

o   We have every right, based on real human experience, to assume that if interconnecting linkages were pursued in active, open-minded research, a new, more complete and accurate image of humanity would emerge — one including the existence of psychic linkages.

SUGGESTED PRACTICAL EXERCISES THAT WILL HELP IN EXPANDING PSYCHIC LITERACY

o   The moment one's intellect accepts the existence of interconnecting psychic linkages, a great shift toward psychic literacy takes place — for the intellect can suddenly "see" what psychic stuff is all about. Therefore, take some social time and ask others if they are aware of psychic linkages, such as parent-child telepathic bonding, lovers' telepathic bonding, sensing vibes, and so forth. Remember that the intellect cannot understand something it has no "programs" for, and it acquires these by *observing* activities in others.

o   If you are already aware, or become aware, of such psychic linkages, begin listing them. You will want to identify what kinds they are. Those kinds which are absent will suggest areas you may want to work on.

* * *

Well, we've now reached the point where (sigh) we must undertake to try to unravel a very vexing problem: this has to do with *what* psychic perception is, or what it consists of. Few books do not contain at least one challenging chapter. But we want to try to give our intellects some "program refinements" without which it may not be enabled to hone its perceptual patterns. Remember: "enable" means "to EMPOWER."

XVI

What is Psychic Perception, Anyway?

I'd now like to share with you another of those curious gaps in the study and understanding of psychic stuff to date.

I own about a thousand books on psychic stuff, over five thousand psychic research papers and reports, and a very extensive clippings file. I even own numerous books which do not specifically focus on psychic stuff, but, in various ways utilize the term "psychic perception." Practically everyone uses the term once in a while. "Oh, yes, *that's* psychic perception."

Well, nowhere in all this literature can I find a definition for "psychic perception." You might expect that the *Encyclopedia of Occultism and Parapsychology*, which otherwise contains fifty-one listings beginning with "psychic," might have one. But, no. *Parapsychology: Sources of Information* doesn't have one either.

Am I missing something?

I guess we assume we know enough about what psychic perception is so as not to need a descriptive definition for it. But, is this not somewhat like asking our intellects to drive the psychic car without having any spark plugs? The fact of the matter is that our intellects make their *connections* by having a grasp on what something means.

Get this picture. Our intellects hear the term "psychic perceptions." They then begin searching their files for its definition. Oops, can't find one. The next best thing to do is search the files again for something that *seems* to fit. In this way, then, four billion people can come up with four billion different "definitions." And, still, the intellect doesn't know what it's supposed to *do*, since there is no exact definition to guide it in the first place.

Well, you may say, are not clairvoyance, ESP, telepathy, precognition, etc., forms of psychic perception? Well, yes — or is it no, or maybe? You see, we don't know what those are, either. They are labels for assumed processes whose differences, as we have seen earlier, even parapsychologists cannot describe with any conviction.

One cannot use terms that define nothing to help define "psychic perception," of which we have no definition at all.

You might view all this as unimportant quibbling. After all, we do see psychic perception taking place all the time, do we not? No, we do not. What we see are the *results* of it. For me, there have been at least two reasons for viewing all this not as unimportant, but as something serious.

In the first place, as I understand intellect, it is capable of precision functioning, which is to say, capable of enormous powers — but only if its functioning is precise or can be made so.

Second, when one sets about, as I have done in the past, writing proposals for some kind of psychic research grants to the tune of over a million dollars, one can easily encounter potential sponsors (some of them quite intelligent) who have said, well, we will be very happy to consider your proposal if you can tell us what psychic perception is. At this point, as you might imagine, the total absence of a definition takes on some meaning that the lack of it might not have in everyday situations. When to have or not to have millions actually turns on the definition of a term, and that definition is nowhere to be found, its absence takes on some very large dimensions.

One is reduced to staring, rather moodily, at this empty hole. Well, what's to be done? First of all, get ready to grunt one's way through the yawning hole of a quandary and try to see what lies at its bottom — if it has one.

At the time, a first rather logical step suggested itself: to try to discover what "perception" means — and a great deal of time was spent delving into this matter. Seems easy enough, doesn't it? "Perception" is defined as a mental image, an awareness of the elements of environment through physical sensation, and physical sensation interpreted in the light of experience. All this *seems* clear enough; but, in fact, one ends up on the same shoals of confusion, for in any last analysis these are *results* of processes, not the processes themselves.

I nearly split my brain in working through the rather great volume of scientific reports trying to determine the nature of those processes. Scientists do understand some of the processes involved. But still, they have not yet come to understand *why they result* in perception. In a certain sense, one cannot really blame psychical researchers for not having come up with a definition for "psychic perception" when their brothers and sisters in the perceptual sciences have not really succeeded in coming up with one for "perception" either.

After about three years of pursuing this possibility, it became clear we were not going to get anywhere with it. Now, I happen to be an Ayn Rand enthusiast, the philosopher-author whose caustic but penetrating eye espied some factors in society normally overlooked by a lot of people. In her philosophical tracts and in her best-selling novels *The Fountainhead* and *Atlas Shrugged*, Rand observed that when one is not getting anywhere by following a certain line of thinking, one should "check one's [basic] premises." Remembering this, some bells started going off.

Here we were, ensnarled in the difficulties of identifying perception. Could it be that "perception" was the wrong word, and hence the wrong way of thinking about all this?

As it happened at the time, I was studying the psychic produce of one of this century's most famous clairvoyants, the Dutchman Gerard Croiset. In the terms of the way parapsychologists go about their work, Croiset's psychic proficiencies have been viewed through the usual self-induced fogs of doubt on the part of the researchers. But this doubt was not shared by policemen and other investigators — for Croiset's proficiencies were, according to hundreds who solicited the use of them, turned to good, constructive, i.e., practical use. For, you see, Croiset turned his proficiencies toward helping solve or resolve murders and sex crimes, thefts, to finding missing people and animals, lost objects, and helping to resolve situations regarding fossils and old manuscripts. He was very much concerned with the welfare of children, and in this area his proficiencies seemed to work the best.

I was especially impressed with his proficiency in locating lost children, alive or dead, and was studying the following case at the time I was wrestling with the definition of perception. On Thursday, April 11, 1963, at 4:30 p.m., a young boy named Wimpje Slee had disappeared in the town of Voorburg, outside The Hague. Hundreds of townspeople had looked for the boy, dragging the canals, searching everywhere — to no avail. The boy's uncle finally contacted Croiset, who promptly told him that the youth had drowned, and that his body would be found near a bridge. The next day (April 18), Croiset gave further information. He drew a sketch of the landmarks he saw and indicated that Wimpje had drowned near a small house that had a slanted weathercock on its roof. He added that the body was no longer there but *would* be found on

Tuesday, April 23 between two bridges near the house with the weathercock.

Meanwhile, the Dutch press, well aware of Croiset's psychic proficiencies, published (on April 18 and on April 22) his impressions — thereby enabling readers to check them out. Everyone went out and tried to locate the house with the bent weathercock. At the crack of dawn on Tuesday morning, the house was located and the unfortunate Wimpje Slee was found floating in the Vliet Canal precisely between two bridges near it. Now there are dozens of canals and bridges in Voorburg, so some effort was made to find out how many also had a house with a slanted weathercock between them. None were found. It was also observed that the clairvoyant had predicted the body would be found not on the eleventh or thirteenth day, but on the twelfth — which it was. Croiset added another success to his already long list.[1]

As mentioned above, I was studying Croiset's proficiencies at a time concurrent with our perception imbroglio. I said to myself: "Let's take some kind of perception for granted. But what had Croiset actually done, besides perceive?" After all, if perception includes mental images, well, then we can actually perceive anything we want — for instance, our imaginings, our fears, our fantasies, our visualizations, our fictions, and so forth. Viewed this way, Croiset had *not* perceived any of these. What, then, had he perceived? And especially what had he perceived that all other psychic-types who are proficient also perceive?

It took the better part of a month for my intellect to grunt its way through the possibilities. Finally, early one morning while drinking my coffee and while sitting in my usual cloud of meditative cigar smoke, my intellect finally did its thing. What Gerard Croiset had done was: not *just* perceive, but perceive *the truth*.

PSYCHIC APPERCEPTION

Whoa, now! Perceive the truth? Is this a truism, or a profound discovery? What constitutes truth in human affairs is something that most people are not at all prepared to inspect too closely, although most assume their own intellectualized versions of it are the correct ones — and they usually don't like others fiddling with theirs.

---

[1] Pollack, Jack Harrison, Croiset: The Clairvoyant, The Quality Book Club, London, 1965, pp. 98-99.

Having produced this astonishing resolution, my intellect set to work assimilating it and producing further implications. I actually could sit back, smoke my ubiquitous cigars, and *mentally watch* my intellect putting all the implications together into a new information package.

First, look at the history of psychic stuff. For example, recall the Events provided in the lengthy background-information part of this book. In no case did any of the psychic elements involved "tell" anything other than the truth.

Second, and since the ancients knew more than we do now about psychic stuff, *they* must have had a term that specifically referred to Truth-Telling in its psychic sense. Indeed they had; an archaic one that is now almost completely lost in the archives of human psychic history. This term being: *Soothsaying*, i.e., Truth-Saying and/or Truth-Seeing.

And there we were — now more or less mired in a term that was certain to further enflame the already flammable psychic frontiers. The direct implication was that psychics and psychic arts and crafts practitioners could, if they were proficient, espy truth and, further, speak it. I dare say, this was something that a great many people would prefer *others* never find out. The social-philosophical-religious-scientific implications were awesome — something like having to make a mad dash through an endless forest colonized by millions of bees' nests.

But almost immediately, several things became clear that otherwise seemed occluded in perpetual mystery, one of which was why psychic stuff was so *feared*. It's easy enough to see that hardly anyone wanted soothsayers running loose. Hence, it became somewhat clear why concerted and organized efforts have been mounted to put truth-sayers out of business.

Consider, for example, what has gone down in history as the Salem Witch Hunt whose instigators, as the same history show, saw the "advisability" of getting rid of numerous Salem women who, inexplicably, had suddenly developed truth-saying capabilities.

Consider the case of the unfortunate Friar Girolano Savonarola (1452-1498), one of the first luminaries of the Italian Renaissance, whose ultimate end occurred when he was hung and burnt. This dedicated Christian (at least as regards his interpretation of the Christian purpose) rose to some prominence in Florence by vociferously pointing out the corruption within the Church and thus in society. This was not a small matter, but since people were doing it all the time anyway, this alone was not enough to launch a deadly persecution against him.

Savonarola also, from his pulpits and monasteries, crossed the line between religious and secular matters and rose to become a secular-religious leader in Italy. People were crossing this line all the time, anyway, and to be sure it was something to be borne with circumspection. But Savonarola, the past, present, and future firing his mind, was also a prophet, and an accurate one at that. As a result of his visions and prophecies, he announced (correctly so) the approaching deaths of a few kings, military leaders, and a pope, which was enough to unnerve said parties; he then went on to advise the populace that they need not take the policies and goals of these parties seriously, since soon they would leave their mortal responsibilities to others.

This was too much! Because of the "unwholesome agitation" these advices aroused, persecution began almost immediately, not because those in power doubted the prophecies, but because the population had no need to be informed of such inconvenient truths — even if they *were* truths.[2]

Consider that even today, as we approach the third millennium with the enlightenment we are supposed to have acquired, there has arisen in our postmodern times an *organized network* of self-appointed, anti-psychic "police" whose energetic goal is to debunk not only psychic stuff but anything that (to them) smells of the "paranormal." Why, in our democracy where people are supposed to be able to possess inalienable rights to their own minds, has such an organization arisen? If self-proclaimed psychics were *always* wrong, not only would no one care if they existed, but they would be out of business. No, the great fear regarding psychics is not that they are sometimes wrong, but that they are sometimes right.

And there is another implication, a rather staggering one. Its background is this. In the early 1940s, the parapsychologist, Dr. Gertrude Schmeidler, discovered what henceforth became known as the "sheep-goat effect." As a result of lengthy testing, repeated successfully in several laboratories, it was discovered that people who believed (the "sheep") in ESP scored higher in clairvoyant experiments than those who did not believe (the "goats") in it.[3] No

---

2 Roeder, Ralph, "Savonarola," in The Man of the Renaissance, The Viking Press, New York, 1933.
3 See Schmeidler, Gertrude, "Predicting Good and Bad Scores in a Clairvoyance Experiment: A Final Report," The Journal of the American

one really knew what to make of this discovery. But in the light of the truth-saying implications, was it then to be considered that people who believe in ESP also possessed higher levels of dealing with truths, and that those who did not believe in truths had lower levels of coping with them and thus also had disbeliefs in psychic stuff? You see, implications — uncomfortable ones!

At any rate, obviously, one could not suddenly reactivate a term so archaic as "soothsaying," place it in grant soliciting proposals, and hope to get anywhere thereby. Did a more up-to-date, less flammable term exist? As usual, into the dictionary I plowed — until I found the "right" term: *apperception*.

This is a curious term, one definitely not in popular usage. But since the dictionary says it is not archaic, presumably it is safe enough to utilize it. "Apperception," as it is presently conceived, means "introspective self-consciousness," "the mind's perception of itself as a conscious agent," "a condition in which we are conscious of our own existence and consciousness of our own perceptions," "perception of the sum of things," and "*the recognition of truths*" [emphasis added].

As our months rolled by, it became clearer and clearer that apperception, as truth-seeing, must replace our dependence on the term "perception" in psychic matters. The most fundamental implication regards our direct-sensing systems in that they, by the evidence available, function as "truth-informers."

The second, most fundamental implication is this: if our intellects are not programmed or are misprogrammed regarding sensing the truth-sums of things, then intellectual barriers almost certainly will be erected to filter out inconvenient truth-sums. Were it not for the fact that we can easily observe these filters in people everywhere, this argument might not have much credible ground to stand on. There is even a very ancient, directly applicable adage: "people hear only what they want to hear."

THE FUNDAMENTAL SECRET OF PSYCHIC PROFICIENCY

It appears that our capability of acknowledging and coping with truth is, somehow, directly meaningful to "learning" how to work

---

Society for Psychical Research, 37 (October 1943), pp. 210-221; see also Bhadra, B.H. "The Relationship of Test Scores to Belief in ESP," The Journal of Parapsychology, 30, no. 1 (March 1966), pp. 1-7.

with our psychic elements. The fact that this is an obscure factor, and one never given shape before this present book, is irrelevant. When we do see high-stage psychic proficiencies at work (judgeable, we must remind ourselves, only by their accuracy), their products *always* are truth-seeing and truth-saying.

Therefore, if someone has a low level of psychic proficiency or, perhaps, none at all, such a person should not bewail his or her psychic "inadequacies," but rather suspect the existence of barriers installed in the intellect by self and society that block "truth processing." Certainly it is possible to conceive that the direct-sensing systems of people who are sort of averse to truth-seeing will have to work very hard to deposit some bit of psychic input into their intellects. At any rate, in the context of this present book, the intellect can now get some idea of what to work on.

Altogether, this comprises one of those worrying revolutionary-type things that may or may not fall on fertile soil. I'll be content to leave these implications for others to draw out in their own way, if they choose to do so.

The term "psychic perception" will now be retired from usage in what remains of this book.

WHAT IS PSYCHIC PERCEPTION, ANYWAY?

o We can observe that no definition for "psychic perception" has ever been evolved, even in the disciplines devoted to the study of psychic stuff.

o We should begin to observe that psychic apperception refers to the most communal element identifiable in all successful psychic "sightings," i.e., truth-seeing.

o We must observe that truth-seeing (of any kind) is a sensitive issue and comport ourselves with something akin to caution.

SUGGESTED PRACTICAL EXERCISES THAT WILL HELP IN EXPANDING PSYCHIC LITERACY

o   Since it is much easier to see truth-avoiding and aversions to truth in others than it is in ourselves, and since we do so all the time anyway, try to do so now more deliberately. This will undoubtedly aid in helping your own intellect to locate its own anti-truth barriers. Bear in mind that we do get somewhat upset when we observe others avoiding truths, and it may be that short phases of "agitation" will be experienced. If you understand that they represent intellectual "renovations" along these lines, and that they will shortly subside when the "work" is done, they can be tolerated with some emotional detachment.

* * *

With the meaning of psychic apperception now somewhat in place, we can make a more in-depth foray into the complexities of the psychic labyrinths.

XVII

The Psychic Arts and Crafts

KNOWLEDGE IS POWER

We are familiar with many "Ages:" the Dark Ages, the Age of Superstition, the Age of the Enlightenment, the Age of Reason, the Age of Science and Technology, the Modern Age, the Nuclear Age, the Space Age, and so forth. Napoleon, Elizabeth, and Victoria, such a big impact did they make on the world's consciousness, had entire (but rather short) Ages named after *them*.

Francis Bacon (1561-1626) might have had an Age named after him, too — the Baconian Age; otherwise maybe known as the Age of Intellectualism. During his lifetime, he enjoyed many honors under Elizabeth I and James I. Although he made no discoveries of his own, and, as *The Columbia Encyclopedia* says, really had little influence on science, his character exhibited, as *The Columbia Encyclopedia* says, an extraordinary combination of the philosopher's disinterested love of truth and the politician's love of advancement. The famous author, Alexander Pope (1688-1744) called him "the wisest, brightest, meanest of mankind." Bacon wrote, among other tracts, *The New Atlantis*, a vision of scientific utopia — the possibility of which has vivified scientists and pseudo-scientists alike to this day.

Bacon enunciated, in three words, a concept that burst like a nova of illuminating, intellectual light right at the beginning of the Age of Reason. Ever since, this concept has galvanized countless intellectual furnaces, indeed justifying them as sources of the necessary heat via which mankind might puff its way into future utopias.

These three words were: *Knowledge is power.*

These three words are so axiomatic for us today that their validity can hardly be challenged — without one seeming to have lost one's marbles. Yet, up to Bacon's time, and although knowledge was accepted as pertinent to any kind of power, no one would have thought of exclusively equating power and knowledge. In fact, this would have appeared a simplistic naivete since power derived from many sources besides just knowledge.

But Bacon's somewhat erroneous synthesis laid the foundations upon which was constructed the intellectual idea that the more knowledge one managed to accumulate, the more power one would gain. The best way to gain power, it was quickly seen, was to cultivate intellectual "powers," since intellect seemed to "house" knowledge and, in fact, seemed to be the source of it.

Thus, the Baconian Age of Intellectualism arose, constituting a peculiar paradigm — a pattern of expectation. We might observe we are still much in this Age.

Now, I've no grudge against Sir Francis Bacon and, like many, have enjoyed and been fascinated by his cultural legacy. But surely, becoming enabled to apperceive *truths* is more fundamental to the pursuit of Life than accumulating knowledge which may contain mistakes or misinformation. Anyone's knowledge, we must remind ourselves, is only as good as the information it contains. Also, I quite fail to see how one can have a "*disinterested* love of truth." Can a love of anything be disinterested? Admittedly, truth is truth and apparently truth cares not at all if one is disinterested or not.

At any rate, all the evidence shows that many people, knowledgeable or not, intellectual or not, can and *have* achieved apperceptions of various truths, and that in so doing they have harnessed great powers either for constructive or destructive purposes. Certainly, then, truth is power — at least as well as is knowledge. Too, even if knowledge and truth be powers, it is easy enough to see, as far as observable human experience is concerned, that many have been the knowledgeable and truthful who have bit the bitter dusts of defeat and death. It is really quite easy to show that knowledge and truth may, at times, not be very powerful, or even have power at all. You see, ignorance and lies, too, have power in them, and the fact that this is so is easily enough confirmed.

But if knowledge and truth be powers or not powers, Wisdom is survival! And the wise need to see something that neither knowledge nor truth, by themselves, can see: the future. Knowledge may or may not accumulate in given individuals and cultures. Truths may or may not exist in same. But *everyone* shares for sure in one bit of knowledge and in one bit of truth: unquestionably and unarguably the future *is* coming.

We might continue sporting with Bacon's famous three words thusly: future-seeing is power. And we might remind ourselves: the future is invisible.

THE CRUX OF UNDERSTANDING

The crux of the matter is that knowledge, truth and future-seeing are somewhat indivisible, and, together, equate to what might be called the Primary Psychic Trinity. Intellectualisms that attempt to break apart this trinity always turn out destructively or result in deliberate or inadvertent destructivity.

But, in our present culture, this basic trinity *has* been broken apart in the following, somewhat over-simplified, way. First, at the beginning of our Modern Epoch (c. 1830), human affairs trended in the direction of deciding that the pursuit of knowledge, especially empirical scientific knowledge, was the way to go. To fully launch this direction, which at first was conceived of as a battle between science and religion, events trended in the direction of disenfranchising the powers of religion and its appendages of superstition. Future-seeing, mistaken as superstition, soon bit the skeletal dust of ignominy. Soon the future could not be seen at all.

But these trends, probably quite inadvertently, had a tremendous impact upon philosophy — whose stated goal is to use the human intellect to try to ferret out the truths of things. But, to be effective, philosophy needs to be free to consider all possibilities. Thus, with future-seeing possibilities in cultural disfavor, the truth-isolating purposes of philosophy suffered. Eventually, in the trends, it became decided that philosophy was "ineffective." Thereafter, utopian visions based upon the quite unproven values of empirical knowledge became the rage.

It might then have been predicted that the enterprise of empirical knowledge would begin to suffer from "doubt" — which duly began to manifest with the advent of the Nuclear Age. Thus, our present epoch finds itself in a condition never previously encountered throughout the whole of human history. Our future-seeing potentials are at their lowest ebb in history, we cannot locate truths, and we distrust our own knowledge. Although there may be additional reasons for this miserable state of affairs, certainly one of them is our intellectual predecessors' decision to break apart the Primary Psychic Trinity — leaving us thereby with a peculiar, stress-making cultural inheritance.

THE PSYCHIC ARTS AND CRAFTS

Nothing in this book is being offered up as a cultural panacea that might suddenly "correct" the floating issues involved. But surely a psychic restoration is called for, which is to say, a refocusing on the possibilities inherent in human psychic potentials, and thus on the locatable values and meanings of the psychic arts and crafts.

The major traditional goal of these has always been to future-see, to truth-tell the future, and to integrate what is seen and told with the present and the past.

We can, I think, speed up our intellectual understandings if we modify our conceptions of truth by adding to our psychic language the word *actuality*— the quality or state of being actual. The reason for so doing is that, by observation, truths shift around a lot and, like human nature, are kaleidoscopic in *their* nature. The psychic arts and crafts have as their goal the perceiving of what has been, is now, and will be actual — i.e., *active*. In essence, practitioners of the psychic arts and crafts attempt to perceive more proximate truths relevant to a present or future situation or condition — to see why they are actualizing in the form they are, and how future events will or will not actualize. The term "actuality," therefore, can be used synonymously with truth for the purposes of this book.

I want to emphasize the word *attempt*. We must accept the fact that it is not an easy thing to peer into invisibles in the first place. Even if intellects *do* make the primary, fundamental, and activating decision that invisibles exist, still, apperceiving them remains something of an effort. If it were not for the fact that the invisibles reveal themselves spontaneously, and frequently so, we probably would not even know they exist.

If we can comprehend that the invisibles do exist, it is only a matter of logical deduction that human intelligence can devise ways to monitor them, at least in part. To do so, the ancients were well versed in instituting creative steps to enhance natural intuitive levels found in all humans, especially those who appeared to be better naturally endowed. It is clear that from these enhanced intuitive levels it was soon apperceived that the invisibles "worked" in patterns and cycles, just as visibles did. From something like this came the axiom: "as above, so below."

It was thence but a short step (albeit one taken over longish periods of time) to observe and codify the "working" patterns and cycles of the invisibles. Out of these codifications came what we are calling in this book the *psychic arts and crafts*. But we must remember that the term "psychic" was coined only in the last century. The ancients had no need of a term such as "psychic," which serves to *separate* (and thus to stereotype) the invisible from the visible. For they conceived of the two as one interlocking, interconnected, and interlinked whole.

The "science" of the ancients did, however, tend to view the invisibles as superior to the visibles, since, by their experience, *altering* some invisible factor brought change into the visibles while, by their same experience, altering visible factors without reference to their invisible superstructures seldom brought about changes of any magnitude. Doing so even sometimes worsened situations.

Since the ancients saw no need to artificially separate the two realms of activity, they identified the invisibles via the various professions who designed specialized arts and crafts. We do the same today. For example, we understand the difference between a psychologist, a doctor, and a stock-market analyst, although all three essentially deal in invisible and visible factors. But the categories are different.

Thus, in ancient times, a *prophet* was one who announced what *will* come, i.e., Events beyond human intercession. But an *oracle* was one who announced Events in which human intercession *could* play a role. An *omen-reader* interpreted visible and invisible trends regarding specific issues and changes in worldview or Zeitgeist — the spirit of the times. The function of *shamans* was deliberately to enter the invisibles via certain and precise altered-state-of-consciousness disciplines and catalyze alterations in their arrangements or actualities.

The ancients also observed that certain invisible factors were identifiable by their differing natures, such as fear, hope, death, life, the masculine, the feminine, abundance, scarcity, cruelty, warlikeness, peacefulness, and so forth. They *personified* these isolatable *factors*, calling them *divinities* — different powers or principles "dwelling" within the invisibles. Unfortunately for all of us in this age, historians of later epochs mistranslated "divinity" as gods or goddesses, assuming the personified images themselves were objects of superstitious religious veneration — when, in fact, the ancients possessed no "religions" in the terms we understand them today.

The function of the *Magician* was to evoke, via designed psychic disciplines (often ritualized), these personified powers or principles for purposes that aided human needs or desires. The sole surviving remnant of such evocations we have today is, of course, supplicative prayer.

The unchallenged queen of the psychic arts and crafts was, however, *astrology*. The ancients did not know why the movements of the planets and stars correlated with natural events and the ongoing human drama. They only knew, by observation, that they did. From lengthy observations, they constructed elaborate disciplines whose function was to predict what correlations would be or come into actuality at given times.

WHAT THE PSYCHIC CRAFTS ACTUALLY DO

Essentially, *any* device, vehicle, tool, practice, or discipline that renders invisible information visible to our intellects is a psychic art, craft, or technology. It might be observed that in this sense psychology is a rudimentary psychic practice, for its stated goal is to dig out and fix up invisible factors that are carrying their strange *products* through into the tangible, mental, and objective realms.

Today, we have even a better analogy. In computer lingo, one talks of "entering" or "accessing" a program. One has "access" by finding the key elements that allows one to "enter" a computer program. And, we even talk of "computer illiteracy" and "computer literacy."

This analogy is very apt, for the psychic arts and crafts (if they are mastered) function as access keys or entering methodologies to the programs continuously running in the invisible realms.

The study of handwriting (*graphology*), in the hands of a competent graphologist, can produce amazing information, not only regarding a person's make-up, but how that person will behave now, has behaved and will behave in the future. Now, don't ask me *why* a person's character is somewhat revealed via his or her handwriting. I don't know. But it is clear that such is the case.

For example, in 1967 I met Lila K. Piper, at that time one of America's leading handwriting experts. By 1974, after my psychic research career had commenced, I was thrown in with a lot of people my poor brain couldn't fathom (parapsychology is populated with a lot of very strange types). It was clear to me that I was going to be associated with some of these on a long-term basis, yet they were always doing things I had a hard time dealing with. I felt I needed some information about them to help make sense out of what was going on. Where to turn? Well, I asked Lila to have a go at seeing what their handwriting revealed.

Rather covertly, I obtained samples of the handwriting of three distinctly different people and awaited Lila's pronouncements. Among these samples were one from a person I couldn't get along with at all, and two from persons with whom I was getting along famously. I was shocked when Lila said of the former that she was hard to get along with, but she would prove to be a true friend in tough times — which was how it turned out.

Of the other two, Lila said that one was very self-serving, never took advice, and would eventually suddenly abandon psychic research altogether probably at a time when his strengths were needed the most. Lila admitted he was a "strong person," but that when faced with "odds beyond his capabilities" he would not listen to constructive advice and would abandon "challenges to himself which his own 'advice' has no answer for. He is not the friend you think he is," she concluded. I had already found out this person never took advice, but I felt he was a friend, and I didn't think he was self-serving more than usual. And certainly, it was unreal to me that he would abruptly abandon psychic research — which, as far as I could tell, was the love of his life.

Lila's *written* warning included, "if you do not expand your contacts, when he does abandon the project you will be left without any support at all." Well, based upon this advice I began a program that expanded my own contacts, and when this person eventually *did* execute his *overnight* departure my own house of cards did not collapse totally.

Regarding the second person, Lila warned that he *always* "makes enemies of everyone. He will never admit he has a fault or is at fault. He is a user and is always looking for scapegoats. Yet, on the surface he appears cordial and competent. If you plan a long-term relationship with this man, you must make sure he can always save his face. But even that will not last, for everything he mixes in will collapse, and you will become another scapegoat." Now, I couldn't conceive of any of this at the time. But, as a year or two passed, upsets began to occur, and I found I had to help this man save face. And, to my sorrow, eventually, the worst Lila had predicted *from only this man's handwriting* came to pass.

We all occasionally get caught up in arrangements that are hard to get out of, leaving us to await an unwanted result. For me, this latter situation was one of them. Had I been really alert to all this, I could have consulted this person's horoscope and found the time period the volcano was most likely to erupt. In his natal horoscope, this man has a Uranus/Saturn conjunction (explosive authority) nearly exactly opposite my Mars (intense activity). According to astrological stuff, our relationship was then one to be a contest between his explosive authority and my intense activity. The time eventually came along when the disruptive planet Uranus came across my Mars opposite *his* Uranus/Saturn conjunction. All hell broke loose, and I became a scapegoat just as Lila had predicted. Lord only knows there was enough advance information available — only I was too dull to acknowledge its usefulness. I could have been better prepared than I was and acted quite differently.

Next to handwriting analysis, *palmistry* (the study of lines, mounds, and marks on the hands) gives enormous amounts of information, including probable life-span, indications of health and its dangers, indications of emotional and mental capabilities, and areas of life in which the person will succeed the best or fail the worst. At the present time, palmistry is practically a lost psychic art/craft. But, as we have seen above, the noted clairvoyant-astrologer, Louis Hamon (Cheiro), was an adept in this palmistry. I have no idea why the invisible forces and energies working in us should be imprinted on our hands any more than I know why the growing code for an oak tree is in its seed. But such is the case. Extremely gifted palmists can "work" with these hand indications and perform miracles in gathering intelligence about the invisibles that are most likely to have impact on us.

I'd like to delve into *numerology* at this point, but it is just too complex, and giving the background needed to get a grip on it is beyond the scope of this book. We have encountered Walter Gorn Old (Sepharial) earlier herein. He was the arch-numerologists-cum-astrologer of our modern times, and he used numerology to win horse races (building not a small fortune from this activity) and to succeed in commodities speculations.

Astrology is undoubtedly the queen of the psychic arts and crafts — even counting our own spontaneous psychic factors. The trouble here is that authors feel they have to give an astrology lesson in order for the reader to comprehend what they are talking about. Essentially this is true. But it actually takes at least two years of in-depth study to achieve a grip on what's going on with astrology — and even then, some aspiring astrologers fail in gripping the stuff very well.

So I'll avoid the astrology lessons and say only that, basically, astrology is capable of providing two valuable kinds of information: (1) character analysis and (2) locating strategic times that are either Fortunate or Misfortunate for the individuals concerned. This latter can be expanded to foresee the momentous events concerning nations, societies, and the overall nature of trends in historical events.

There are several problems involved, not the least of which is that most people don't really want to know what is "in" their horoscopes; they only want affirmations about how great they are and how fortunate they will be. Generally speaking, people don't want to hear astrologically brutal things that displease them or make them apprehensive, even though most horoscopes show mixes of brutal and benevolent aspects. I believe this arises from our uncertainty as to whether such disasters are inevitable or whether they can be averted. In any case, it leads to the working maxim in astrology that the astrologer should tell the person only what they are "ready to hear" — which often is not very much.

Another thing to be considered is that some people do not "respond" to their horoscopes very well — as if some other more dominant non-astrological influences are at work in their life. Most astrologers feel that *everyone* has a horoscope — but there are "strong" horoscopes and "weak" ones. Some people "respond" like clockwork, and dramatically so, while others can live unperturbed through astrological aspects what would make mincemeat out of others. Yet, the occasions when astrological workings can be accurately compared to events and times in a person's life far exceed those in which they cannot.

THE ASTROLOGY OF A MASS MURDERER

Here is one of those unquestionably clear examples. I've chosen an especially brutal example involving sex, atrocity, sadism, and torture. Sad as it is, this horoscope, when put together, contains hardly any benevolent aspects and seems to show how far *down* human invisible elements can take someone — in the absence of forewarned human intervention.

I've selected the case of Dean Allen Corll (born on Christmas Eve, December 24, 1939) who, in 1973 in Pasadena, a suburb of Houston, Texas, was discovered to have murdered thirty-one or more boys after submitting them to heinous sexual outrages and tortures. A brief biography of Corll is provided in *The Encyclopedia of Modern Murder* by Colin Wilson and Donald Seaman.

Corll was born in Indiana and apparently suffered a lot within a family situation that was most undesirable. He seemed nevertheless to grow up to be a rather placid type, having a few unfruitful excursions with girls. Corll enlisted into the Army in 1964, and it is probably in the Army he "turned into a fag," as one of his friends was later to comment. In 1969, when he was thirty, he seemed to suffer a personality change and became morose and hypersensitive. Nevertheless, he developed an "inexplicable" magnetic charisma and began spending time with young boys, organizing glue-sniffing parties. When the boys fell unconscious from inhaling the glue, he handcuffed them to boards until they regained consciousness.

Then, for several days thereafter, he subjected them to horribly sadistic sexually abusive acts of all kinds. After killing his victims, he wrapped the bodies in clear plastic and secreted them in three or more mass graves. On August 8, 1973, one of his intended victims did everyone a favor by pumping six bullets into him, but the victim himself, it turned out, had been one of his accomplices in obtaining and murdering several of the boys. The ages of the boys ranged from nine to seventeen. The whole of this took place in a three-year period.

Is all this gross enough? Yes. Well, if astrology holds true, Corll's horoscope should show clear indications regarding his nature. Apparently, on the surface, Corll seemed kind enough, and apparently suffered from no guilt, hugged his toy Snoopy Dog until his demise, and led young boys around in some sort of hypnotic way. After his death, no one could figure out how he could lead so many boys to their revolting dooms or why he should have done so, anyway, considering how many boys there are out there who willingly join in homosexual encounters.

Sociologists and psychologists would determine that Corll was a product of his unfortunate childhood and probably solidify their "wisdom" around this hypothesis. Granted, there is some truth in this, for if the young Corll had lived in a family situation that was supportive of him, he might have developed differently — and it is part of our psychic climate to believe that this makes sense. His mother had three husbands, and clearly Corll was deficient in experiencing masculine support and leadership and family stability.

But then it is also true that many people come from similar environmental circumstances and do not turn into mass killers.

Thus, we might have a look at his horoscope and perform an astrological autopsy. Somewhere near the front of this book, I mentioned that often we use the phrase "he was born a bad seed." Well this, indeed, is a sorry thing to say about someone. But then we do have bad seeds amongst us, do we not?

In popular astrology, too much attention is given to the Sun sign — i.e., one of the twelve parts of the Zodiac in which the Sun is found at the time of the person's birth. The Sun sign is important, to be sure, but is actually only the tip of the tip of the iceberg. Each planet has a plus or minus (positive-negative) meaning. But so does each degree of the 360-degree Zodiac, most of which also have a double plus-minus significance. Thus, when a planet is found at such and such a degree, that planet's meaning must be interpreted against the meaning of the degree in which it is found. For the purposes of Corll's horoscope, I've referred to two books: Ester V. Leinbach's *Degrees of the Zodiac* (which was published in 1972, so we can be sure she did not publish this book with Dean Corll in mind), and Adriano Carelli's *The 360 Degrees of the Zodiac*, published in 1977.

If we look at the superficial aspects of Corll's horoscope, it might at first look like a lot of others. We see that the most powerful planetary aspect element involves Neptune, the planet signifying drugs, hypnotic-like qualities and betrayal. This planet is opposite the aggressive planet Mars (masculinity, violence). We also see that the powerful planet Saturn (authority, decay, death) is badly aspected to his Venus (love, tenderness, the feminine), indicating he would not get along with females.

We could conclude, from just these aspects, that Corll was most likely to be homosexual, and be argumentative and capable of violence. But plenty of people have these same aspects, and they, by themselves, do not equate to mass murder. Thus, we have to dig deeper.

Dean Allen Corll was born with his Sun at two degrees Capricorn. Capricornian males (like their Cancerian counterpart females) are overly sensual, are on the constant lookout for sexual opportunities, and like extended sexual sessions. A certain high percentage of them are bisexual. But Capricorn is a macho, authoritarian, and strangely somewhat unromantic sign, ruled by Saturn.

Sexual outlets would, therefore, be something of prime importance for Corll. Since it was early seen that he did not respond to females, his other recourse would be males. The Army, of course, was ideal for this. Despite the propaganda the military normally puts out, the Army is essentially a male society, and in these there *always* develops a higher-than-normal degree of homosexual opportunities and encounters. We must assume, then, that while in the Army, Corll found his "erotic paradise."

But none of this makes an insensitive, wanton *mass killer* out of anyone. Thus, let's dissect Corll's horoscope completely to see what can be seen — in all its astonishing, unambiguous clarity.

Corll's Moon is at the fourteenth degree of Gemini, this indicating a tendency to lie about everything and anything, leading the person into being tricky and dishonest while at the same time denoting a clever mentality. The Moon is, among other things, the symbol of frequent change, moods and feelings of inferiority.

We find his Jupiter (the symbol for expansiveness and gambling) at zero degrees Aries, this degree denoting one who can maintain a clear conscience about all he becomes involved in *no matter what it is*. This degree denotes an overstressed sense of self, a pride easily perverted into haughtiness, into encroachment upon the rights of one's neighbors (the majority of Corll's victims came from his own neighborhood), fiery passions, a deep righteousness, and a clear conscience no matter what.

Corll's Mars (the symbol for violence, aggressiveness, and energy) is at twenty-three degrees Pisces, this degree denoting a leaning toward emotional values and sensuous living along with a misconception of true values of relationships and a clinging to false values.

We find Corll's Mercury (symbolizing thought and intellect) at twelve degrees Sagittarius, this degree almost assuring us that sexual excesses are likely.

We find Corll's Uranus (the planet of quick and often violent change) at the eighteenth degree of Taurus. This degree was, in Corll's horoscope, very near the north node (the point where a planet is most distant from the Sun) of Mars, and denotes clear-cut violence and sadism, as well as a struggle between the powers of life and the powers of death. This degree is considered savage and warlike and, like zero degrees Aries, is sometimes called the degree of the "executioner."

We find Corll's Saturn (the chief symbol of unyielding authority and death [the skeleton with a scythe]) at the twenty-fourth degree of Aries. The visual symbol of this important degree is that of an almost naked woman (lust) and indicates peaks of creative energy which, unchanneled, result in excesses of vulgar and obscene sexual activity. The expression "sexual need" never has fitted so well as in this degree. It is more than a need. It is an inescapable necessity, something fatal. Male subjects with a planet at this degree will have trouble with the female sex, will not strive too high, and will be content with eking out a living (Corll was quite content eking out a living by working at the Houston Lighting and Power Company).

Now, we come to the two outermost planets — the baleful, hypnotic Neptune and the death/rebirth planet, Pluto. Corll's Neptune (the planet of drugs, hypnosis, charisma, mediumship) is at the twenty-fifth degree of Virgo. If the rest of the horoscope's aspects are good, then this degree may automatically bestow qualities of leadership, as it did in the case of Queen Elizabeth I, whose Sun was at that degree. But if numerous other aspects in the horoscope are negative, then, although it implies hypnotic qualities that will enthrall followers, it will manifest in *pathological* drives to bolster the ego.

Finally, we come to Pluto, who governs death of things, even in the best of horoscopes. Corll's Pluto is at the second degree of Leo — the visual symbol of which is a rudderless ship, prey to the waves. This degree denotes one devoid of moral strength and all that goes with *that* — and the danger of "shipwreck" ahead, i.e., death.

Thus, clearly and unambiguously, the invisible energies and forces at work within Corll aimed at sadism with a clear conscience. From even the most benevolent astrological viewpoint, it is hard to see how Corll could, on his own, surmount these dreadful aspects. It is true that if *some* of these aspects are present in a given horoscope, they will be, in astrological terms, counterbalanced by others that are more fortunate or benevolent. It is almost unthinkable that Corll's sadism did not show up while he was a child — but it is conceivable that it was ignored as just "childish stuff that he would grow out of." Any competent astrologer would have been shocked by this horoscope — if any had erected it.

Thus, Dean Corll was a sadistic time bomb awaiting ignition. When, then, would this ignition manifest? Well, it could have ignited any time, but, astrologically speaking, there is one sure epoch that could be depended upon to set it off.

According to *The Encyclopedia of Modern Murder*, in 1969, when he was thirty, Corll suffered a profound personality change, becoming morose and hypersensitive. All astrologers will recognize this as the time of the Saturn "return" — when the planet Saturn, on its trip around the heavens, returns to the place it was when the person was born. In Corll's life, this profound astrological event took place in March 1969. The Saturn Return is very hard in everyone's life, indicating a time when the old will cease, and the person has either an opportunity to decline in energy or to try to start a new kind of life.

This is especially hard on men, many of whom kill themselves or attempt suicide at the time of their Saturn return. Corll's Saturn is at the awful twenty-fourth degree of Aries, indicating that if energies are not creatively channeled they will result in an excess of destructive sexual activity. Combined with Corll's other dismal aspects, this sexual activity will take on murderous and execution-like potentials. The preponderance of the evidence shows that Corll never had any support or guidance in constructively channeling his energies. With all the other *distinctly malevolent* aspects his horoscope shows, he bit the destructive dust and sent along thirty-one-plus young boys ahead of him.

Now, to be honest, to determine all this ahead of the time when Corll's abysmal mass-killer nature was confirmed by its grizzly results would test any astrologer's competence; indeed, even if they correctly saw the aspects and what they implied, they would be loath to pronounce such a completely negative prognosis. Yet, taken from astrological sources, here is a *complete* personality profile of Corll, which is unambiguous and accessible via astrology, that "explains" many of the sorrowful destructive factors at work within him.

The authors of *The Encyclopedia of Modern Murder* refer to Jack Olsen's biography of Corll, *The Man with the Candy*, in which Olsen "makes it clear that he [Corll] was a man who never grew up." I can venture a second opinion: something grew up all right — but *what* was it?

I was quite shocked in reading Corll's biography in *The Encyclopedia of Modern Murder* when the authors, seemingly out of nowhere, compared him to, of all people, the famous author Marcel Proust — another "oversensitive homosexual" who had a distinctly sadistic streak and enjoyed "watching rats being tortured to death." I made haste to dig up Proust's horoscope, and Bingo! Proust had *his* Neptune at the fatal twenty-fourth degree of Aries just as Corll had his Saturn there. Proust had his Pluto at the eighteenth-nineteenth degree of Taurus where Corll had *his* Uranus — all this equating to sadism, torture and killing.

All this set me on a search for other famous "sadists" who might have similar aspects in *their* natal charts — among whom I found Adolf Hitler. Hitler's horoscope is, of course, one of those most scrutinized in history. In 1934, Hitler's horoscope was being very favorably interpreted by many German astrologers, but one, a certain Count Finckenstein, concluded that, "He's a homicidal maniac!" and that Germany had sold itself into the hands of a murderer. Not only does Hitler's natal chart show his Mercury still in association with the fatal twenty-fourth degree of Aries, but his Uranus at the ascendant is at nineteen degrees Libra — almost the only degree that contributes to the development of fascism and criminal tendencies.

Also, I immediately suspected that the infamous monk, Gregory Rasputin, who so greatly influenced Russian history and who was a known sadist and a heterosexual voluptuary in excess, *must* have a planet at the twenty-fourth degree of Aries — which he did; the sensual, hypnotic, betraying planet Neptune.

Similar astrological elements can also be found in horoscopes of heterosexual mass murders — for example, those of Theodore Bundy (who murdered over twenty girls) and Norman John Collins (seven girls). In the latter case, Collins was known to have psychological "problems" shortly before he began his killing sprees, but psychologists concluded that he seemed completely normal.

Isn't all this just awful? Well, let's switch to something more positive.

THE ASTROLOGY OF FORTUNE

As mentioned above, the degrees of the Zodiac all have meaning, positive and/or negative. Some are worse, a few or which we have seen in the case of Dean Allen Corll who had *not one* Fortunate aspect in his entire horoscope. But, as I have mentioned earlier and will again later, there are Fortunate invisible energies and forces as well as the Misfortunate ones. And if this is so, we would expect those who have some of the most supreme astrologically Fortunate aspects also to succeed supremely in life.

For example, in his horoscope, Robert Redford has Saturn at the fourth degree of Aries. This degree is almost entirely benevolent, indicating that Redford will rely on instinct which guides him beyond what wisdom normally provides for many others. His Neptune is at the sixteenth-seventeenth degree of Virgo, indicating altruism (which Redford is rather noted for), but a penny pincher who will accumulate great wealth, along with a keen awareness of public superstitions and weaknesses which can be used for cool profit. He is likely to enjoy a luxurious old age surrounded with friends — if he cultivates them. If not, he may end up lonely surrounded only by his accumulated wealth.

Samuel Goldwyn, the famous, ultra-rich movie magnate, who started out as Samuel Goldfish, a glove salesman, also had his Uranus at this same Fortunate degree of Virgo.

Jacqueline Kennedy Onassis, although having a horoscope that promises great tragedy, has her Neptune at zero degrees Virgo, which denotes, among other things, a certain dignity even when relegated to the lowest position. This degree combines the two basic characteristics of Leo and Virgo, and it is a degree of service and of kingly (in her case, queenly) elegance. A person with this degree placed in high position (in her case, on her horoscope's midheaven) will gain the greatest "kingdom."

Diana, Princess of Wales (and future Queen of England), although having several threatening aspects in her horoscope yet has her Sun at the best of all possible places, the ninth degree of Cancer. The north node of Jupiter has been at this degree for quite some time and indicates an abundance of very steady and reliable luck. Couldn't you just eat your heart out? Well, eat it out some more.

Aristotle Onassis, who started out at the age of sixteen with, he claimed, only $60 in his pocket, made his first million by the age of twenty-five, and later became one of the world's richest men. He had nothing less than his Jupiter at this same extremely Fortunate ninth degree of Cancer which bestows very steady and reliable luck.

I could go on and on. But, have I made some kind of point by now? It is completely unclear to me why psychical researchers and parapsychologists have *refused* and persist in refusing to explore the possibilities in these kinds of psychic arts and crafts. Perhaps you can figure it out. In any event, astrology is headed in new directions, as we shall see ahead, and a type of astrology has found a completely scientific basis which can hardly be denied — unless one also wishes to deny the foundations upon which science rests.

SPONTANEOUS SOOTHSAYING

Outside the disciplined psychic arts and crafts, people in general experience spontaneous drops of invisible information, i.e., spontaneous soothsaying — which even practitioners of the psychic arts and crafts sometimes can only await to happen. These occur in a wide spectrum of anything from modest hunches and gut feelings through dreams up to and including elaborate visions. I have included several examples of these kinds already, so I needn't elaborate much here. The trouble here is that, like the more disciplined arts and crafts, dreams and other spontaneous occurrences need to be *interpreted*. Seldom do they deliver information in clear-cut forms the intellect can readily understand — although, as we have seen, sometimes they do.

Although given individuals learn to work with psychic elements, our culture, as a whole, has completely lost the traditional abilities needed for analyzing and finding the "truth" in the cryptic contents of gut feelings, hunches, dreams, and elaborate visions. The ancients had several titles for such interpreters who could figure out what spontaneous psychic intrusions were wanting to say.

The ancient soothsayers held forth at oracular sites or buildings specially constructed for their purposes. These variously were referred to as sleep temples, healing temples, or dream temples. Few attempts have been made to reconstruct and get an idea of their exact functions. But, it seems obvious enough to me, they were tasked with psychic-type information *management*. As we have seen, it is clear the ancients accepted the existence of invisible energies and forces and felt obliged to try to monitor their invisible workings. Apparently, a large part of this monitoring took place in the sleep/healing/dream temples. In Greek and Roman times, it is known that at least four hundred of these temples existed, and if we add the Middle East and Egypt, perhaps a thousand or more — to say nothing of India and China, etc.

As I understand it, at least three things went on in these temples. The first was dream analysis, undertaken on the assumption that one's personal psychic factors were trying to alert the individual to some important, forthcoming event or time.

Second, "healing" must have been a kind of psychic psychotherapy whose methods are completely lost to us now. But apparently, it was held (and demonstrated) that anyone who was ill also possessed the knowledge within self to cure — and that in a trance or dream-like state akin, I suppose, to shamanistic practices, the cure could be elicited and acted upon.

Third, certain activities must have focused on hypnotic-like, subliminal-suggestion-like activities — which, I might point out, are being rediscovered and marketed today as subliminal programming.

At any rate, dream interpretation at least was big stuff, and if soothsayers were good at what they did, it is easy enough to see why they were considered valuable. That they were good, generally speaking, is patently clear since people, then as now, being the practical creatures they are, would not have tolerated them if they had not been good. But people then as now listened to soothsayers and dream-clues when they wanted to and ignored them if the information was "inconvenient."

For example, while the young Julius Caesar was struggling up the lines of the Roman bureaucracy, he had a dream of raping his own mother. He took his dream to his soothsayers for interpretation. If we today took such a dream to a psychoanalyst they would certainly believe (a la the Freudian stereotyping system) that we harbor suppressed desires to screw our mother — which may or *may not* be true. At any rate, Caesar's soothsayers did their thing and arrived at the conclusion that Julius Caesar was "destined to conquer the earth, our Universal Mother" — which he shortly did at the time.

As far as I can tell, people have been snickering over this "prophecy" ever since, especially in our modern times, and somehow manage to avoid getting together the dream and the soothsayers' interpretation with the fact that Caesar *did* conquer the "world" of his time. Yet, Caesar was only human, and when his own wife dreamt that he would be murdered if he went to the Senate on the morrow, he ignored her as well as several other soothsayers and went to his assassination — much as did Abraham Lincoln when he ignored his *own* dream about such an event.

OMEN READING

Yet another category of accessing psychic-type information has to do with what used to be called *Sortes* or *sortilege* which means *divination* by lots. A rudimentary form of this is casting stones and reading the "omens" they seem to signify. In ancient times, this was extended to "reading" fresh livers, chicken entrails, blood spills, the smell or patterns in excreta, moles or birthmarks, etc., and in some cases even sperm ejaculations and menstruation discharges. Omens could also be seen in weather patterns, flights of birds, rock formations, chance encounters, and what have you.

The I Ching yarrow sticks and the Tarot cards, always fashionable in some quarters, are not thought of as *Sortes*, but actually are. In my experience, consulting the I Ching or the Tarot cards sometimes produces surprising and accurate results, but more often the results remain ambiguous until "read" in conjunction with other clues that can be arrived at via the types of psychic arts and crafts reviewed above.

* * *

It should be somewhat obvious by now that if we utilize every psychic technique we can, it is quite probable we can gain a decent idea of the master plan of our hidden psychic agendas. The evidence is somewhat clear that highly achieved psychic "readers" (soothsayers) utilized not just one technique, but a combination of two or more, and, so to speak, played them off against each other to arrive intellectually at a kind of total result.

Few that I know try to utilize this multi-disciplinary psychic approach. If someone is interested at all in becoming a psychic-type practitioner, they tend to specialize in one of the arts or crafts and thence try to view the portents through the one window of the specialization. When a person gets an itch to consult some psychic-type practitioner, generally they are experiencing some kind of immediate, tangible crisis and want an "answer" for it. I know of three people who toss the I Ching sticks when they get up each morning to get an idea of what the day has in store for them. I know one person who does the same with numerology — computerized numerology, at that. I know of two people who have even turned their computers into a *Sortes* generating machine on the assumption that the inscrutable invisibles can work through a computer as well as through entrails, or the I Ching sticks. Hey! If it works, I'm certainly for it.

But to do the job right takes more than shallow, sporadic efforts and exclusive expertise in only one area. If there are hidden master agendas, as clearly I am proposing there are, then we have to adopt the largest overview possible and utilize a mix of all the techniques available in order to *map out* what is involved.

The trouble is that this takes, first, a lot of knowledge, and thereafter a lot of work — all of which is very time-consuming and *must be carried out over a long period of time.* It is easy enough to see why the ancient soothsayers worked full-time and had to have centers to work in. It is quite conceivable that they worked in groups (a psychic clinic, so to speak), each member specializing in one or more psychic arts or crafts activities, and the whole of their "results" combined into one informative package. We do know that when the ancients consulted oracles they usually consulted more than one and then tried to establish a consensus. We hardly do anything of the kind today, rarely seeking a "second opinion" on even the most important matters we seek psychic counsel on. In the larger overview, we are probably missing the bigger picture that a *combined* effort could clarify better.

THE PSYCHIC ARTS AND CRAFTS

o We can observe that a Primary Psychic Triad exists in which knowledge, truth, and future-seeing are combined into an inseparable whole.

o We can observe, admittedly with some effort and a good deal of introspection, that our present culture has contact with and knowledge of this important triad.

o We might observe that if we work to recombine the possibilities of these three categories of power, our intellects will develop a broader, more integrated base to calculate from.

* * *

We have reached a point where we now must turn our attention to contemporary discoveries that not only tend to validate the actual existence of our direct-sensing potentials but altogether are laying the foundations for the coming psychic renaissance. These contemporary discoveries are taking place in several different disciplines as they are presently conceived. But it is easy enough to see that in the not-so-far future these discoveries will *converge* — more or less creating a new *science* of the invisibles. At this point, then, and to begin closing this book I'll review the most important of these discoveries.

XVIII

The Electromagnetic Future

MEET THE GEOMAGNETOSPHERE

When I first began working in parapsychology in 1969, I did so much under the assumption that psychic proficiencies were powers of the mind. This assumption, as we have seen, was generally shared by all psychical researchers for several decades. Although I felt there may be other "agents" behind psychic stuff, still the hypothesis that they were functions of mind was not completely unsuitable. As functions of the mind, however, it was generally held that nothing "outside" the mind could affect psychic processes, and that if they were affected the causes must be *in the mind* itself.

In 1974-75, however, as our testing progressed we began bumping into a curious phenomenon that grew into tremendous implications. This "bump" revolutionized my overview of psychic stuff altogether.

By 1975, my colleagues and I at Stanford Research Institute had, on a daily basis, accumulated something like a million examples of ESP (telepathic and/or clairvoyant) showing up in experimental trials. I myself had been a direct participant in many of these. These experiments were always done with the most rigorous controls that could be conceived, all of which had to be approved in advance by impersonal "committees" of invisible advisors tucked away in obscure recesses of various bureaucracies. Moreover, the security of these controls was daily overseen in person by representatives of our clients.

The daily results of these sessions were immediately turned over to a battery of statisticians who, with their million-dollar computers, analyzed the hell out of them. Since we had long been able to eyeball the fact that the presence of successful ESP was more evident on certain days and less or even non-existent on others, it was finally decided to ask the computers to generate a list of the best and worst days.

With this rather long list in hand, we then had to analyze by hand the experimental notes of each experiment in an effort to see what variables, if any, were present on the "off" and "good" days. Due to the extraordinary protocols established and the number-by-number routines that eventuated from them, it soon became evident that external conditions changed very little, if at all. However, one of the pre-session protocols required the subjects to itemize their physical and emotional status before the experiment began and also required them to note if and when these changed during any given session.

In this way we could account for the effect on success rates if a person was suffering from headaches, hangovers, the flu or, in the case of women, menstrual cramps. Surprisingly, these factors did not seem to negatively influence the production of successful ESP performance. Neither did whether the subject felt "on" or "off" seem to have anything to do with anything.

On the other hand, what quickly became obvious was that if the subject was hungry or developed a need to relieve themselves, the statistic promptly bottomed out. Needless to say, we were able to remedy these situations by adding to our checklist certain "convenience" questions and to immediately stop a given experiment for needed breaks.

But, still, this left about three-fourths of our sessions unaccounted for, especially the negative ones. We then called for and received long lists of experimental sessions from *other* laboratories and analyzed them the same way — to find that they too contained better and worse days, which in some cases correlated exactly with ours.

After all was said and done, the only alternative left was to suspect the existence of invisible environmental influences common across many subjects and many locations —something that was clearly operating *outside the mind*.

No one could imagine what these might be, and so I assumed the task of trying to get a grip on them. The question I asked myself was: "What could influence everything and everybody on the same day?" It was not until 1978 that I found even a plausible explanation.

My first task was to try to correlate our low-ESP days (of most interest) with human behavior in general. Fortunately, I had a clever assistant who knew just where to go to get mass human-behavior statistics. These revealed that there were days in which mass psychological behavior was "unsettled," and many of these days corresponded to our "bad" days.

For example, hospital and police statistics show that on certain days more people come in for "treatment" than usual, and that police have to deal with increases in mayhem on certain days. Certain days have more car accidents than others, and so forth. There were noticeable correlations between our low-ESP days and days of heightened hospital and police activity. Even more, there were more earthquakes and volcanoes erupting on our low-ESP days, as well.

Progress, yes? Somewhat. Clearly certain days had "vibes" universally shared in strange ways. But then this left us with the question as to what "disturbed" the vibes of the world in such a broad way. Well, there could be only one thing so globally influential, and it floats over our heads all day: the Sun.

In 1978, when I came to this conclusion, the prevailing scientific attitudes held that even if the Sun erupts and sends solar particles and plasma outward, and that these collide electromagnetically with the ionosphere and the whole geomagnetosphere that surrounds earth, the overall effects are so "small" that they could not conceivably cause effects in living organisms. Yet, with the help of my assistant, I could make a hasty correlation that showed high solar activity corresponded with not all but certainly a large part of our "off" days.

I wrote a proposal that suggested some time and money be spent accumulating proper computer programs, additional staff, and a "solar" library to explore the possibilities with an overview goal of proving or disproving the effects of the sun on ESP performance. Other than the work entailed, all this sounds simple enough, doesn't it? Well, I was astonished when this proposal was rejected on the grounds that the prevailing attitude in science held that there was no evidence that the electromagnetism of the Sun affects human or animal life at all.

I can be a stubborn case at times. Not to be defeated by mere scientific attitudes, I set up my own personal research program along these lines and was able to invoke unofficial interest in this project, for, in 1979, I came across a strategic Soviet publication which hinted at the nature of what energized Soviet psychotronics into existence in the first place.

The English translation of *Electromagnetic Fields and Life*, by the Soviet high-energy physicist A.S. Presman had become available as early as 1970.¹ But since normal parapsychological research activities do not include dealing with the Sun, we all had managed to avoid knowing of its existence. Since World War II, Presman had been studying the effects of electromagnetic fields on living organisms, and, since 1966, had given special courses on this subject in the Department of Biophysics, Moscow University.

Further, in 1978, the Soviet academician A.P. Dubrov published a book entitled *The Geomagnetic Field and Life: Geomagnetobiology* in which copious evidence is given that links human psychic (yes, psychic!) performance to the Sun and electromagnetism.²

The implications contained in these two books seemed to me to be all too clear. If Soviet scientists indeed had demonstrated that biophysical organisms are linked to, and therefore respond to, invisible geomagnetic conditions, then these same conditions probably also "carry" invisible information. Beyond the obvious advantages to psychic "transmitting" which thus would be potentially available, instruments designed to interfere with or influence such invisible conditions might also be used to great advantage.

It seemed not at all unlikely that these possibilities were what galvanized the Soviets to undertake massive psychotronic researches. If so, this provides at least part of the answer to the earlier mystery of why they had set up psychic research programs seemingly in defiance of their own ideology.

At any rate, parapsychological expectations in the United States are locked into such a limited belief situation as to be almost totally incapable of factoring the activities of the Sun into psychic research expectations. Although I didn't get very far officially with my own "my solar project," I continued it personally and have maintained it to this day. As we shall see, solar research has led directly into other significant developments that, taken together, are calling forth the coming psychic renaissance.

But this first act was not yet over with. When one of my colleagues told the noted physicist Michael A. Persinger of Laurentian University in Canada (who, as might be now be

---

[1] See, Presman, A.S., Electromagnetic Fields and Life, Plenum Press, New York, 1970.
[2] See, Dubrov, A.P., The Geomagnetic Field and Life: Geomagnetobiology, Plenum Press, New York, 1978.

expected, has a deep interest in psychic stuff) of our unofficial discoveries in this regard, he took it upon himself to survey a large spectrum of past ESP trials and correlate their results with solar activity. Persinger eventually published several papers in which it was clearly established that decreased geomagnetic activity somehow enhances telepathic, clairvoyant, and, even, dream activity, while increased solar activity correlates with decreases.[3]

Here, then, is a completely new element (but only one of several) that, in my opinion, is destined to reinvigorate the emergence of new interests in psychic stuff. What this means in practical terms is that dependable psychic functioning is more frequent during quiet electromagnetic periods and more undependable during disturbed periods. But it also implies that parapsychologists will have to become solar experts!

Already work along these lines has been undertaken and is certain to invigorate and influence new discoveries regarding psychic stuff. For example, researchers James R. Johnston and Jean Millay[4] and Julieta Ramos[5] have published papers regarding brainwave phase synchronization giving good evidence that when the electromagnetic environment is upset, it is harder for our brainwaves to remain synchronized. Obviously, if we are to think straight and experience dependable psychic factors, these can best take place if our minds are not being made mush by the electromagnetic environment. It's as simple as that, and the implications on behalf of increasing dependable psychic-factor activity are enormous. Here, in one fell swoop, is an entirely new basis for a new understanding of psychic proficiency, and the implications are enormous.

If we can take the hint here, then it is proper to assume that the invisible environment has a lot to do with the emergence of psychic performance. The Russian electromagnetic bioinformation transfer theory, backed up by experimental evidence, does one thing no other theories about psychic matters have been able to do. It links

---

3 Persinger, Michael A. and Schaut, George B., "Geomagnetic Factors in Subjective Telepathic, Precognitive, and Postmortem Experiences," Journal of the American Society for Psychical Research, Vol. 82, July 1988.
4 Johnston, James R. and Millay, Jean, "A Pilot Study in Brainwave Phase Synchronization," PSI Research Review, March 1983.
5 See, Grinberg-Zylberbaum, Jacobo, and Ramos, Julieta, "Patterns of Interhemispheric Correlation During Human Communication," International Journal of Neuroscience, Vol. 818, 1978, pp. 289-346.

us and our psychic systems to the geomagnetic environment and thus to the cosmos as well.

And it does one more thing: it resurrects the idea so familiar in the wisdom of the ancients — that all things visible and invisible are, after all, interconnected. As above, so below.

THE ELECTROMAGNETIC FUTURE

o We can observe with the dawning understanding that solar and other cosmic electromagnetic phenomena do have impacts on human behavior, a new relationship between man and cosmos is beginning to be constructed. We can theorize that much of our behavior will soon be seen to be linked with these subtle forces and energies.

o The implication is, of course, that "cosmic connections" do exist. Obviously, most of this kind of information is still in the heads and research reports of specialists who are investigating what is involved. But, increasingly, magazines are beginning to popularize much of it, and will hopefully do so more frequently in the future.

SUGGESTED PRACTICAL EXERCISES THAT WILL HELP IN EXPANDING PSYCHIC LITERACY

o   Keep an eye out for articles that report on these special kinds of phenomena and linkages so as to keep your psychic literacy updated.

o   Try to note when you are feeling well and energetic and when not. Look around you if these states are being experienced by others. We often feel alone and guilty when we feel this way or that, but in fact the feelings may well be the result of a general geomagnetic condition which is affecting more than just you.

o   If it interests you to do so, try to observe increases in dramatic activities during the full moons — if you already haven't. Soon your intellect will begin to understand that your energy and mood levels are attributable to more than just your own internal situations. Noticing this will help strengthen the integration between your direct-sensing systems and your intellect.

XIX

The Bioelectric Human

Dr. Harold Saxton Burr was a member of the faculty of Yale University School of Medicine for forty-three years, teaching anatomy and neuroanatomy. Earlier in his distinguished career, he published in 1935, a paper entitled "The electro-dynamic theory of life" in which he discussed experimental evidence that seemed to suggest that living organisms were possessed of electric (or electronic) structures having a great deal to do with their functioning, their well-being, and their illnesses.[1]

One of the major ideas in this historical document was the possibility that if some electrical/electronic sector of the organism was damaged, then the physical aspects of the body suffered. The implication was that if the *electrical* malfunctioning could be corrected then the *physical* aspects would correct themselves, too. Indeed, in 1935, Burr published another paper entitled "Experimental findings concerning the electro-dynamic theory of life and an analysis of their physical meaning."[2]

Again, in 1938, yet another paper was published entitled "Bio-electric properties of cancer-resistant and cancer-susceptible mice," which did more than just suggest that cancer-resistant mice also had ideal bioelectric conditions.[3] The implication was that when the bioelectric states of the mice were in a deteriorated condition, the mice got cancer.

To shorten the story here, in 1972, Burr published an absolutely fascinating book entitled *Blueprint for Immortality: The Electric*

---

[1] Burr, H.S. and Northrop, F.S.C., "The electro-dynamic theory of life," Quarterly Review of Biology, 10, pp. 322-333, 1935.

[2] Burr, H.S. and Northrop, F.S.C., "Experimental findings concerning the electro-dynamic theory of life and an analysis of their physical meaning," Growth, 1, pp. 78-88, 1937.

[3] Burr, H.S., Strong, I.E., and Smith G.M., "Bio-electric properties of cancer-resistant and cancer-susceptible mice," The American Journal of Cancer, 32, pp. 240-248, 1938.

Patterns of Life[4] in which he described in detail the clinical evidence supporting his contention that the human organism and, indeed, *all* life forms are structured on and conform to an electronic blueprint — which he called a "life field" or L-field. He goes on to describe the importance that L-fields and bio-organic electric potentials have to medicine, psychiatry, and agriculture (which are beyond the scope of this book).

Now, the importance here is this: We are all familiar with magnets which attract and repel bits of metal and with compasses whose needle points to north. Magnets and compasses can only do their thing because they possess electromagnetic fields that *extend* beyond the confines of their physical structure and interact with other electromagnetic fields. *Anything* electric, be it a wire or a human body, thus not only possesses internal electric structure but also EM fields that extend some distance outside the physical body proper. These fields, of course, interact with other smaller or larger fields they come in contact with. The gist here is that when such fields interact, they can be said to be "communicating."

Ah, yes, perhaps you are beginning to grasp my gist here, and are beginning to intuit how all this has something to do with psychic stuff. Well, nothing is for sure yet, but people are working away at the prospects.

Most certainly the Soviet psychotronic researchers are. While Burr did not exactly make the psychic connection (or at least say so in his book), certain Russian researchers soon did. To wit, the noted researcher, A.P. Dubrov, who in his book[5] describes in clinical detail his research into the active nature of the electromagnetic fields and their interconnectedness with the geomagnetic situations discussed in the previous chapter. On page 184 of his book he states, unequivocally, that the effect of the geomagnetic field on the central nervous system indicates that there is a relationship between geomagnetic activity and several psychic diseases, and that increases or decreases in solar activity are direct causes of disturbances in human psychic activity.

The implication, then, is that research into the bioelectric nature of humans irrevocably opens the door to a new form of

---

4 Burr, Harold Saxton. Blueprint for Immortality: The Electric Patterns of Life, Nevil Spearman Publishers, London, 1972.
5 Dubrov, A.P., The Geomagnetic Field and Life: Geomagnetobiology, Plenum Press, New York and London, 1978.

psychic research. It is, in fact, impossible to discuss the one without considering the other — in that the human, as an electromagnetic being, most certainly *must* possess bioelectric information capabilities.

Also out of the Soviet Union, in 1979, the definition of "bio-information" received extensive clarification in *Electromagnetic Bio-Information*, edited by Fritz Albert Popp.[6] The science of bio-information is the study of how information is transferred via electric and magnetic energies within biological organisms, between organisms, and to places distant from them. In this book, experimental evidence of this kind of transfer was given by eleven independent bio-information researchers. It therefore became clear that the Soviets (all research in the USSR must be approved and funded by the government) had initiated a vast, multi-disciplinary bio-information research plan possibly as early as the conclusion of World War II.

Within the context of American and Soviet relations as they pertained until just recently, the implications were nothing less than awesome. Apparently, under the umbrella term "bio-information," the Soviets accepted the actuality at least of telepathy, ESP, clairvoyance, and possibly more.

Now, bio-information (also known as "biological resonances") is defined as sensitive reactions in biological systems induced or produced by electromagnetic waves. It is specifically stated in almost all reports that nature seems to utilize such waves for regulatory purposes, or, more generally, for communication within and between living systems. When the word "nature" is evoked in association with these processes, the understanding draws very close to what I've been calling "our direct-sensing systems" in this book.

In the American scene, however, since psychic stuff was still seen in the context of modern parapsychology (which contained no equivalent electromagnetic bio-information overview), American psychical researchers were missing the bio-information boat. However, other researchers not directly connected to parapsychology *were* making headway.

In fact, among others, Dr. Robert Becker, of the Department of Orthopedic Surgery, State University of New York, had been

---

6 Popp, Fritz-Albert, Ed. Electromagnetic Bio-Information: Proceedings of the Symposium, Marburg, September 5, 1977, Urban & Schwarzenberg, Munich, 1979.

researching bioelectric stuff for some thirty years. In 1977 he presented some of his laboratory data in a paper entitled "An application of direct current neural systems to psychic phenomena."[7] He pointed out that psychic phenomena are not accepted by organized science because it knows of no mechanisms by which they can exist. He went on to point out the lack of logic involved in this, because all these phenomena, whether accepted or not, still are related to some function of the nervous system, and, to varying degrees, represent the mind-body problem. They all represent processes of control and communication within the individual, among individuals, and between individuals and their physical environments.

In his 1985 book, *The Body Electric*,[8] however, Becker comes more aggressively to the point. Why, he asks, if certain living organisms can sense, as is now proven, each other's electromagnetic fields, should we not anticipate finding that psychic functions, such as ESP, telepathy, and clairvoyance, are shared by *all* species? Although he admits that the study of biofields is yet in its infancy, still he points out that pigeons have magnetic detectors thousands of times more sensitive than any technological instrument we have thus far developed. Then there are dogs, cats, and even pet birds who find their way home over hundreds of miles; and, I might add, mothers who sense when their child is in danger.

Becker, bless his heart, even dares the anti-psychic cliques. Pointing out that there is a "curious dogma" in science that considers that what is not understandable doesn't exist, he then observes that mainstream science has dismissed psychic phenomena as delusions or hoaxes simply because they are rarer than sleep, memory, pain, growth, or consciousness — which are all inexplicable in traditional scientific terms — but which must be accepted because they are too common to be denied. I might point out that psychic phenomena actually are not so rare, as we have seen in this book. But mainstream science ignores them anyway.

Becker then goes to bat for psychokinesis. The biofield, he says, lends itself to theories of psychokinesis. The material world, at least in so far as physics has penetrated it, consists of atomic structures

---

7 Becker, Robert O. "An Application of Direct Current Neural Systems to Psychic Phenomena," Psychoenergetic Systems, Vol. 2, pp. 189–186, 1977.
8 Becker, Robert O. The Body Electric: Electromagnetism and the Foundations of Life, William Morrow, New York, 1985.

held together by electromagnetic forces. If some people can *detect* fields from other organisms, why shouldn't some people be able to *affect* others by means of their linked fields — and heal them?

Why not indeed? If some people, I might ask, can affect others, why shouldn't they be able to affect *themselves*, too? Please, at this point, recall the John Traynor and the fish-skin Events described earlier herein.

BEYOND TIME AND SPACE

Well, onwards. The new discipline of studying human electromagnetic (bioinformation) energies being still in its infancy, so far its precepts have not been expanded to include extradimensional and interdimensional possibilities. Do human bioinformation possibilities include cracking through the matter-time barriers? The answer to this comes from another advancing field of inquiry, that of physics: and the answer is a probable yes.

The quantum physics popularizer, Fred Alan Wolf, devotes the entirety of his recent book, *Parallel Universes*,[9] to this question. Wolf doesn't yet actually utilize the term "psychic," but his "space warps," "time warps," "imaginary space," and "spacetime" are equivalents for it.

He talks, for example, of lucid dreaming as an activity which marks the overlapping of parallel dimensions, in which consciousness (or bioinformation potentials) can exist simultaneously.

He points out that "time is invisible," and that it is now a legitimate physics precept that things do not exist in a single universe but in a series of parallel ones, and that the mind can and does live in parallel worlds, as well.

He asks if (and practically states that) the future influences the present — in Chapter 27, entitled "Quantum 'two-timers' and more messages from the future," the topic of "talking to yourself in the future" is thoroughly examined. And in so doing he plunks his readers down in the middle of one of the major topics in this present book, that of psychic precognition and/or prophecy.

---

9 Wolf, Fred Alan, Parallel Universes, Simon and Schuster, New York, 1988.

THE NEW SCIENCE OF THE ELECTRONIC BIOPSYCHIC HUMAN

Thus is a new science of life being born. One in which a consideration of psychic stuff is not only completely unavoidable but is a must. This new science of life differs radically from the science of the past in which even the mention of psychic stuff was ideologically anathema. There are, of course, a few dozen books seeking to describe some aspect of this new science; but it is not the purpose of this present one to review them all. In these books there is something of a scramble to use replacement terms for psychic ones, since mainstream science is still negatively sensitized to their usage. But the replacement terms in all cases are actually referring to psychic phenomena of various kinds.

The new science, therefore, is bringing into existence the rudiments of a new psychic science; and, in fact, it is impossible to grasp the meaning of this new science if its psychical aspects are not overtly considered as being, perhaps, its centerpiece.

The emergence of these new ideas (and the books that appear as a result) arouses something of a hullabaloo in the traditional currents of science upon the grounds that if these new ideas be true, then everything science has stood for in the past is in error. But this is only an alarmist attitude somewhat detached from observing the actual and main goal of science — discovery. Error there may be in "traditional" science, but only in part. After all, a fact can be nothing more nor less than a fact. By its own definition, science can stand for nothing else than facts.

But facts can be *interpreted* in different ways. Hardly any facts science has so far discovered will fall just because a new science is emerging which is discovering new facts. But past facts will, indeed must, be reinterpreted in the light of the new understandings. To seek to prevent reinterpretation can only be seen as authoritarian exercises now almost totally unjustifiable.

A new image of humanity and our potentials is being uncovered, defined, and described. The fact that this image is also a *psychic* image comes as something of a surprise to some, considering past anti-psychic attitudes. But it is an image that more fully reincorporates human psychic experience, which, as we have seen, has been recorded (and in many cultures honored) since time immemorial.

THE BIOELECTRIC HUMAN

- We can observe that a new and extremely important aspect of humanity has swept into human awareness: the knowledge that we are not composed only of matter, but of electromagnetic structures (or blueprints) as well.

- We should expect, therefore, that the limiting images of humanity we get from conventional attitudes in science will have to be altered to incorporate these salient bioelectromagnetic discoveries and their implications.

- We should observe that it is already known that these bioelectric blueprints are of extraordinary importance to medicine, psychology, biology, chemistry, physics, creativity, human well-being, and, of course, psychic stuff.

- We should observe that bioelectromagnetism probably is an important "bridge" between our physical bodies and the realms of invisible energies and forces, and that via this bridge, information which is subtle in its nature flows in and out of our direct-sensing systems.

SUGGESTED PRACTICAL EXERCISES THAT WILL HELP IN EXPANDING PSYCHIC LITERACY

o   Assuming you accept the idea that your direct-sensing systems really exist, take a few moments several times a day to relax quietly and try to focus on them. Doing so will help strengthen the links between these direct-sensing systems and your intellect. Don't be too surprised to find that this linkage is weak at first. It is in many people. In doing this simple exercise, do not try to be telepathic or clairvoyant, etc. These are intellectual concepts that may or may not have anything to do with how your direct-sensing systems actually perceive or interact with bio-information. Learn to recognize your direct-sensing systems in their *own* terms, and not upon terms that, admittedly, are artificial intellectual labels.

o   Ask others if they are aware of their own direct-sensing systems. If they are, get their feelings about what they do for them.

o   If you are up to it, select one of the books in the bibliography having to do with bio-information. Harold Saxton Burr's *Blueprint for Immortality: The Electric Patterns of Life* is written in easy-to-understand terms without over-simplifying its context. Further, it is in print and relatively easy to obtain.

XX

Scientific Astrology

It is easy enough to foresee that the new sciences of solar geomagnetics and bioelectrical biology represent two areas of discovery that can hardly remain completely independent of each other. Indeed, long before I ever heard of them, various inter-blending scientific societies had already begun to form: for example, the International Society of Biometerology, the Society for Biological Rhythm, and the Foundation for the Study of Cycles.

The history of the development of the natural sciences was characterized not by trends toward mutual interactions but by increasing specialization — pursued to such a degree that even scientists in the same discipline developed difficulties in mutual understanding. Scientists claimed their "turfs," so to speak, and, in fact, often took "political" stances to safeguard their turfs' boundaries. For example, biologists had no mutual interactions with physicists, nor chemists with those who studied electromagnetism. And parapsychology was ghettoized in its own "irrational turf."

However, apparently the Age of Interrelated Scientific Fields is now upon us. Scientists in diverse branches of science are beginning to "intercommunicate," as it is politely put — not, I suspect, because they necessarily want to, but because it has now been unavoidably realized that progress in one field of science never fails to have repercussions in all the others. The topics of the New Physics, molecular biology, chemistry, and bioelectric dynamics, for example, are all now recognized as intimately interlinked and have begun to develop together into what some call a "symbiotic" state.

Since all these must in some form begin to deal with bioelectric and bio-information communication processes (i.e., psychic-type processes), it is clear that a new field will join the symbiotic state, a field perhaps so precisely defined that it may be called *biopsychic*.

OK. So we can now foresee a time when symbiotic scientific activity certainly will increase regarding those kinds of psychic phenomena that deal with information processing — i.e., the kind we have considered in the first part of this book. But what of the psychic arts and crafts? Shall they, too, have a renewed place in the scientific future? Apparently so, at least as regards a new form of astrology.

And, as I use this last chapter to round out the backbone of this book, I can say that this last topic just tickles me pink! The proponents of anti-psychic scientism have always treated astrology, in any form, with absolute mockery and derision. They justified this type of treatment by two assumptions: that the planets could not possibly have any direct or indirect effects on living organisms on Earth; and that astrology, being the "confused interpretative craft" that it is, could never be brought into the scientific fold with regard to accepted scientific methodologies.

But if certain astrological phenomena could be demonstrated via accepted scientific methodologies, what then?

SYNCHRONICITY AND COSMIC "ARRANGEMENTS"

Several decades ago I set to work reading through the collected works of the famous Swiss psychoanalyst, Carl Gustav Jung. I was suitably over-awed with the breadth and depth of the great man's thinking — especially when it transcended the then prevalent "normal" psychological theories everyone was expected to bow down to. Jung, I think, posed the ultimate problem *vis a vis* psychic matters when he tried to identify an area of study called synchronicity (the study of coincidences). To illustrate what he meant by synchronicity, he gave an absolutely charming example of it.

Then, only a few years ago, I again came across this same example in a delightful article in *Science*, February 1985, authored by Rudy Rucker, entitled "The Powers of Coincidence: Do hidden forces link seemingly synchronous events?" The example goes thusly.

A Monsieur Deschamps, when a boy, was once given a piece of plum pudding by a Monsieur de Fortgibu. Ten years later, in a Paris restaurant, he saw the same kind of plum pudding and ordered a piece. The restaurant could not accommodate him since the pudding had already been ordered by M. de Fortgibu. Many years later, at a party, the same plum pudding was offered as a delicacy. M. Deschamps remarked that the only thing lacking was M. Fortgibu. At that moment, the door opened, and an old man in the last stages of disintegration walked in — Mr. Fortgibu, who had got hold of a wrong address and burst in on the party by mistake.

Events like this one happen all the time, but since no one knew how to explain them they were called coincidences — which is normally interpreted as chance or random events. However, "coincidence" actually means "occupying the same space of time," and/or "harmonious" or "rhythmic." People who have puzzled their brains over these matters have been able, they think, to identify two types of coincidences — meaningful and unmeaningful. But beyond that no one has gotten very far — except for astrologers.

In his *Science* article, Rucker used the above example to launch his short article into a consideration of whether or not invisible energies and forces link synchronous events, for if they do then they all would be meaningful. Rather, they would be meaningful *arrangements*.

It is somewhat difficult to see how plum puddings could have such cosmic meaning; unless, somehow, the links of causation are carried down into levels that are beyond our capability to make sense of. One implication that can be drawn from this is that the universe entire, and all things in it, are interconnected in some gigantic "patterning" — a skein of objects, events, and experiences both macro and micro, encounters with history, and apparently, even encounters with plum puddings.

Further, these "links," once established at the universal causation level, imply (in the words of Schopenhauer) "a most wonderful pre-established harmony." This harmonious patterning, I should add, would exist whether or not we realize it does.

Now, the traditional applications of the psychic arts and crafts always focused on trying to puzzle out what the invisibles were up to, and the uncontested queen of these arts and crafts was always astrology, since, astrology studies not planets *per se* but causal chains. Thus, we must now have a last look (in this book at least) at astrology to try to determine if it will be a part of the dawning psychic renaissance.

THE ASTROLOGICAL CONNECTIONS

In the 1940s, a French psychologist, Michel Gauquelin, somewhat irritated by astrological craziness and feeling that astrology was "utterly worthless" and could not be demonstrated experimentally, decided to use scientific methods to prove it so. To this end, he collected the birth times of 576 notable French physicians and set to work to see what was what in their horoscopes.

To his surprise, his statistics showed a large majority of physicians were born more often in the two hours after the rise and culmination of Saturn and Mars — a result that could not be attributed to chance alone. (Remember it has already been established in this book that, in astrological terms, Saturn "rules" medicine, hospitals and healing, while Mars "rules" physical vitality.)

Assuming there must be some hidden flaw in his doctors' data, he switched to statistically analyzing the birth times of sports champions — only to find one of his strongest effects. An overly large majority of them were born specifically shortly after the rise and/or culmination of Mars. (Remember, Mars signifies physical activity.)

Gauquelin thence embarked on what was to become his life's work: statistical research regarding the interrelationships of birth times and career choices. Many years of collecting evidence showed, beyond any reasonable statistical doubt, that the large majority of sports champions and exceptional military leaders tend to be born when Mars predominates in the natal chart, i.e., at the ascendant or mid-heaven. The majority of politicians and famous actors have Jupiter at the ascendant or mid-heaven. Scientists have Saturn at those points, while the majority of successful artists have the Moon.

Eventually, Gauquelin and his wife Françoise had statistically analyzed sixty thousand natal charts and were able to reconfirm the original results. He found other "effects." For example, we tend to be born when the planets are approximately in the same positions as they were when our parents were born. He analyzed the natal positions of the planets with regard to temperament, especially establishing planetary factors apparently related to "weak" and "strong" will. For example, many sports types who do not have Mars in a significant place in their natal chart do pursue sports careers anyway but don't get very far. Writers are stronger willed when the Moon is rising or culminating and thus have a better will to succeed.

Gauquelin quickly points out that although the planets apparently do correlate statistically with our basic temperaments, other factors must also be taken into consideration. In his opinion, the planets neither dictate nor directly influence our career choices.

Further, his enormous statistical archives show that these particular correlations seem only to apply to superstars and not to ordinary persons or to those who have failed in life. Gauquelin remains somewhat detached from traditional astrology, claiming it contains baskets-full of erroneous interpretative methods (which is true in my opinion, too). But what he is referring to here is strong and weak natal charts — instantly recognizable to accomplished traditional astrologers but not commonly acknowledged by average astrologers plying their trade to the general public. After all, it would not be good business to tell someone they had a "weak" chart.

At any rate, you get the idea here. For the first time in history, astrology found itself possessed of a quite large statistical basis. This basis did not, and perhaps cannot, confirm the entirety of astrological lore, and in fact is in disagreement with some of it. Nonetheless, what henceforth became known as the "Gauquelin Effect" rests on statistics accumulated by proven scientific methods.

When the news of the Gauquelin Effect began to be noticed by mainstream science as early as 1955, it was ignored. Gauquelin found that astrology can only thrive in the lower-class media but certainly not in science. However, Gauquelin is a lean, mean fighting machine. He felt, and rightly so, that for the first time in the history not only of science but of astrology itself, someone had finally presented a real scientific investigation conducted on a grand scale. He had proposed a methodological guide giving practical explanations of how to study this difficult subject while avoiding errors which previous researchers had not managed to avoid. So, he persisted, and began publishing books.

The response was immediate and large. Subsequently, when mainstream science had recovered from the shock of realizing it could no longer avoid the issue, well, the proverbial feathers hit the fan. Yet mainstream science was now caught between a rock and a hard place. It could hardly deny evidence accumulated via its *own* trusted statistical methods without at the same time being seen as an authoritarian overlord in which science says what the overlord decrees. Therefore, there was nothing to be done except to let Gauquelin proceed.

However, the noise of the hullabaloo also reached the citadels of scientism in which astrology was viewed with the contempt normally otherwise reserved for the lowest of the pseudoscientific scum. Shortly, Gauquelin found his plate rather full at having to deal with anti-astrological scientistic cliques determined by means fair or foul to dispose of the Gauquelin Effect.

In the United States one of these cliques, calling itself a "scientific committee," determined to accumulate "their own" statistics fully anticipating that the Gauquelin Effect would not appear in "their more honest" work. Duly, they found themselves able to announce the total absence of the Effect and exhausted themselves in demeaning Gauquelin as a blemish on the professions of science.

However, the "committee" which conducted this this second set of birth-time analyses contained one person who suddenly and without forewarning defected from it, absconding with relevant research documents. These documents proved that the Gauquelin Effect had appeared in the "committee's" impartial analysis, and with the same magnitude. A scientific decision was therefore taken that the "committee" should fake its own statistical results and claim that the Effect was not present in them.[1] Were it not for the defector, Gauquelin would have been professionally ruined and his work relegated to the bin of pseudoscience forevermore — or until (and if) another investigator conducted a similarly large body of work.

Via this rather rocky road, eventually science will have to begin incorporating at least statistical astrology into its bulwark of accumulating facts.

Now if, for example, every time a sports champion is born, the planet Mars is mostly on the ascendant or mid-heaven of the child's astrological chart, are we not looking at something that resembles M. de Fortgibu turning up every time M. Deschamps eats a certain kind of plum pudding? In other words, a synchronicity, a pattern of some kind, a *repeating pattern* — a *cycle*! Yes, we most certainly are.

If it is a cycle we are looking at, would we not expect planetary correlations to turn up in that somewhat esoteric science called the study of cycles?

---

1 This fiasco received considerable press coverage. Its details may be found in several sources. See Gauquelin, Michel, Birth-Times: A Scientific Investigation of the Secrets of Astrology, Farrar, Straus & Giroux, New York, 1983, pp. 109-114. Also, Rawlins, Dennis. "Starbaby," Fate, October 1981, pp. 67-98. It may also be noted that Fate, bless its heart, publishes continuing updates on anti-psychic machinations.

THE ASTROLOGY OF CYCLES

Referring back to a situation discussed earlier, in which it had become apparent that activities of the Sun were disrupting our ESP research at Stanford Research Institute, one of the questions that needed to be considered was this: was it possible to predict ahead of time when the Sun was going to become active? If so, we could increase successful results by working only on days when the Sun would not be upsetting things — and go to the beach on days it was.

Alas. Although it took some time and effort to find it out, no one really knew how to predict what the Sun was going to do. True, the National Oceanic and Atmospheric Administration Environmental Research Laboratories at Boulder, Colorado, which monitors the Sun continuously, made attempts to predict Solar activity two weeks ahead of time. But they struggled to be consistently correct at it. What to do? Well, as they say, when there is a real need, sometimes the universe provides.

Not long after this disappointing discovery, I was in New York taking a week's leave from the rigors of ESP research in California. I went shopping in the August heat in an occult bookstore — naturally, one of my passions. I noticed a small announcement tacked on the bulletin board to the effect that one John Nelson, whom I had never heard of, was going to talk about the planets and, further, according to the notice, was just about to do so.

Now, it was HOT and sweaty. Moreover, it was New York's rush hour. And anyway, I had already heard a lot of astrological nuts talk about the planets. What more could I learn? Yet before I knew what I was doing I had flung myself in a taxi and was transported to the hotel where this lecture was going to take place. Once in the room, I saw there were only six other rather glum types present. My heart sank. This was going to be a bomb.

Nelson was slender as a reed, in his sixties and rather damp from his taxi ride from the airport. I could tell he was disappointed by the small turnout. And I was disappointed for his sake, too. He seemed quite a decent, but meek fellow. He began his talk, and barely fifteen minutes later the hairs on my arms were standing erect — for it was clear that John Nelson was an Avatar from the Future. And, further, he had at least part of the answer to my problems with the mighty Sun. He was to become one of my dearest friends and my Instructor, and I his willing long-term student.

His story is thus: For most of his life he worked as a radio propagation analyst for RCA Communications which was once the largest shortwave radio communication organization in the world. However, radio broadcasting suffered badly from the same thing our ESP experiments did — solar eruptions and sunspots. Whenever the Sun was acting up, radio broadcasting became full of static and noise and sometimes completely impossible. In 1946, it became clear that the shortwave radio industry needed a reliable magnetic storm forecasting service so that advance preparations could be made for alleviating the effects of these periodic disruptions.

RCA asked John Nelson to undertake research on this topic and to try to figure out a forecasting method. Although other researchers, both in government and observatories, were working on the problem, no progress had been made. After two years of careful research, Nelson came to the conclusion that solar eruptions and sunspots were only a small part of the answer. His data told him that there were patterns in the disruptions that repeated themselves not exactly, but approximately. It was evident to him that some natural forces besides the disruptions themselves were in some way involved.

He was able to conclude that whatever it was affecting the Sun had something to do with the solar system itself — and the most likely candidates in the solar system were the planets. They revolved around the Sun in a gigantic dance of variable patterns. Could *the planets* be responsible for Solar disruptions?

Shortly, Nelson was able to provide at least a partial answer: yes, they are. When the planets "arrange" themselves in certain patterns, the Sun erupts. Soon he was able to construct a satisfactory forecasting service for RCA which was dependable eighty-five percent of the time. In April 1951, RCA released to the news media a detailed account of Nelson's research regarding the planetary position effects that he had found. This news release thence generated considerable interest in the field of astronomy. But it did put that science dangerously close to forbidden astrology and so the reactions overall were, as it was said, mixed and, even, heated.

Skeptical astronomers argued that the planets were too small and too far from the Sun to possibly have any effect on its behavior. Nelson countered by saying that he agreed the planets had very little, if any, effect upon the *main* body of the Sun, but that they could have considerable effect in the solar *atmosphere* where sunspots existed. Here, in the very unstable electrified area of the Sun's surface, a very small force from the planets could produce an avalanche effect and create turbulence in the solar atmosphere which resulted in solar storms and sunspots. These then produced solar showers that, upon reaching Earth's ionosphere, disturbed it and made shortwave broadcasting difficult.

A considerable scientific debate ensued. Meanwhile, the shortwave industry world-wide, government agencies, observatories, and other interested parties (such as a legion of stock market analysts) began subscribing to Nelson's monthly forecasting sheet and continued to do so until his untimely death.

Although Nelson had published, in 1978, his forecasting techniques in a small book entitled *The Propagation Wizard's Handbook*,[2] still his methods were somewhat complex. I begged to become his student in order better to understand all the aspects involved and thus discovered that Nelson had not included certain salient factors in his book — mainly the ones he continued to discover in later years.

For example, on his monthly forecasting sheets there began to appear certain check marks against certain days. When I called to ask what they meant, he told me they were for the benefit of certain "other" clients which, I discovered, were stock market analysts. Nelson had been able to extend his forecasting to include days on which the market would move up or down significantly. Now, is this not a *practical* application of knowing about the movements of the planets?

Although Nelson always winced at the word "astrology," and insisted his methods had nothing to do with it, he was soon seen by many astrologers as one of "their" darlings; for, in fact, his techniques for planetary forecasting at least resembled a *type* of astrology and, since they were statistically and practically usable, a type of science and technology, too.

Nelson and Gauquelin were the first to confirm that the motions and arrangements of the planets do indeed affect earth and life and conditions upon it — admittedly not in the way traditional astrology says they do, but in ways that are undeniably akin to

---

[2] Nelson's book The Propagation Wizard's Handbook, has long been out of print. A competent version of it has been issued under the title Cosmic Patterns: Their Influence on Man and His Communication, by the American Federation of Astrologers, 6 Library Court, S.E., Washington D.C., 20003.

astrology's central hypothesis: that the planets and their changing, cyclic arrangements do correlate with activities on Earth. However, they were not the first to suspect that such was the case.

In the early 1930s several German astrologers began to suspect that planetary arrangements had something to do with sunspots, and speculation that this might be the case occurred even earlier. Prior to 1965, various researchers had demonstrated scientifically several "planetary" connections with living organisms: that living beings regulate their rhythms of life according to the movements of the Sun and Moon; that the composition of human blood varies with cosmic influences; and that chemical tests showed that planetary influences and cycles affect the water content of human cells.

Indeed, the Soviets must have developed their bio-information sciences directly as a result of taking these verified phenomena seriously — while in the West these scientifically-achieved discoveries were suspended in doubt because of the "astrological" implications.

As mentioned above, if, then, planetary arrangements do correlate with cycles, we should expect to find that these correlations are also visible in cycles characterizing other phenomena besides birth times and short-wave radio disturbances.

Indeed, the Foundation for the Study of Cycles, founded by Edward R. Dewey in 1941, began to plot planetary correlations to certain kinds of cycles as early as 1955.[3] Specific planetary arrangements can be correlated to cyclic activity of earthquakes, volcanoes, weather patterns, naturally to the sunspot cycles, lynx abundance, grasshopper outbreaks and other wildlife cycles, rhythms in tree growth, airplane traffic, cotton, steel, and cigarette production, and, of course, stock prices, gold and silver cycles, building booms, wars, fashion changes, and periods of war and peace.

Clearly then, enabling ourselves to correlate this kind of stuff opens the future to a type of forecasting, a type of future-seeing, via a kind of "astrological" proficiency.

But the case for planetary influences has opened even wider. Artificial satellites launched into space have confirmed that space is

---

3 See Dewey, E.R., "A Key to Sunspot-Planetary Relationship," in Cycles — Selected Writings, Edward R. Dewey, Ed., Foundation for the Study of Cycles, Inc., Pittsburgh, 1970, pp. 254-259.

not empty, as once was completely believed to be the case, but rather is permeated with an infinite number of waves and frequencies which emanate from not only the planets, but the stars, too, which affect our planet and all life forms on it.

In a sense, then, the "intuition" of the ancients was correct when they assumed that human life is interconnected with the cosmos by invisible threads.

WHY WE NEED TO KNOW ABOUT ASTROLOGY AND CYCLES

Now, you might ask *why* we should involve ourselves with all this exceedingly complex astrological stuff in the first place? I've even heard a few people say something like this: "well, what's gonna happen is gonna happen, and there ain't nothin' we can do about it."

I started hearing certain people say this when I was a child. I heard it said in the hallowed halls of the United Nations when I worked there. I've even heard a few "astrologers" say it, these apparently not having understood the "work" of astrology at all.

Although this kind of outlook obviously contains portions of fatalism and pessimism, it must be admitted that it contains a little realism, too. Look at it this way. Sometimes people who *know* they can't cope with something are the best ones to identify and describe that something and perceive its outcomes. On the other hand, perpetual optimists who are always busy smiling and "coping" are just those who cannot see anything else outside their optimistic vistas.

Both pessimism and optimism, but especially pessimism, exist because a certain illiteracy also exists. Illiterate people are those who, more or less, must accept certain amounts of fatalism in their philosophy — because they know they are not up to understanding what must be dealt with. This is perhaps the greatest curse, and Fate, of the illiterate.

But the same must be true on larger scales. For example, if humanity as a whole is also illiterate in a given area, then what's going to happen will, and humanity can only stoically, if morosely, observe this "realism."

In 1728, the Chevalier de Ramsay, having noted one of these "areas," said of it: "The History of former times is like that of our own. Human Understanding takes almost the same Forms in different Ages, and loses its Way in the same Labyrinths."[4] The Chevalier de Ramsay indeed spoke sooth, which is to say, announced a certain realism — and one which, I think, should take on great meaning as we approach our very difficult future.

At any rate, we can't very well cope with things about which we are illiterate. In this book we have seen that our direct-sensing systems can and do alert us to dangers or opportunities which our intellects themselves otherwise fail to perceive. The term "alert" implies that a *future* situation is being forecasted. And the fact that an enormous amount of people have experienced these spontaneous, direct sensing inputs attests to the realism that the future *can* be forecasted in many ways.

Yet, when our direct-sensing systems fail us, to what methodologies might we turn? Well, obviously, those that study the invisibles, those that forecast their cycles — and their synchronicities. For example, in Jung's anecdote at the front of this chapter, by the third time M. Deschamps had encountered that certain plum pudding, he noted that M. Fortgibu should also turn up — which he actually did. This is, of course, a mini-cycle, but it *is* a cycle nonetheless — in that certain events always come together as a cycle.

Michel Gauquelin's massive amounts of data regarding birth times and planetary arrangements clearly shows that Mars and/or Saturn are present at the horoscope's cardinal points when doctors or scientists are born. *Perhaps it is the other way around*: when the twos planets are at the cardinal points of their horoscopes, we might expect doctors or scientists to be born — much as M. de Fortgibu turns up in relationship to M. Deschamps' plum puddings.

Gauquelin probably has not discovered yet that when Mars is in the zodiacal sign Virgo, wars get going more often than when Mars is in any of the other eleven zodiacal signs. In other words, here is an *alert* staring us in the face, and one that will allow forecasting years and decades ahead of time. The fact that wars come and go on a cyclical basis had definitely been demonstrated by those who study cycles; and some of the same people have noted the Mars connection as well.

If Saturn or Mars is in a strategic place in the horoscope of scientists and doctors (near the mid-heaven in the case of Albert

---

[4] The Chevalier de Ramsay, A Discourse Upon the Theology and Mythology of the Ancients in the Travels of Cyrus, Vol. II, p. 78, 1728.

Einstein), then it is also possible to note that when an intuitive is born, Pluto and/or Uranus often will be found at one of the four cardinal points in their horoscope. When a politician is born, Jupiter will be found to be strategically placed many times more than can be expected by chance. And, when that politician chances to be running for high office, if the selfsame Jupiter is crossing that person's mid-heaven at the time of the elections, he or she will probably be elected to that office, as we have seen.

But these planetary phenomena are not just planetary phenomena. For, you see, the planets *move* in a great waltz of interlocking *cycles* — and living organisms dance to their tunes. If someone really wants war to manifest, astrologically speaking the planetary waltz will obviously help them. But if wiser people might observe the planetary and cyclical war possibilities here, such might be avoided by the exercise of great tact and reticence. However, none of this need have caught anyone by surprise, since the placement of Mars in the zodiac can be forecast years ahead of time.

The point here is, of course, that if we can anticipate cycles we can take precautions to avert their observably related effect or, perhaps, take advantage of them. This, then, is why we need to become literate about all this kind of stuff — at the individual as well as at the larger social levels. Such, in fact, is the stated purposes of those who do study cycles and those who do study astrology, in whatever form. The presence of certain mixes of invisible energies and forces can be revealed through these arts and crafts. It is entirely feasible that humanity really need not lose "its Way in the same Labyrinths."

THE INESCAPABLE CONCLUSION

The purpose of these last chapters has been to pull together various psychic factors that will project our psychic literacy toward the future. These psychic factors are being derived not from tradition or history, from myth or beliefs or opinions, but rather from contemporary and completely respectable scientific activities which increasingly are revealing the rudiments of human psychic potentials. There can be little doubt that these new discoveries will increasingly converge and result in a new science of psychic matters.

It is this expectation that illuminates the need for increases in psychic literacy overall and even suggests a certain urgency. Indeed, if our bio-information (direct-sensing) potentials in some way *can* perceive such "other realities" as the future, then our intellectual capabilities of understanding the implications are of extraordinary importance. Only an increase in psychic literacy will aid our intellects to grasp the implications and supreme importance of our psychic potentials.

One question has remained unanswered. How were the ancients enabled to conceive of and accept invisible matters that are generally visible to us today only via acceptance based on scientific methods? There are at least two possible answers to this.

First, it is clear that they did not deny human experience. To them, apparently, if humans experienced something, then it "belonged" to nature and the natural orders. Our modernist culture more or less has rejected the value of human experience, distrusting it if it could not be seen to conform to the rigid and arbitrary expectations of scientism.

But, second, the ancients had views of existence and of human frailties that were gradually abandoned in the seventeenth and eighteenth centuries. Implicit in a great deal of our modern thinking has been the idea that what is inaccessible to our physical senses cannot exist. Indeed, this view protects those who hold it from ever being proved wrong in that they simply believed that our sense organs are our only source of knowledge. The mind, duly conditioned to this view, then acts to prevent other knowledge from being revealed to it.

As the occult researcher David Conway, points out: "Ancient thinkers were aware of this danger and it worried them, for they believed that the acquisition of knowledge depends to a large extent on the disposition of the knower, requiring him to adapt to the type of information available to him. His 'adequacy' (*adaequatio rei et intellectus*) was the term they used to describe this process and, though doubtless ready to admit that our sense organs are more or less adequate to acquaint us with physical reality, they realized too, that other types of reality might lie beyond their reach. It was important therefore that the *possibility* of these should never be rejected. As Heraclitus put it: if we do not expect the unexpected, we shall be sure not to find it."[5]

---

[5] See Conway, David, Secret Wisdom: The Occult Universe Explored, Jonathan Cape, London, 1985, pp. 58-59.

It is a sad mark on our recent cultural history that we, today, are now obliged to rediscover and accept — and catch up with — this ancient wisdom.

At any rate, the processes for doing so are now underway, and the acceptance of "other types of reality" will, as it did in the case of the ancients, lead to deeper interests in discovering how other realities impact on our lives. Although we today are still hooked on scientific credibility and dare make no conclusions about anything that has not first been scientifically "approved," it is starting to be suspected that at least some of these other realities are accessible via direct psychic apperception — a long-accepted fact for the ancients.

However, the new sciences reviewed above are bringing into existence not only a scientific credibility regarding invisible information-communication processes in the human organism, but also a scientific study of the invisible elements connected with planetary positions and terrestrial cycles and their various phenomena. None of these new developments are dissimilar to the psychic arts and crafts.

The inescapable conclusion, then, is that a psychic renaissance has begun. And it is a *scientific* and technological development most of all!

SCIENTIFIC ASTROLOGY

o   We can observe that the advent of computers has enabled statistical researchers to analyze incredible amounts of data that before were unmanageable. Submitting as many as sixty thousand birth times to computer analysis has revealed direct correlations between planetary placement at birth and the eventual choices of professions.

o   We can observe that direct relationships between certain planetary positions and solar activity has been confirmed. The relationship between certain planetary positions and natural phenomena on earth and between human activities and behavior has also been scientifically confirmed.

o   Thus, we should observe that based on these confirmations a type of astrology does exist — and thus a new science of astrology is coming into existence.

o   We can observe that the ongoing science of the study of cycles has also noted certain astrological connections to cyclic activity of many different kinds, including phenomena that are distinctly human, such as war, peace, stock investing, and so forth. The unavoidable implication is that even human activities are somehow influenced by astrological factors.

SUGGESTED PRACTICAL EXERCISES THAT WILL HELP IN EXPANDING PSYCHIC LITERACY

o   In a quiet moment, make a list of your intellectual attitudes concerning astrology and its potentials. Study them carefully, trying to spot the time they were programmed into your intellect, and upon what basis.

o   In conversation, ask others what *their* attitudes are regarding the *usefulness* of astrology.

o   Make an effort to discriminate between popular "newspaper" astrology and "functional" astrology.

o   Select one or more of the astrological texts listed in the bibliography and read them at leisure. Especially, consider reading those published by Michel Gauquelin (see bibliography).

* * *

IF WE DO NOT UNDERSTAND THE PARAMETERS INVOLVED, WE KNOW WE ARE ALMOST CERTAIN TO MAKE GRAVE MISTAKES AND/OR WILL ACHIEVE VERY LITTLE. BUT, TO THE DEGREE WE UNDERSTAND THE NATURE OF ALL THE PARAMETERS INVOLVED, AND DELIBERATELY STRIVE TO INCREASE THAT UNDERSTANDING, WE CAN ALMOST DEPEND ON ACHIEVING MIRACLES. UNDERSTANDING IS THE KEY ELEMENT IN ALL THIS. IT IS EASY ENOUGH SAID THAT, NEXT TO PERCEPTUAL ABILITIES, UNDERSTANDING IS PROBABLY THE PREMIER ABILITY IN THE VAST ARRAY OF ALL HUMAN ABILITIES.

* * *

Conclusion

In the first part of this book I reviewed in anecdotal form various kinds of psychic stuff that are prevalent in our present culture which are not unlike what has been experienced in the historical past. In so doing I was obliged to review the existence of powerful anti-psychic attitudes also prevalent in our modern culture, since the way in which psychic phenomena are viewed is dependent not only on their verifiable existence but the cultural treatment of their verification by anti-psychic attitudes.

The kinds of psychic phenomena I reviewed were selected based upon the criteria that they (1) have an extraordinarily long history of occurrence, and (2) they have value and practical meaning regarding human needs. Psychic capabilities can and should be interpreted *only* in the light of the meaning and value they hold for the human experience.

Anti-psychic sentiments have been very powerful in the modern epoch, and in view of the strength and duration of these sentiments it is something of appreciative wonder that observation of these phenomena did not pass permanently out of human interests. I have attempted to demonstrate why they did not do so. Interest in psychic matters continues to renew itself solely because creative people in pursuit of their goals actually depend on psychic inputs as valued sources of information unobtainable by any other means.

All the psychic phenomena reviewed in this book have also been demonstrated as having value and meaning to the one thing that can never be ignored — human survival. Thus interest in and curiosity about psychic possibilities will never pass completely out of human considerations, no matter how the socially dominant attitudes view them.

The realization that psychic stuff is important and useful to human survival is perhaps the only realization that will stimulate a true and accurate interest in achieving psychic literacy. If observation of the phenomena is governed by any other specialized interests, interpretations of the meaning and value of the psychic "mainframe" will soon derail into boxed and limited intellectual speculations.

It has been asserted that the study of psychic phenomena is meaningless if they cannot be interpreted in the light of biological chemical-mechanistic principles.

Certainly we should strive to match up psychic and biological operations everywhere we can. But our understanding of these material principles — just as of psychic principles — is bound to be incomplete and partially erroneous. Yet the search for truthful principles rightly proceeds in all fields of unconventional as well as conventional investigation. And this incompleteness of theory and data is not confined to investigators of biological chemical-mechanistic principles. For over a hundred and fifty years now, modern pro-psychic enthusiasts have continuously worked under the assumption that psychic capabilities were functions of the human mind, and that the mind was centered in the physical brain. They did so with full knowledge that the working definitions of the mind were certainly questionable and suspiciously incomplete. Even so, the modern psychic research paradigm was erected upon this assumption, and its expectations were derived from it.

The psychic vocabulary used reflects this assumption. Telepathy was mind-to-mind transmission of information from brain to brain. Clairvoyance was the perception by the mind of distant information beyond contact of the physical senses. Precognition was the mind transcending the time barrier. The accepted definitions of these terms thoroughly locked expectations in the psi-mind-body hypothesis. And these definitions thoroughly infested not only pro-psychic scientific attitudes but popular ones as well. The fact that during this 150-year period very little progress was achieved in resolving psychic issues *in any way* certainly suggests the basic hypothesis was in error — which should have been understood much earlier.

However, correction to the hypothesis had to wait upon discovery of the essential electromagnetic nature of biological organisms, a discovery that logically might have taken place in parapsychology but did not. Rather it took place in physiology, a sector of scientific inquiry not at all prepared at first to cope with the psychical implications of biological electromagnetism. And, in large part, this discovery did not take place in the United States or the scientifically cultivated West but in the Asian regions that together comprise much of the Soviet Union.

Chimerically, the discovery therein of the bio-information potentials of biological electromagnetism was quickly realized to be of such import that this development was probably one of the first elements to begin altering the ideological dialectical materialism upon which the Soviet Union had been founded in the first place.

All this, of course, represents a cultural saga of some magnitude barely skimmed across in this book, whose future chapters must be written in the special ways only learned hindsight can give.

Bio-information electromagnetic potentials can no longer be discussed without also considering the substance and meaning of the psychic capabilities of organisms. Hence, the basic psychic hypothesis which has endured for 150 years must now undergo redefinition in the light of bio-information theory. Past psychic terminologies certainly must be abandoned, to be replaced by new terms more in keeping with ongoing bio-electromagnetic discovery. All this equates to the emergence of a new psychic science which may not even have retained or preserved the word "psychic."

What this book then represents more than anything else is a descriptive transition from the modernist psychic paradigm of the immediate past to the new emerging one of the immediate and farther future. However, the new paradigm, beyond its purely scientific aspects, will have to acknowledge the most basic meaning of bio-information capabilities in terms of human experience.

I have cast the contents of this book in popular terms rather than in parapsychological or scientific ones because I believe it very important for the popular intellect to be able to conceive of these issues and the changes they portend, and because the greatest reservoir of understanding human psychic experience lies neither in the elite environments of parapsychology nor in science but with the people. The humanitarian advances that can result from the saga explored in this book are enormous, as is the meaning of it to our present and ongoing "consciousness revolution."

In my mind, the best way to support the birthing of these humanitarian and consciousness potentials is for the people in general to increase their psychic literacy. My long experience within the active parts of the saga itself placed me in a good position to be able to view the whole of it. And thus this book resulted.

As many readers will by now have observed, I've focused only on certain specific kinds of psychic stuff—those that are most pertinent to the coming bio-information transformation, and thus to the dawning psychic renaissance. These specific kinds of psychic stuff all deal with and are carriers of *information*, specifically information having meaning to survival in various ways, ranging from death crises up to financial prosperity. There are, of course, other kinds of psychic phenomena. I have omitted some of them because they need yet another book for full treatment, and I've omitted others because, in my opinion, there are phenomena labeled "psychic" which in reality are not.

However, we are quickly approaching a transformation in which attempts to distinguish between what is and what is not psychic probably will no longer be fruitful. This transformation will entail acknowledgment that the human organism is not a biological one, but a *biopsychic* one. Thus, with the exception of survival issues, the standards even I am presently using to judge will probably have become irrelevant. You see, even I will have to continuously update my own psychic literacy — or, should I say, bio-information literacy.

The developmental course of this transformation will cling very closely to the practical issues and applications of psychic stuff as these are discovered, recovered, or realized. Not only scientific discovery will determine the shape of the scientific psychic renaissance, because the future exigencies of human survival and prosperity may play a dominant role. After all, people whose direct-sensing systems and intellects have achieved good integration will always be in a better place to grasp survival issues. And these necessarily will not be only scientists, but also leaders, communicators, artists, providers, teachers, and people trying to make it in life.

And at any rate, the coming Age of Practical Necessity is most likely also to be an age in which the people more actively assume the burdens of clearing the avenues for human biological, cultural, and *psychic* survival. Already it is clear enough that the people are determined no longer to dwell under scientocracy or politocracy and are increasingly more determined to assume the challenges of their own inherent capabilities and merits.

This is how it should be, and I, for one, wish them well and much success.

BLESSINGS.

INGO SWANN

Afterword
Ingo's Psychic Renaissance

Dean Radin, PhD
Chief Scientist
Institute of Noetic Sciences, Petaluma, California, USA
September 29, 2018

Ingo Swann was one of the most celebrated and rigorously tested psychics in recent times. As such, his Psychic Literacy manuscript, published here for the first time, provides a valuable snapshot of his unique perspective on parapsychology as of 1989. As I write this Afterword, nearly 30 years have passed since Ingo finished his manuscript. This raises a number of interesting questions: How has parapsychology fared in the intervening three decades? Has the psychic renaissance he was anticipating been achieved? Do we have a better understanding of what's going on behind the scenes with psychic effects, which refers to the invisible forces, agendas, and purposes that Ingo described? Is the scientific evidence stronger today than it was back then? Are psychic abilities more accepted by the general public and in scientific circles? And have parapsychologists begun to embrace esoteric topics like astrology?

The answers to these questions vary in ways that Ingo would have appreciated. He knew that psychic abilities would not become broadly embraced based only upon personal or scientific evidence, but rather — as with all controversial and taboo topics — acceptability is strongly moderated by fads and fashions in history, culture and sociopolitics. When the timing is right, these factors can conspire to vastly accelerate progress. In 1989, most people would have laughed at the idea that in a mere 30 years same-sex marriage and legalized recreational marijuana would be the law of the land in the United States and nearly all other developed countries. But after decades of grassroots preparation, one day we wake up and previously unthinkable taboos are "suddenly" broken.

With this in mind, as far as Ingo's vision of the psychic renaissance goes, the cultural shift is underway, but only if you know where to look. From a scientific perspective, which is reflected in the "serious" mainstream media, parapsychology is still mostly treated as entertainment or as silly pseudoscience. On the other hand, from the perspective of popular culture, psychic themes remain dazzlingly lucrative, as seen in the endless television shows and superhero movies that capitalize on psychic tropes. The sensational success of "paranormal fiction," like the Harry Potter franchise, also demonstrates that public interest in psychic abilities remains as popular as it has ever been. But while the orthodoxy stubbornly maintains the status quo, Ingo's vision is slowly but surely coming into focus.

Consider, for example, an article that appeared in the May 2018 issue of American Psychologist, the flagship journal of the American Psychological Association (APA), the principal US-based professional organization for academic and clinical psychologists. In that issue, the lead article was entitled, "The Experimental Evidence for Parapsychological Phenomena: A Review." The author was Etzel Cardeña, professor of psychology at Lund University in Sweden. After analyzing 10 classes of experiments exploring psychic effects ("psi" for short), Cardeña's conclusion was unequivocal: "The evidence for psi is comparable to that for established phenomena in psychology and other disciplines." That this article appeared in the conservative voice of academic psychology — which among scientific disciplines has traditionally been the most skeptical about psychic abilities — cannot be overstated. It represents an academic sea change in topics that are appropriate for serious debate.

Another sign that we are in the midst of a cultural shift is a statement by University of California statistics professor Jessica Utts. In 2016, Utts was President of the American Statistical Association (ASA), the world's largest organization of academic and professional statisticians. In her Presidential Address, she mentioned that one area she had studied in detail on behalf of the US government was parapsychology. She said: "The data in support of precognition and possibly other related phenomena are quite strong statistically and would be widely accepted if they pertained to something more mundane." Her opinion was offered in a matter-of-fact way to a mainstream scientific audience, and unlike the hysterical calls for witch-burning that such a statement might have evoked in past years, it was received with mildly raised eyebrows.

A third sign is the endorsement of my 2018 book, Real Magic (Penguin Random House). In that book I explored the esoteric lore about magic and compared those ancient practices to what we investigate in parapsychology. Connections between the esoteric traditions and psychic phenomena are obvious, as Ingo mentioned. But until very recently that relationship was strictly avoided by most parapsychologists because it was embarrassing to even mention that psychic ability lay at the core of all of the esoteric traditions. And yet, even with the social pressure in academia that causes most psi researchers to dodge this connection, I was grateful to receive endorsements by two Nobel Laureate scientists, by a program director of the National Science Foundation, by scientists who won major prizes from the National Institutes of Health and the National Academy of Sciences, and by numerous other prominent scientists and scholars. That indicates the psi-taboo is weakening.

A fourth sign can be seen in a big international science conference sponsored in 2018 by the pharmaceutical company Merck, of Darmstadt, Germany. That conference, held in honor of Merck's 350th anniversary as a company, including 35 invited speakers, 30 of whom were world-class scientists and entrepreneurs working at the leading edges of their fields, and 5 were Nobel Laureates. I was one of the invited speakers, and I was specifically asked to speak about the relationship between science, magic, and psychic phenomena.

These signs indicate that Ingo's renaissance is proceeding apace. Some of the emerging cultural openness to psychic phenomena is probably due to the widespread adoption of practices like meditation and yoga, but the acceleration is also attributable to two other reasons: First, the scientific evidence is much stronger today than it was in 1989; and second, we have far better ways of assessing if results in laboratory studies are in fact repeatable.

When Ingo was writing Psychic Literacy, meta-analytical techniques were relatively new, and they were just beginning to be applied to the literature of parapsychology. Meta-analysis is a statistical method for objectively measuring if experimental effects are repeatable by integrating study outcomes across many similar experiments. As the article in American Psychologist showed, questions about repeatability of psi effects has been settled in the affirmative for at least 10 classes of psychic experiments. Ingo was pessimistic about scientific progress in parapsychology because until the rise of meta-analysis, the goal of most researchers was to find the one perfect psychic experiment that anyone could easily replicate. Today we know that that Holy Grail was an illusion, and that establishing repeatability across experiments is a more efficient and realistic way to establish the authenticity of an effect.

What about our understanding of invisible forces, agendas, and purposes? Here too notable progress has been made by acknowledging that just like all other forms of perception and cognition, psychic abilities appear to bubble up to awareness from the deep unconscious. In recognition of this, researchers devised new and more efficient experimental methods. Ingo's development of a remote viewing training scheme was part of this trend. Earlier forced-choice protocols, like the ESP card tests pioneered by J. B. Rhine, were superseded by Ingo's (and others') free-response methods, and by the use of unconscious physiological and behavioral methods. While ESP card tests were effective in demonstrating psychic abilities, they were also intensely boring, so it wasn't surprising that performance in those tests was difficult to sustain.

By contrast, the newer types of experiments were designed to tap into some of the invisible factors that Ingo was writing about; they did this by using the unconscious mind to perform psychic tasks. These tests had the advantage of not forcing the subject to consciously "be psychic" on demand, they also avoided the problem of statistical biases that occur in repeated forced-choice tests, and in some tests the entire experiment would consist of a single trial, which significantly reduced the problem of boredom. These newer experimental methods (that is, as of Ingo's 1989 manuscript) included the following:

Ganzfeld telepathy, which uses a mildly altered state of consciousness to enhance mental awareness of subtle psychic impressions. In a typical experiment, a "sender" is given a photographic target randomly selected out of a pool of 4 photos, and then she is asked to telepathically send it to a "receiver" who is isolated by distance and shielding. After the sending period, the receiver is asked to select which of four possible photos the sender was trying to mentally send. Under this design, if telepathy did not exist, the best she could do would be to select the correct target 1 in 4 times, for a 25% "hit rate." But after 108 published studies, consisting of over 4,000 individual test sessions, the overall hit rate was 32%. Because so many repeated experiments were conducted, this seemingly modest increase over the chance-expected hit rate is associated with mind-bending odds of 10,000 trillion to one.

Presentiment tests, which measure unconscious fluctuations in human physiology prior to being exposed to a future, randomly selected stimuli. After 26 experiments were published, involving physiological measures such as heart rate, skin conductance, pupil size, and electrical brain activity, a meta-analysis was reported in 2012. The overall odds against chance were determined to be 100 million to one. An updated meta-analysis, published in 2018, found another set of 19 published studies and confirmed the positive results of the earlier analysis.

Implicit precognition, a time-reversed effect based on an idea borrowed from social psychology, called priming. In a conventional priming study, you are shown an emotional word like "happy," and then you see a photo with either happy or sad content. You are asked to press a button as soon as you decide that the emotions of the word and photo either match or mismatch. Most people are faster when making decisions about matched emotions than mismatches. In the implicit precognition experiment, this temporal order is reversed, such that the photo is shown first, and then the subject decides if it is displaying happy or sad content, and then the priming word is shown. The idea is that the priming word shown in the future will influence how fast the initial decision is made. A 2016 meta-analysis of 90 repeated experiments exploring this time-reversed effect, which was reported from 33 labs around the world, resulted in odds against chance of over a billion to 1.

Ingo would have been deeply satisfied to know that advances in experimental methods were helping to bring about his envisioned renaissance. But what would he have thought about those super-skeptical scientists who pooh-pooh psychic abilities as pseudoscientific nonsense without bothering to study the evidence? Such people are still among us, of course. But given the results of the latest meta-analyses, and the slow but sure transformations in cultural and scientific acceptance, what sustains these extreme skeptics?

The simple answer is that people believe what they want to believe. Some people will never accept the existence of psychic phenomena regardless of the strength of the evidence or even their own experience. But it's also possible that some people — especially academics — who are quick to publicly denounce parapsychology do so not because they don't believe in psi, but because they feel that if they were too openly sympathetic they might lose their job. To test the idea of an "anti-psi taboo" that constrains what people feel comfortable to admit, we conducted an anonymous survey among adults in the United States to find out what kinds of psychic effects people have actually experienced first-hand, and not what they profess to believe.

To do this, we formed a list of 25 different kinds of psychic phenomena, ranging from intuitive hunches, to telepathy, clairvoyance, precognition, and beyond. In a random selection of 283 members of the general population, we found that 94% reported that they had personally experienced at least one of the 25 psychic effects, and on average they reported 7.7 such experiences. Then, among 175 randomly selected scientists, we found that 93% reported at least one of the 25 psychic effects, and on average 8.7 experiences. This outcome supported our suspicion that a very large majority of the population, including scientists, had personal psychic experiences. But scientists in particular learn to not to talk about them, because they feel it isn't safe to do so. The echoes of the Inquisition, which cruelly reinforced the taboo that prohibits public admission of psychic gifts, ended centuries ago. But its effects continue to reverberate in the modern academic world.

Finally, have parapsychologists begun to embrace esoteric topics long associated with psychic phenomena, like astrology? For many active psychic researchers today (but not all), this remains a bridge too far. The struggle to gain academic acceptance depends largely on perceived credibility, and while the astrological analyses described by Ingo are fascinating and may well lead to important insights someday, adding astrology to parapsychology's toolbox would make an already combustible topic dangerously explosive. At some point, when the "woo-woo taboo" finally dissolves, it is likely that many ancient methods of divination, including astrology, will play an increasingly important role within the range of topics that parapsychologists will be inclined to investigate. There is already fledgling interest in how conventional geocosmic variables correlate with psychic performance, including geomagnetic fields, solar wind, and lunar cycles.

In sum, looking back at Ingo's *Psychic Literacy* with the benefit of hindsight, I can say with confidence that some portions of his vision are in the process of unfolding. The new Age of Enlightenment he was imagining may take another 30 to 60 years to come to full fruition, assuming that present cultural and scientific support continue their current trends. With that support, it seems increasingly certain that Ingo's vision will become a reality.

Glossary
WORKING TERMS AND NEW CONCEPTS
USED IN THIS BOOK

ALIGNMENT

"Align" means to be in or come into precise adjustment or correct relative position. In this book, "alignment" is majorly used with regard to adjusting our intellectual equipment into correct relative positions regarding psychic phenomena and their "workings." (See INTELLECTUAL SPECULATION.)

ANTI-PSYCHIC SYNDROME

A "syndrome" is a group of signs or symptoms that occur together and characterize a particular response pattern which, in psychology, is normally referred to as an abnormality. In this book, "anti-psychic syndrome" is utilized to indicate pattern-response prejudices and intellectual attitude formations that avoid observing psychic factors, or deny their existence altogether, and which actively seek to extend these same prejudices or attitudes into a larger public.

BIOELECTRICAL RHYTHMS

It has now been determined that all living processes are closely associated with bioelectrical processes. The question is under study regarding whether or not the electromagnetic fields generated by living organisms themselves have control and information functions. It appears that they do, and that they do so in rhythm with local electromagnetic environments and terrestrial and cosmic electromagnetic rhythms. Since it is now known that information can be exchanged via these same mechanisms, such knowledge supports the greater psychic hypothesis.

BIOFIELD

Recent research has established that all terrestrial animals, including the human species, possess electromagnetic fields that extend outside the physical body, and that these biofields also have effective means of communication exchange. The state of biofields at any given time can be correlated with electric and magnetic atmospheric fields, electromagnetic oscillations, and atmospheric ions. Such communication exchanges are completely analogous to traditional interpretations of psychic communication exchanges. (See BIO-INFORMATION, BODY ELECTRIC.)

BIO-INFORMATION

A term derived from Soviet research regarding possible mechanisms involved in the interaction between electromagnetic radiation and biological systems — often also referred to as "biosignals." The science of determining the exact nature and information content of biosignals is in its infancy, but it has been established that at least some of this content includes information completely analogous to psychic-type information. (See PSYCHIC CAPABILITIES.)

BIOPSYCHIC

Refers to the capability of biological organisms to receive, emit, and exchange information via mechanisms independent of the normally accepted five senses.

BODY ELECTRIC

The sum of all the bioelectrical processes and their electromagnetic fields in a living organism which direct intra-biological activity, process electromagnetic information, and communicate with other electromagnetic fields external to it. Many of these processes equate to capabilities normally identified as psychic.

COSMIC ACTIVITY

Various kinds of radiation originating in areas beyond the terrestrial environment, particularly in the Sun, and brought to Earth in various ways, such as by the solar winds and by planetary vibrations and oscillations, which in various ways impact on and "cause" effects in inorganic matter and organic systems. It is now clear that such activity is important to Earth's living organisms — an assumption which has traditionally been fundamental to astrology.

CYCLE

An interval of time during which one sequence of a recurring succession of events or phenomena is completed; a course or series of events that recur regularly and usually lead back to a starting point; a repeating reactive rhythm or oscillation of any kind. Intervals of time between repetitions in a cycle can vary from nanoseconds to millennia.

DESTINY

In this book, "destiny" refers to any progression of human activities that is in some way brought about or affected by invisible energies which is constructive. Such activities appear to draw on free, life-supporting energies which may be either visible or invisible, and which culminate in constructive ends. (See FATE.)

DIRECT-SENSING CAPABILITIES

In this book, "direct-sensing capabilities" is used with reference to the sensing any information not directly available to the five major physical senses on the one hand or not directly available to intellectual perception on the other. The term nearest in meaning is "intuition," i.e., the power or faculty of attaining to direct knowledge or cognition without rational thought and inference.

However, this book seeks to extend understanding and literacy beyond the confines of old labels by introducing terms that are more in keeping with observable processes. We possess many direct-sensing capabilities that cannot be included within the scope of the term "intuition." (See INTELLECT and OBSERVER METHOD.)

ELECTRO-MAGNETOSPHERE

A "sphere" produced by an electromagnetic field. This term is usually used with regard to Earth's electromagnetic field which extends some distance into space and which interacts with other cosmic electromagnetic fields, such as the Sun, the planets and, presumably, the stars.

FATE

In this book, "fate" refers to any progression of human activities that is in some way brought about or affected by invisible energies which is destructive or leads to destructive culminations. Such activities appear to be bound up with visible and invisible forces which "drive" actions toward destructive or unhappy results. (See DESTINY.)

HUMANISTIC

Anything that contributes to extending human self-realization and enlarging human potentials in a positive sense — as contrasted to "anti-humanistic," i.e., anything that prevents the acquisition of knowledge concerning the true parameters of human potentials.

INFORMATION GLUT

The present-day proliferation of information which seems increasingly to exceed our individual, social, scientific, or cultural capabilities of intellectually being able to assimilate or constructively integrate it, leading to a variety of intellectual breakdowns.

INTELLECT

The power to know as distinguished from the power to feel or will. Intellect is thought of as the capacity for knowledge, especially via rational or intelligent thought. However, any given intellect is only as good as the quality and extent of the knowledge it contains.

INTELLECTUAL SPECULATION

Any temporary sifting of information which attempts to develop an understanding of something without "closing the doors" to future developments or future rethinking on the subject. However, much intellectual speculation does function upon a "closed door" basis and seeks to interpret facts and phenomena without acknowledging their larger relationships and implications.

INTELLECTUAL STEREOTYPE

An intellectual idea conforming to a fixed or general pattern, especially a standardized mental picture held in common by members of a group and representing an oversimplified opinion, affective attitude, or uncritical judgment.

LIFE-SERVING

Anything that positively serves the enlargement of the survival potentials of living organisms and the maintenance of such potentials. (See DESTINY.)

MATTER/TIME BARRIER

A "point" beyond which our physical senses cannot perceive information and which acts as a "barrier" to our abilities to perceive unless we shift awareness to include psychic perception of information which, as it were, lies "outside" physical perception of matter and time. (See PSYCHIC CAPABILITIES.)

OBSERVER METHOD

The process by which we come to realize, know, or sense through consideration of observable facts whether or not these conform to what is believed.

OCCULT BARRIER

"Occult" means "to cover up" and refers to anything hidden, secret, or concealed, including things that cannot be detected or seen by the physical senses or the rationalizing intellect. In this sense, OCCULT BARRIER refers to obstacles to knowing made up of secreted, concealed, hidden, or not-revealed information.

PARADIGM

A pattern, especially of thinking or of attitudes, which describes how things are viewed by most people at any given time, and from which certain expectations are derived. Sufficient accumulation of new information which cannot be accommodated by a given paradigm necessitates its replacement by a new one.

PARAPSYCHOLOGY

The term "parapsychic" was coined by the French psychical researcher Emile Boirac (1851-1917) for "all phenomena produced by living beings or as a result of their actions, which do not seem capable of being entirely explained by already known natural laws and forces." Although the term caught on in Germany, it was never extended into general usage, but rather was translated into the term "parapsychology" as popularized by the late Dr. J.B. Rhine in the United States. PARAPSYCHOLOGY is a transition term that represents a shift of emphasis regarding how psychic stuff should be researched. The general goal of the earlier psychical researchers was to observe psychic phenomena and report on their findings. Most of these findings necessarily collided with conventional science paradigms, which found them dubious.

The goal of parapsychologists was to "make psychical phenomena safe for science" by adopting acceptable scientific research methodologies, mostly by conducting statistical analyses of laboratory tests. Since most psychical phenomena "evade" direct statistical analysis, parapsychologists drifted in the direction of experimenting only with those that might be statistically accommodated. Generally speaking, they have failed in their attempts to make psychic stuff safe for science, since science still regards even their selected phenomena as dubious. (See PSYCHICAL RESEARCH, PSYCHOTRONICS, PSYCHOENERGETICS.)

PSYCHIC CAPABILITY

In this book, "capability" refers to a state pre-existing before a proficiency is developed, but upon which a proficiency can be constructed. A proficiency culminates in highly refined abilities, which, in turn, manifest as effects controlled by will, i.e., end products. During the last one hundred years, terms such as "telepathy," "clairvoyance," "precognition," etc., have all come to denote certain abilities and capabilities. This book strives to point out that these are end products of proficiencies, rather than the proficiencies or their underlying capabilities themselves. The human organism apparently possesses numerous (perhaps thousands of) psychic capabilities that have not been identified — and none of which *can* be identified by seeking to compress them into the available terminology. Rather than do so, then, in this book the older existing terms are generally abandoned, and terms more descriptive of the apparent capability-processes involved are utilized instead. For example, our organisms appear to be able to link to the future and transcend the matter-time barrier — hence the term "future-seeing" is utilized instead of the older term "precognition" which is generally defined as the mind perceiving the future. Insofar as we understand the mind, no basis for this definition has been discovered. The mind perceives only what it can perceive, and so the crucial distinction is that our perception extends beyond what the mind is capable of perceiving.

PSYCHIC DYSFUNCTION

Impaired psychic functioning, the inability to actively sense or utilize psychic information being provided by one's direct-sensing systems. Psychic illiteracy also may be considered dysfunctional.

PSYCHIC GAP

Any void in individual, social, scientific, or cultural understanding regarding psychic matters: also, any such void that is "filled in" with rationalizations whose "explanations" are not consistent with observable facts regarding psychic stuff.

PSYCHIC LITERACY

A condition of intellectual mobility regarding psychic matters that encompasses a maximum of personal experience, direct and indirect observations, intellectual learning, larger rather than smaller amounts of background information, and the ability to perceive spoken/unspoken contexts.

PSYCHIC REALISM

The ability to observe psychic phenomena and their apparent "workings" independently of intellectual, moral, political, religious, scientific, or cultural pro or con prejudices.

PSYCHOENERGETICS

A term coined in the United States in the late 1970s which is roughly equivalent to the new Soviet term "psychotronics," for the similar purposes of avoiding the semantic difficulties arising from the terms "psychical research" and "parapsychology."

Both "psychoenergetics" and "psychotronics" represent a shift in emphasis regarding not only how psychical phenomena are to be studied, but to what ends, with a particular focus on practical applications of psychic activity irrespective of whether or not such activity fits accepted scientific theories. (See PSYCHICAL RESEARCH, PARAPSYCHOLOGY, PSYCHOTRONICS.)

PSYCHOTRONICS

A term coined in the U.S.S.R. and the East Bloc countries in the early 1970s, presumably to avoid the semantic difficulties represented by the terms "psychical research" and "parapsychology." Essentially, however, it implies an extension of parapsychology by indicating the relationship of humanity to the universe, particularly the interaction with other physical bodies and matter and with "fields of energy, known or unknown." By this definition, PSYCHOTRONICS comes closest to how I am using the term "psychic" in this book. (See PSYCHICAL RESEARCH, PARAPSYCHOLOGY, PSYCHOENERGETICS.)

PSYCHICAL RESEARCH

Formal, organized attempts to research the general scope of psychical phenomena, instituted in 1882 with the founding of The Psychical Research Society in London. This term remained in general usage until the mid-1930s but fell into disuse and disfavor thereafter. (See PARAPSYCHOLOGY, PSYCHOTRONICS, PSYCHOENERGETICS.)

SCIENCE

Systematized knowledge of the world and existence, as distinguished from ignorance and misunderstanding, such knowledge being attained through a formal process of empirical, experimental discovery and verification. Scientific knowledge generally refers to discovering general truths and the operation of general laws.

SCIENTISM

A dogmatic belief in conventional scientific knowledge as it is currently defined, in accord with a preconceived philosophical outlook — usually materialistic and anti-psychic in nature — that is characterized by a tendency to reject paradigm-challenging evidence.

SUCCESSFUL LIFE, THE

The result of operating at the fullest, most constructive potential possible for any given person. The successful life operates on the assumption that the amount of happiness is, in the longer run, greater than the amount of unhappiness, and that the individual can correct situations that tend to prolong the latter. Perception of visible and invisible energies and forces that impact on one's life is almost mandatory for pursuing and establishing the successful life.

SYNTHESIZE CONTEXTS, TO

To bring together, intellectually, the obvious and the not-so-obvious so as to form a whole of understanding that is greater than the sum of its parts.

Bibliography

In terms of literacy problems, bibliographies are something of a difficulty considering today's information glut. If I were to include all the printed materials used to conceptualize this book, the bibliography would be about 70 pages long. This would be of no service to general psychic literacy. Therefore, I've had to select. I've included sources most pertinent to the content of this book. Books on psychic matters that will be of service to "beginners" are marked with a single asterisk. Those describing some aspect of the New Sciences are marked with a double asterisk. Most books listed probably can be obtained through any general, or occult, metaphysical, or New Age bookstore.

***

Arieti, Silvano. *The Intrapsychic Self.* Basic Books, Inc., New York, 1967.

Ayer, A.J., *Philosophy in the Twentieth Century.* Vintage Books, New York, 1982.

Bandler, Richard, and Grinder, John. *The Structure of Magic.* Science and Behavior Books, Inc., Palo Alto, CA, 1975.

*Barker, Stan. *The Signs of the Times: The Neptune Factor and America's Destiny.* Llewellyn Publications, St. Paul, MI, 1984.

*Becker, Robert O., and Marino, Andrew A. *Electromagnetism and Life*, State University of New York Press, Albany, 1982.

**Becker, Robert O., and Selden, Gary. *The Body Electric: Electromagnetism and the Foundations of Life*, William Morrow, New York, 1985.

*Bentov, Itzhak. *Stalking the Wild Pendulum: On the Mechanics of Consciousness.* Wildwood House, London, 1978.

**Bergler, Edmund. *The Superego: Unconscious Conscience*, Grune & Stratton, New York, 1952.

**Blakemore, Colin, and Greenfield, Susan, Eds. *Mindwaves: Thoughts on Intelligence, Identity, and Consciousness*. Basil Blackwell, Inc., New York, 1987.

Bollingen Series XXX — 3. *Man and Time*, Pantheon Books, New York, NY, 1957.

Boswell, Rolfe. *Prophets and Portents: Seven Seers Foretell Hitler's Doom*. Thomas Y. Crowell Company, 1942.

Brown, Daniel P. "A Model for the Levels of Concentrative Meditation," *International Journal of Clinical and Experimental Hypnosis*, Vol. XXV, No. 4, 1977, p. 236-273.

**Burr, Harold Saxton. *Blueprint for Immortality: The Electric Patterns of Life*. The C.W. Daniel Company, Ltd., London, 1988.

**Bush, Vannevar. *Science is Not Enough*. William Morrow & Co., Inc., New York, 1967.

Carelli, Adriano. *The 360 Degrees of the Zodiac*. The American Federation of Astrologers, Inc., Tempe, AZ, 1977.

**Carrel, Alexis. *Man the Unknown*. Harber & Brothers, New York, 1935.

Carter, C.E.O. *An Encyclopaedia of Psychological Astrology*. The Theosophical Publishing House, London, 1970.

"Cheiro" (Louis Hamon). *Cheiro's World Predictions*. London Publishing Co., London, 1927.

"Cheiro" (Louis Hamon). *Fate in the Making*. Harper & Brothers Publishers, New York, 1931.

Cirlot, J.E. *A Dictionary of Symbols*. Philosophical Library, New York, 1978.

*Conway, David. *Secret Wisdom: The Occult Universe Explored*. Jonathan Cape, London, 1985.

**Cousins, Norman. *The Pathology of Power*. W.W. Norton & Company, New York, 1987.

**Cozzi, Steve. *Generations and the Outer Planet Cycles*. American Federation of Astrologers, Inc., Tempe, AZ, 1986.

Curti, Merle. *Human Nature in American Thought*. The University of Wisconsin Press, Madison, 1980.

Day, Harvey. *Seeing into the Future*. Thorsons Publishers Ltd., London, 1966.

Dean, E.D., and Sherwood, H.C. "Dollars May Flow from the Sixth Sense," *Nation's Business*. April 1967, p. 64-66.

Dean, E. Douglas, et al. *Executive ESP*. Prentice-Hall, New York, 1974.

Devore, Nicholas. *Encyclopedia of Astrology*. Philosophical Library, New York, 1957.

**Dewey, Edward R. *Cycles — Selected Writings*. Foundation for the Study of Cycles, Pittsburgh, PA, 1970.

**Dewey, Edward R., and Mandino, Og. *Cycles: The Mysterious Forces that Trigger Events*, Manor Books, 1973.

Dingwall, Eric J., Ed. *Abnormal Hypnotic Phenomena: A Survey of Nineteenth Century Cases (in five volumes)*. J. & A. Churchill, Ltd., London, 1967.

Dixon, N.F., *Preconscious Processing*. John Wiley & Sons, New York, 1981.

Dixon, N.F., *Subliminal Perception: The Nature of a Controversy*. McGraw-Hill, London, 1971.

Dobin, Rabbi Joel C. *The Astrological Secrets of the Hebrew Sages*. Inner Traditions International, Ltd., New York, 1977.

**Dubrov, A.P. *The Geomagnetic Field and Life: Geomagnetobiology*. Plenum Press, New York, 1978.

**Dubrov, A.P., and Pushkin, V.N. *Parapsychology and Contemporary Science.* Consultants Bureau, New York, 1982.

**Dunne, J.W. *The Serial Universe.* Faber & Faber Limited, London, 1934.

**Dunne, J.W. *"Intrusions?."* Faber and Faber, London, 1955.

*Ebon, Martin, Ed. *The Psychic Reader.* The World Publishing Company, New York, 1969.

*Ebon, Martin. *Psychic Warfare: Threat or Illusion?.* McGraw-Hill Book Company, New York, 1983.

**Edelman, Gerald M., and Mountcastle, Vernon B. *The Mindful Brain: Cortical Organization and the Group-Selective Theory of Higher Brain Function.* The MIT Press, Cambridge, 1978.

*Ehrenwald, Jan. *The ESP Experience: A Psychiatric Validation.* Basic Books, Inc., New York, 1978.

Eiseley, Loren. *The Unexpected Universe.* Harcourt, Brace & World, Inc., New York, 1969.

Ellenberger, Henri F. *The Discovery of the Unconscious.* Basic Books, Inc., New York, 1970.

**Epstein, Gerald. *Waking Dream Therapy: Dream Process as Imagination.* Human Sciences Press, New York, 1981.

**Epstein, Gerald. *Healing Visualizations: Creating Health Through Imagery.* Bantam Books, New York, 1989.

**Fedynskii, V.V., Ed. *The Earth in the Universe.* National Aeronautics and Space Administration, the National Science Foundation, Washington, D.C., 1968.

**Feldman, David Henry. *Nature's Gambit: Child Prodigies and the Development of Human Potential.* Basic Books, Inc., New York, 1986.

**Ferguson, Marilyn. *The Aquarian Conspiracy.* J.P. Tarcher, Inc. Los Angeles, 1980, 1987.

**Ferguson, Marilyn. *The Brain Revolution: The Frontiers of Mind Research*. Taplinger Publishing Company, New York, 1973.

Fodor, Nandor. *Freud, Jung, and Occultism*. University Books, Inc., New Hyde Park, NY, 1971.

Forman, James Henry. *The Story of Prophecy: In the Life of Mankind from Early Times to the Present Day*. Tudor Publishing Company, New York, 1940.

**Gauquelin, Michel. *Birth-Times: A Scientific Investigation of Astrology*. Farrar, Straus & Giroux, New York, 1983.

**Gauquelin, Michel. *The Scientific Basis of Astrology*. Stein and Day, New York, 1969.

**Gauquelin, Michel. *Written in the Stars*. The Aquarian Press, Wellingborough, Northamptonshire, England, 1988.

*Gawain, Shakti. *Creative Visualization*. Bantam Books, New York, 1982.

Geley, Gustave. *From the Unconscious to the Conscious*. Harper & Brothers Publishers, New York, 1920.

*Gittelson, Bernard, and Torbet, Laura. *Intangible Evidence*. Simon & Schuster, Inc., New York, 1987.

*Glass, Justine. *They Foresaw the Future: The Fascinating Story of 6000 Years of Fulfilled Prophecy*. G.P. Putnam's Sons, New York, 1969.

*Goldberg, Philip. *The Intuitive Edge: Understanding and Developing Intuition*. Jeremy P. Tarcher, Inc., Los Angeles, 1983.

Goodavage, Joseph, F. *Astrology: The Space Age Science*. Parker Publishing Co., Inc., West Nyack, NY, 1966.

Graven, Jacques. *Non-Human Thought*. Stein and Day, New York, 1967.

*Greene, Liz. *The Astrology of Fate*. Samuel Weiser, Inc., York Beach, ME, 1984.

Greenhouse, Herbert B. *Premonitions: A Leap Into the Future.* Bernard Geis Associates, New York, 1971.

*Gribbin, John. *Forecasts, Famines, and Freezes.* Walker Company, New York, 1976.

**Gribbin, John. *Time-Warps.* Delacorte Press, New York, 1979.

Grim, John A. *The Shaman.* University of Oklahoma Press, 1983.

Hampden-Turner. *Maps of the Mind: Charts and Concepts of the Mind and its Labyrinths.* Macmillan Publishing Co., New York, 1981.

Hardinge, Emma. *Modern American Spiritualism.* University Books, New Hyde Park, NY. 1970.

Hayles, N. Katherine. *The Cosmic Web: Scientific Field Models & Literary Strategies in the 20^h Century.* Cornell University Press, Ithica, NY, 1984.

Haynes, Renee. *The Society for Psychical Research — 1882-1982: A History.* MacDonald & Co., London, 1982.

Heidegger, Martin. *Being and Time.* Harper & Row, New York, 1962.

Heline, Corinne. *Occult Anatomy and The Bible: Healing and Disease in the Light of Rebirth and the Stars.* The Rosicrucian Fellowship Press, Oceanside, CA, 1940.

*Hewish, A. *Seeing Beyond the Visible.* American Elsevier Publishing Co., Inc., New York, 1979.

*Hill, Napoleon, and Stone, W. Clement. *Success Through a Positive Mental Attitude.* Prentice-Hall, Inc., Englewood Cliffs, NJ, 1960.

Hillman, James. *Re-Visioning Psychology.* Harper & Row, New York, 1975.

*Hirsch, E.D., Jr. *Cultural Literacy.* Random House, New York, 1988.

**Hoffer, Eric. *The True Believer*. Harper & Row, New York, 1951.

Hogue, John. *Nostradamus & The Millennium*. Doubleday & Company, Garden City, NY, 1987.

Holden, James H., and Hughes, Robert A. *Astrological Pioneers of America*. The American Federation of Astrologers, Tempe, AZ, 1988.

Hooper, Judith, and Teresi, Dick. *The 3-Pound Universe: Revolutionary Discoveries about the Brain from the Chemistry of the Mind to the New Frontiers of the Soul*. Macmillan Publishing Company, New York, 1986.

Howe, Elic. *Astrology: A Recent History Including the Untold Story of Its Role in World War II* (also published as *Urania's Children*). Walker and Company, New York, 1967.

Hudson, Thomson Jay. *The law of Psychic Phenomena: A Working Hypothesis for the Systematic Study of Hypnotism, Spiritism, Mental Therapeutics, Etc.* (1896) republished by Hudson-Cohan Publishing & Communications Company, Salinas, CA, 1979.

*Inglis, Brian. *Natural and Supernatural: A History of the Paranormal*. Hodder and Stoughton, London, 1977.

*Inglis, Brian. *Science and Parascience: A History of the Paranormal — 1914-1939*. Hodder and Stoughton, London, 1984.

*Kalweit, Holder. *Dreamtime & Inner Space: The World of the Shaman*. Shambhala, Boston, 1988.

Kitagawa, Joseph M., and Long, Charles H., (Eds.). *Myths & Symbols: Studies in Honor of Mircea Eliade*. University of Chicago Press, Chicago, 1969.

*Krippner, Stanley. *Human Possibilities: Mind Exploration in the USSR and Eastern Europe*. Anchor Press/Doubleday, Garden City, NY, 1980.

Lamon, W.H. *Recollections of Abraham Lincoln, 1847-65*. A.C. McClurg and Co., Chicago, 1895.

Lay, Wilfrid. *Man's Unconscious Spirit*. Kegan Paul, Trench Trubner & Co., Ltd., London, 1921.

Le Bon, Gustave. *The Crowd: A Study of the Popular Mind*. The Viking Press, New York, 1960.

Leinbach, Esther V. *The Degrees of the Zodiac*. L.N. Fowler & Co., Ltd., London, 1973.

Lonsdale, William. *Star Rhythms: Readings in a Living Astrology*. North Atlantic Books, Richmond, CA, 1979.

Lundsted, Betty. *Planetary Cycles: Astrological Indicators of Crisis & Change*. Samuel Weiser, Inc., York Beach, ME, 1984.

Luria, A.R. *The Mind of a Mnemonist*. Basic Books, Inc., New York, 1958.

**MacClaine, Shirley. *Dancing in the Light*. Bantam Books, New York, 1985.

MacIver, R.M. *Power Transformed*. The MacMillan Company, New York, 1964.

*MacKenzie, Andrew. *Riddle of the Future: A Modern Study of Precognition*. Arthur Barker Limited, London, 1974.

**Maslow, A.H. *The Farther Reaches of Human Nature*. The Viking Press, New York, 1971.

Mauskopf, Symour H., and McVaugh, Michael R. *The Elusive Science: Origins of Experimental Psychical Research*. Johns Hopkins University Press, Baltimore, 1980.

*McConnell, R.A. (Author & Publisher). *An Introduction to Parapsychology in the Context of Science*. University of Pittsburgh, 1983.

*McConnell, R.A. (Editor & Publisher). *Parapsychology and Self-Deception in Science*. University of Pittsburgh, 1983.

McDonald, J. "How Businessmen Make Decisions," *Fortune*. August 1955, p. 84-87.

Meerloo, Joost A. *Along the Fourth Dimension*. The John Day Company, New York, 1970.

Merlau-Ponty, Jacques, and Morando, Bruno. *The Rebirth of Cosmology*. Alfred A. Knopf, New York, 1976.

Merrel-Wolff, Franklin. *The Philosophy of Consciousness Without an Object: Reflections on the Nature of Transcendental Consciousness*. Crown Publishing Group, New York, 1983.

Mihalasky, John. "The Role of Precognition in Risk-Analysis," *The Engineering Economist*. Summer 1972, p. 55-62.

Montgomery, Ruth. *A Gift of Prophecy: The Phenomenal Jeanne Dixon*. William Morrow & Company, New York, 1965.

Moore, Thomas. *The Planets Within: Marsilio Ficino's Astrological Psychology*. Bucknell University Press, London, 1982.

Morrish, Furze. *Outline of Astro-Psychology* Rider and Company, London, 1952.

**Nelson, J.H. *Cosmic Patterns: Their Influences on Man and His Communication*. American Federation of Astrologers, Washington, D.C., 1974.

*Nicholson, Shirley. *Shamanism*. The Theosophical Publishing House, Wheaton, IL, 1987.

Nye, Robert A. *The Origins of Crowd Psychology*. SAGE Publications Ltd., London, 1975.

Osborn, Arthur W. *The Future is Now: The Significance of Precognition*. University Books, New Hyde Park, NY, 1961.

Osty, Eugene. *Supernormal Faculties in Man*. Methuen & Co., Ltd., London, 1923.

**Peat, F. David. *Synchronicity: The Bridge Between Matter and Mind*. Bantam Books, New York, 1988.

**Peck, M. Scott. *The Road Less Travelled: A New Psychology of Love, Traditional Values, and Spiritual Growth*. Simon and Schuster, New York, 1978.

Pendell, Elmer. *Why Civilizations Self-Destruct*. Howard Allen, Cape Canaveral, FL, 1977.

Penfield, Wilder. *The Mystery of the Mind: A Critical Study of Consciousness and the Human Brain*. Princeton University Press, Princeton, NJ, 1975.

**Phillips, Stephen M. *Extra-Sensory Perception of Quarks*. The Theosophical Publishing House, Wheaton, IL, 1980.

Pietsch, Paul. *Shufflebrain: The Quest for the Hologramic Mind*. Houghton Mifflin Company, Boston, 1981.

*Playfair, Guy Lyon. *If This Be Magic*. Jonathan Cape, London, 1985.

*Playfair, Guy Lyon. *The Indefinite Boundary*. St. Martin's Press, New York, 1967.

*Playfair, Guy L., and Hill, Scott. *The Cycles of Heaven: Cosmic Forces and What They are Doing to You*. Avon Books, New York, 1979.

Podmore, Frank. *Mediums of the 19th Century*. University Books, New Hyde Books, NY, 1963.

*Pollack, Jack Harrison. *Croiset the Clairvoyant*. Doubleday & Company, Garden City, NY, 1964.

**Popp, Fritz-Albert. *Electromagnetic Bio-Information*. Urban & Schwarzenbert, Munich, 1979.

Popper, Karl R., and Eccles, John C. *The Self and Its Brain: An Argument for Interactionism*. Springer International, 1977.

Presman, A.S. *Electromagnetic Fields and Life*. Plenum Press, NY, 1970.

*Prince, Walker Franklin. *Noted Witnesses for Psychic Occurrences*. New University Books, New Hyde Park, NY, 1963.

Purucker, G. de. *Occult Glossary: A Compendium of Oriental and Theosophical Terms*. Theosophical University Press, Pasadena, CA, 1972.

*Puthoff, Harold, and Targ, Russell. *Mind-Reach: Scientists Look at Psychic Ability*. Delacort Press, New York, 1977.

Rucker, Rudy. *Infinity and the Mind: The Science and Philosophy of the Infinite*. Bantam Books, New York, 1983.

Russel, Eric. *Astrology and Prediction*. Drake Publishers, Inc., New York, 1972.

Saraydarian, Torkom. *Symphony of the Zodiac*. Aquarian Educational Group, Sedona, AZ, 1988.

*Schmeidler, Gertrude. *Extra-Sensory Perception*. Atherton Press, New York, 1969.

Schwartz, Berthold Eric. *Parent-Child Telepathy*. Garrett Publications, New York, 1971.

"Sepharial" (Walter Gorn Old). *An Astrological Survey of the Great War, Being an Examination of the Indications Attending the Outbreak and Presumptive Effects of the Conflict*. W. Foulsham, London, 1914.

"Sepharial" (Walter Gorn Old). *Cosmic Symbolism*. David McKay, New York, (n.d.).

"Sepharial" (Walter Gorn Old). *The Great Devastation: A Prophecy of Times that Are Coming Upon Europe*. London, 1915.

**Sheldrake, Rupert. *A New Science of Life: The Hypothesis of Formative Causation* (Ed. note: now published as *Morphic Resonance: The Nature of Formative Causation*). J.P. Tarcher, Inc., Los Angeles, 1981.

**Sheldrake, Rupert. *The Presence of the Past: Morphic Resonance and the Habits of Nature*. Times Books, New York, 1988.

Shumaker, Wayne. *The Occult Sciences in the Renaissance: A Study in Intellectual Patterns.* University of California Press, Berkeley, 1972.

Sinclair, Upon. *Mental Radio.* Werner Laurie, London, 1951.

Smith, Frank. *Insult to Intelligence.* Arbor House, New York, 1986.

*Smith, Huston. *Beyond the Post-Modern Mind.* The Theosophical Publishing House, Wheaton, IL. 1982.

Snider, Denton J. *Feeling Psychologically Treated and Prolegomena to Psychology.* Sigma Publishing Co., St Louis, 1905.

**Snow, Chet B., and Wambach, Helen. *Mass Dreams of the Future.* McGraw-Hill Publishing Company, New York, 1989.

Soal, S.G., and Bowden, H.T. *The Mind Readers.* Doubleday & Co., Garden City, NY, 1960.

Swann, Ingo. *Natural ESP: The ESP Core and Its Raw Characteristics.* Bantam Books, New York, 1987.

Szasz, Thomas S. *The Manufacture of Madness: A Comparative Study of the Inquisition and the Mental Health Movement.* Harper & Row, New York, 1970.

Tabori, Paul. *Pioneers of the Unseen.* Taplinger Publishing Company, New York, 1972.

*Talamonti, Leo. *Forbidden Universe: Mysteries of the Psychic World.* Stein and Day, New York, 1975.

Tantum, William H. (Ed.). *The Doomed Unsinkable Ship.* 7 C's Press, Inc., Riverside, CT, 1974.

*Targ, Russell, and Harary, Keith. *The Mind Race: Understanding and Using Psychic Abilities.* Villard Books, New York, 1984.

Terletskii, Yakov Petrovich. *Paradoxes in the Theory of Relativity.* Plenum Press, New York, 1968.

Tester, Jim. *A History of Western Astrology*. Ballentine Books, New York, 1987.

Thass-Thienemann, Theodore. *The Subconscious Language*. Washington Square Press, New York, 1967.

*Time-Life Books. *Mysteries of the Unknown (Series)*: Alexandria, VA: *Psychic Powers* (1987), *Cosmic Connections* (1988), *Mind Over Matter* (1988), *Psychic Voyages* (1988).

Ulman, Montague, and Krippner, Stanley, and Vaughan, Alan. *Dream Telepathy*. MacMillan Publishing Co., New York, 1973.

Underhill, Evelyn. *Mysticism*. E.P. Dutton, New York, 1961.

*Vandenberg, Philipp. *The Mystery of the Oracles*. MacMillan Publishing Co., New York, 1979.

*Vaughan, Alan. *Patterns of Prophecy*. Turnstone Press, London, 1974.

*Warcollier, Rene. *Mind to Mind*. Creative Age Press, New York, 1948.

*Watson, Lyall. *Beyond Supernature*. Bantam Books, New York, 1988.

Webb, James. *The Flight from Reason*. MacDonald, London, 1971.

West, D.J. *Eleven Lourdes Miracles*. Gerald Duckworth & Co., Ltd., London, 1957.

**White, John, Ed. *Psychic Warfare: Fact or Fiction?*. The Aquarian Press, Willingborough, Northamptonshire, 1988.

Wieman, Henry Nelson. *The Directive in History*. The Beacon Press, Boston, 1949.

**Wilber, Ken, and Engler, Jack, and Brown, Daniel P. *Transformations of Consciousness; Conventional and Contemplative; Perspectives on Development*. New Science Library, Shambhala, Boston, 1986.

Wilkins, Hubert, and Sherman, Harold. *Thoughts Through Space*. Creative Age Press, New York, 1942.

Williams, John K. *The Wisdom of Your Subconscious Mind*. Prentice-Hall, Inc., Englewood Cliffs, NY, 1964.

Wilson, Colin. *Mysteries: An Investigation into the Occult, the Paranormal & the Supernatural*. G.P. Putnam's Sons, New York, 1978.

Wilson, Colin. *Religion and the Rebel*. Salem House, Salem, NH, 1984.

*Wilson, Colin. *The Psychic Detectives*. Mercury House, San Francisco, 1985.

**Wilson, Robert Anton. *Cosmic Trigger*. Falcon Press, Phoenix, AZ, 1977.

*Wilson, Robert Anton. *Prometheus Rising*. Falcon Press, Phoenix, AZ, 1986.

*Wilson, Robert Anton. *The New Inquisition: Irrational Rationalism and the Citadel of Science*. Falcon Press, Phoenix, AZ, 1986.

**Wolf, Fred Alan. *Parallel Universes*. Simon and Schuster, New York, 1988.

**Wolf, Fred Alan. *Star Wave: Mind, Consciousness and Quantum Physics: An Original Interpretation of What Quantum Physics Tells Us about the Human Mind*. MacMillan Publishing Company, New York, 1984.

Yates, Frances A. *The Art of Memory*. University of Chicago Press, Chicago, 1966.

Zain, C.C. *Mundane Astrology*. The Church of Light, Los Angeles, 1963.

Zelenski, Countess. *Noted Prophecies Concerning the Great War and the Great Changes to Follow*. Yogi Press, Chicago, 1917.

**Zukav, Gary. *The Dancing Wu Li Masters: An Overview of the New Physics*. William Morrow, New York, 1979.

THOSE WHO CAN CONQUER MATTER, ENERGY, SPACE AND TIME,
CAN TRANSFORM THEM INTO UNBELIEVABLE THINGS.

About the Author

Ingo Swann (1933-2013) was an American artist and exceptionally successful subject in parapsychology experiments. As a child he spontaneously had numerous paranormal experiences, mostly of the OBE type, the future study of which became a major passion as he matured. In 1970, he began acting as a parapsychology test subject in tightly controlled laboratory settings with numerous scientific researchers. Because of the success of most of these thousands of test trials, major media worldwide often referred, to him as "the scientific psychic."

His subsequent research on behalf of American intelligence interests, including that of the CIA, won him top PSI-spy status. His involvement in government research projects required the discovery of innovative approaches toward the actual realizing of subtle human energies. He viewed PSI powers as only parts of the larger spectrum of human sensing systems and was internationally known as an advocate and researcher of the exceptional powers of the human mind.

To learn more about Ingo, his work, art, and other books, please visit: **www.ingoswann.com**.

Other Books from Ingo Swann:

Everybody's Guide to Natural ESP
Master of Harmlessness
Penetration
Penetration: Special Edition Updated
Preserving the Psychic Child
Psychic Sexuality
Purple Fables
Reality Boxes
Resurrecting the Mysterious
Secrets of Power, Volume 1
Secrets of Power, Volume 2
Star Fire
The Great Apparitions of Mary
The Windy Song
The Wisdom Category
Your Nostradamus Factor

A BioMind Superpowers Book
from Swann-Ryder Productions, LLC,
www.ingoswann.com

www.ingramcontent.com/pod-product-compliance
Lightning Source LLC
Chambersburg PA
CBHW020137130526
44591CB00030B/78